Hotels
An International Survey

Herbert Weisskamp

Hotels

An International Survey

Frederick A. Praeger, Publishers

New York · Washington

BOOKS THAT MATTER

Published in the United States of America in 1968
by Frederick A. Praeger, Inc., Publishers
111 Fourth Avenue, New York, N.Y. 10003
All rights reserved
Copyright in Stuttgart in 1968 by Verlag Gerd Hatje, Stuttgart, Germany
Library of Congress Catalog Card Number: 68—31 525
Printed in Germany
Translation into English: Herbert Weisskamp

Contents

Inhalt

The boom

For over ten years there has been a boom in hotel building all over the world. The full extent of the boom is not known: it has its origins in the growth of air travel and the consequent arrival in Europe and elsewhere of droves of American tourists, who increased the pressure on hotels which were already crowded and outdated. The emergence of new nations in Africa and Asia has also fostered a host of hotel projects in places where comfortable accommodation was formerly almost non-existent. Once-dreaded outposts of diplomacy soon began to boast a jet airport and a luxury hotel belonging to one of the international chains, and all over the world the new facilities seemed to stimulate demand rather than satisfy it. So much so, that the Big Three in the hotel world are now building or operating hotels from Aruba to Abidjan, from Dacca to Dar-es-Salaam, from Port-of-Spain to Porticcio to Pago-Pago. Cervantes' saying "the road is better than the inn" is no longer true, even of the most remote corners of today's world.

Though the boom has already gone on for some time, it seems bound to gather even greater momentum. Lower air fares, the universal adoption of the American habit of holding conventions, and the ambition of less important cities to possess prestige hotels, will all maintain the boom; and in the world of tomorrow with its abundance of leisure time, tourists will be even more numerous. Anyone with doubts about the future of the hotel business should remember that even in such places as Copenhagen, London, Frankfurt, Zurich, Amsterdsam, Bangkok, Santiago or Hamburg, it is difficult to find a hotel room at any time of the year.

So far, the boom has mainly been a success story for the US-type hotel, offering an American brand of comfort and prestige, and spread abroad by the wide range of American society which it attracts. All the big hotel chains are owned by US corporations.

Up to now, the participants in the boom have been developers and financiers, governments and city authorities,

1. Ski Hotel Borgafjäll in Southern Lapland. Exterior view. Architect: Ralph Erskine.

1. Skihotel Borgafjäll in Süd-Lappland. Außenansicht. Architekt: Ralph Erskine.

industrial giants like Alcoa, airlines (KLM with their Midway Houses were pioneers, followed today by PanAm and TWA, who both operate international hotel chains) and oil companies, for whom hotels may be either investments or part of a sales drive. Great names like the Rothschilds, the Aga Khan, the Rockefellers and even the Vatican, have been involved, but architects, oddly enough, have largely remained in the background.

The names of architects are never given in press releases about new hotels (architects being generally less than newsworthy nowadays) and are not even known to the men who manage the hotels after they are built. Not even the most distinguished names in architecture are used for publicity, while the life-history of a hotel manager and his family—his "dynastic relations"—are recounted to the last detail in brochures. Hotel corporations are quite capable of hinting that today's hotel is superior to its guests, but seem incapable of admitting that today's architect has taste superior to that of most guests.

Architects and clients

Only a few eminent architects have ever built a hotel. Frank Lloyd Wright designed the Imperial Hotel in Tokyo: its survival in an earthquake renewed his fame. Richard Neutra has built several resort motels in California (see pages 126 and 130) and planned Hilton hotels in Brazil; Arne Jacobsen has been responsible for an entirely unified design in his native Copenhagen (see page 46).

Admittedly, many hotel jobs are handled by architects whose speciality is the rapid turnover of work of doubtful architectural merit, and whose efforts have filled places like Miami Beach and parts of the Mediterranean coast with a hotchpotch of crude, slick clichés. Admittedly, hotels are often marred by the disastrous errors that have also ruined some US embassies—gestures in the direction of the local vernacular or nostalgia for a glorious past. Admittedly, hotels are hardly "total works of art" in the Wagnerian sense, for though their architecture, like Wagner's scores, may bear up the whole, it will also be dominated by action, by décor and by stage-management.

Is the conclusion then to be that hotels can never make great architecture? Certainly not. Outstanding hotels have been designed by architects in Mexico, Spain and the USA, in Denmark and Israel; while Gio Ponti's work in Rome and Sorrento has shown how hotel architecture can be both arresting and highly personal.

If hotels are seldom good subjects for purist architecture, they do at least offer a chance to build something impressive, to create a pleasant relationship with the landscape or with large sheets of water (waterside hotels can be seen far away, and have an inviolable view), and to arrange the game of life for humans at leisure or busily occupied.

But there still remains the apparent lack of understanding between architects and developers. There is uneasiness on both sides. Hotel people see the architect as a puritan who sticks rigidly to his austere modern style, and refuses to give them the ornate or glamorous interior, the trappings of delight, elegance or romance which they hanker for; and the famous architect, better able to get his own way, may seem even more of a peril. In some cases, too, the fact that professional fees represent a considerable slice of the capital invested by the developers, may cause them to choose run-of-the-mill architects who are prepared to turn out a quick job at a fraction of the established fees.

From the other side of the fence, architects find that hotel managers place too much emphasis on décor and "stage-management", demand over-designed exteriors which disrupt the essential outline and texture of buildings, and leave only elevations and lobbies to architects, handing over the "interior façades" to unspeakable decorators who horse around with chandeliers, fake antiques and folksy bric-à-brac. Architects feel that they are allowed too little control of the design process, with the consequence that most hotels end up as trivial or flashy stage sets, draped heedlessly over a structural frame. But they should bear in mind an observation which appeared in the magazine "Der Baumeister": "Purists and those who demand modern or nothing, will never find fulfilment in hotel design. But a little playfulness, a light touch, even a little embellishment, can hardly diminish the architectural distinction of a hotel, if the design is good in the first place."

The architectural standard of the big US-type hotels has gone up considerably of late—several recent projects like the Tel-Aviv Hilton (see page 20) are milestones in the architectural development of their own countries. Architects should convince their clients that there is no reason why their work should lack exuberance, whether of sense or spirit; and hotel executives should remember that all kinds of uncompromising buildings—from glass boxes to sculptures in raw concrete—have already proved themselves to be both financial and functional successes.

One strong point of the gifted architect is his ability to get the very best out of site and climate. Ralph Erskine's Borgafjäll Hotel in South Lapland (Fig. 1), built to an extremely tight budget, shows what brilliant site planning can achieve. "The hotel was placed on the edge of a gravel pit and together with the surrounding terrain, composed as a giant 'ground sculpture' in the hope of finding harmony with the mountain skyline and the spiral forms of the windblown snow. Wind screens are moreover built to direct the wind to gouge out and build up the snow in sculptural forms. The ground sculpture the hotel forms also gives the 'home slopes' for ski practice which are lacking in the immediate surroundings, ski runs starting on the roof" (Erskine).

When Richard Neutra was at work on several Hilton hotels in Brazil, one of his first ideas was to give the new capital of Brasilia (Figs. 2 and 3) something it greatly needed: a variety of shaded spaces for outdoor living, including an open auditorium which would share a stage with the ballroom. For the proposed Hilton hotel in Rio de Janeiro (Fig. 4) his planning began with the approach to the hotel from Galeão and Santos-Dumont airports. Instead of being jolted along crowded streets and twisting coastal avenues, guests would be able to take motor boats and gay ferries and short—cut across the bay from the airport. Arrival, rapid and spectacular, would be at Arpoador Point, which is flanked by the beaches of Copacabana and Ipanema, with the Tijuca Mountains, the Corcovado and all Rio for a backdrop. Neutra suggested that the hotel should be enlarged to act as a reception center for arriving tourists, under the name of Rio Reception Room.

Architecture versus decoration

In matters of site planning, disagreement between architect and client appears to be rare—it arises more often in the no man's land which lies between modern architecture and interior "decoration". It should be obvious that the restrained, distinctive and distinguished exteriors of good modern architecture can never combine satisfactorily with flashy or frivolous interiors.

The architect can capitulate and become one of the decorating team: the results may be like Yamasaki's Century

Plaza Hotel in Los Angeles (Figs. 5 and 6)—a well-planned building whose large but pleasantly-proportioned interior is weighed down by an excess of over-visible decoration. Yamasaki seeks "delight, serenity and surprise." They may be present in his "music-filled sunken plaza" but they do not inhabit his "transitional décor—a harmonious blending of the best of traditional and contemporary designs"—groaning under a thousand chandeliers and caparisoned with countless hand-made combinations of cloth, wood, leather, metal and ceramic.

The guest may enjoy the "important entrance" created for the "important person" he is; he may enjoy becoming "enfolded into a more intimate situation as he approaches the registration area"; he may enjoy being "virtually surrounded with concern", by the "total environment based on a guest-oriented philosophy" which is being sold to him, but one is entitled to doubt whether such decorative lushness can ever have anything esthetically worth while to offer today's traveling public.

The architect can give a little ground to the interior designer, and still remain in control of the most important elements—the flow of interior space, strength or subtlety of rhythm, the overall color scheme, the intensity and sequence of the lighting, the views, the interplay of open and enclosed spaces. If he refrains from excessive Brutalism or extravagance of form, and keeps his tones subdued or neutral, he may induce the designer in his turn to refrain from showy permanent finishes and to confine his strongest colors, textures and patterns to fabrics, whose very replaceability makes them less disruptive.

Architects have on occasion shown an imaginative creativity as high-spirited as that of any of their colleagues in interior design. Ralph Erskine painted his wooden Borgafjäll Hotel in slightly clashing primary colors to make it stand out like the wooden toy it is, and to lend a splash of intense color, like that of a Lapp costume, to the monochrome winter landscape. Gio Ponti has made his Parco dei Principi hotel in Sorrento (Figs. 7 and 8) a summation of the ceramic art of the Salerno region—on floors and walls a profusion of dark and light blue patterns recalls the sea a hundred meters below at the foot of the sheer cliff.

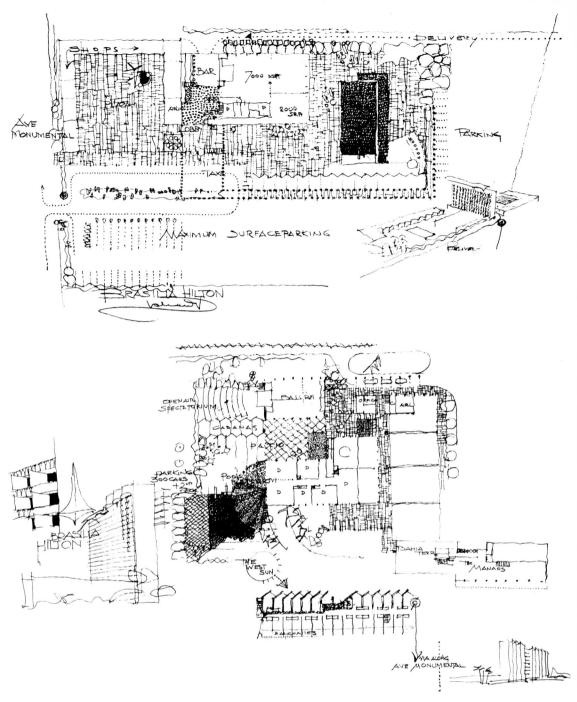

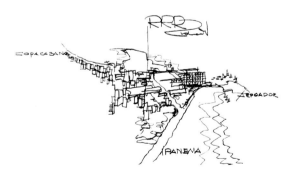

2, 3. Design sketches for a Hilton Hotel in Brasilia. Architects: Richard J. Neutra with Herbert Weisskamp.
4. Hilton Hotel Rio de Janeiro. Layout sketch with proposed reception center (Rio Reception Room). Architects: Richard J. Neutra with Herbert Weisskamp.

2, 3. Ideenskizzen für ein Hilton-Hotel in Brasilia. Architekten: Richard J. Neutra mit Herbert Weisskamp.
4. Hilton-Hotel Rio de Janeiro. Lageplanskizze mit dem vorgeschlagenen Empfangszentrum (Rio Reception Room). Architekten: Richard J. Neutra mit Herbert Weisskamp.

If architects can be as lively as interior designers, the designers can in their turn produce architectural interiors which are both subtle and restrained. One example is the Golden Door restaurant at Kennedy airport (Figs. 9 and 10) by the Knoll Planning Unit and the design department of the Brass Rail restaurant chain. This huge room of nearly 2000 m² is divided into eight dining sections, defined by long sofas and planting troughs and each seating some 40 persons. Surrounded by low-keyed colors (off-white ceiling, beige upholstery, soft-colored carpet), the sections are differentiated by red, blue or beige coffered ceilings with lights in the coving. A warm, diffused general illumination comes from recessed down-lights, and the glow of the coves can be varied by separate dimmers for each section.

Soft light, a characteristic of many American restaurants, could well be used to subdue over-decorative walls and bric-à-brac, and to concentrate interest on table settings, flowers, plants or food preparation at waiters' stations.

The three Irish hotels built by the Intercontinental Hotel Corporation (see pages 98–107) prove that great things can be done by interior designers with a talent for creating intimate atmosphere and skill in handling simple materials (in this case wood, linen, tweed and limestone) and who work within a disciplined and restrained architectural framework.

Where such ideal partners cannot be found, architects can make use of structure, both inside and out, to dominate the excesses of decoration. Structure has been successfully used as a primary element of design, both by Edward Killingsworth on his Kahala Hilton (see page 196) and to an even greater degree by Skidmore, Owings & Merrill in the Mauna Kea Beach Hotel (see page 203), where structure is itself the principal decorative and space-defining element.

The role of architects in hotel design—by no means a minor one, even by today's standards—will become increasingly important. As the boom makes itself felt in medium-sized cities, more and more jobs will go to architects of regional reputation; the task of fitting a hotel sympathetically into a townscape or a landscape, the desire to reflect regional character and to create congenial interiors, the lack, eventually, of clearly defined standards, will make real architecture possible.

Hotel types

Present-day hotels cannot easily be classified, since the only clearly-defined type is the international luxury hotel generally associated with the name of Hilton or Intercontinental. Outside this type, which may be found today even in such remote places as Kabul, Katmandu and Peshawar, categories have become blurred; individual projects are influenced by factors as diverse as function, size and site, budget and by-laws. This book reflects the breadth of types and of approaches to design, and includes some examples that simply refuse to be categorised at all.

International luxury hotels for businessmen and tourists used to conform to a given size of 500 to 1200 rooms. Recently, their sizes have fluctuated from 2150 rooms (New York Hilton) down to a minimum of 275 rooms (Hilton hotels in Amsterdam (see page 42) and Rotterdam: fully-fledged big-city hotels in spite of their smaller size). Many international hotels of today have a "compact" size of 300–400 rooms. The Hilton group and their international competitors have also developed a smaller luxury hotel, often found in resort areas, of 150–300 rooms, with a minimum of 100 rooms (Barbados). The Hilton Inns (see page 119)—a term preferred to the more ordinary motor hotel—have from 150 to over 300 rooms, while airport hotels (Paris-Orly, Quebec) have a capacity of 275 rooms. The American-style luxury hotel that has had so much influence all over the world, has small apartments and large public rooms: guest-rooms may have little in the way of costly finishes, but the lounges, bars and restaurants have lavish interiors. This follows the sound theory that anything special in the guest-rooms has to be repeated many hundreds of times, while a rich display in a public room is seldom duplicated. Very few new projects would qualify as luxury hotels if judged by the standards for room size (including bathrooms) laid down by Harold Sleeper in his book "Building, Planning and Design Standards":

minimum 21 m², depth 5,50 m, width 3,80 m
average 26 m², depth 6,55 m, width 4,05 m
luxury   32 m², depth 7,15 m, width 4,75 m

The plan of a typical apartment (Figs. 11–13) is likely to show a coat closet at a right angle to the corridor and a bathtub (sometimes shorter than 1,50 m) parallel with the corridor and the long axis of the building. This layout achieves a minimum width for each apartment and, since every saving of space is multiplied many times over, permits the greatest possible number of units to be fitted into a building of given length. Examples typical of many other projects are the Vienna Intercontinental and the Washington Hilton.

Where the width of the standard unit is not vital, more interesting solutions can be tried, as in the Hotel de France, Conakry (Fig. 14) and several projects shown in this book. The desire to have guest-rooms that are not mere sleeping-boxes, but can be lived in, and to create a sense of separation between the sleeping and living areas, has led architects to relocate the bathrooms (Fig. 16) or to add a sitting space at an angle to the window (Fig. 15); minute in size but with a generous view. The original plans for the Century Plaza Hotel by Minoru Yamasaki showed a variety of unusual unit plans (Figs. 17 and 18), graded from small to small-medium, and from large-medium to large apartments. Bathrooms were on the exterior of the building, reducing the noise level and the air-conditioning load. Rooms were separated by partitions unbroken by connecting doors, and by sound-proof wardrobe/TV/dressing table units. Guests were not only given a choice of double, twin or day beds, but also of sofa-and-chair or all-chair seating. In the final stage of planning, however, a decision was taken in favour of a conventional plan.

The overall plan of bedroom wings can be straight or staggered, L-, T-, or Y-shaped (Figs. 19 and 20), a hollow square (see page 88) or a single (Fig. 21) or double (Fig. 22) curve. Essentially, however, every international luxury hotel follows a similar tripartite functional pattern of guest-room slab, public rooms, and service areas. Public rooms are connected with the apartments by a vertical shaft, while service areas, though strictly segregated from the guest and public sections, are interlocked with them so that the service can reach any room in the guest areas, only from a different direction and through a different door from that used by guests. Perfect service is invisible but omnipresent, much like modern heating and ventilating systems. Large sections of the service plant, especially the food preparation and cooking sections, are industrial in character, manufacturing semi-finished and finished products which are tested and costed to the last ingredient at a central headquarters thousands of miles away.

The huge volume of the public rooms and service sections will invariably require a large floor area near ground level, several times greater than that of any one floor of the guest-room slab. The broad base, also known as the "pancake", has produced the podium or pedestal type of hotel with its inherent formal problems (Fig. 23). The guest-room part is easy to design as a clean-cut cube or slab (Fig. 24): it contains a repetitive series of equal or similar units, the total of which is normally a multiple of the 15 apartments served by a chambermaid. Experimental solution like the Tamanaco Hotel in Caracas (operated by the Intercontinental Hotels Corporation) with its step-

ped down wings have proved a failure functionally, as the work of chambermaids on several floors cannot be coordinated properly.

The formal problems occur where the tall slab meets the flat base, and a forest of columns penetrates through the public or service areas. Solutions to the problem are many: this book shows quite a variety. The high-rise slab can be placed beside instead of above the podium (see page 98); the multiple loads from above can be redistributed by longitudinal beams, taking up the full depth of an intermediate floor which also houses some of the services machinery (this is the usual solution; see Tel-Aviv Hilton, page 20); the supporting structure can form a shallow cushion under the multi-storey slab, and extend into the cross-walls above (Rome Hilton, see page 62). The number of columns within the slab building can be greatly reduced by structural means (Royal Hotel, Copenhagen, see page 46; Denver Hilton, see page 36). In many cases it will be possible to integrate the main columns and their simple rhythm quite successfully with the more open layout of the public rooms and to develop the podium freely, as witnessed by a hotel in Teheran designed by Foroughi, Zafar, Sadegh and Ghiai (Fig. 25). The largest of recently built hotels, the New York Hilton, suffers from an excess of columns penetrating the podium floors (Fig. 26). Its main lobby, reached from the narrow sides and pierced by heavy columns, is easily clogged by group arrivals and the problem is made worse by the fact that there are no adjacent lounge spaces, merely indoor promenades. The constant coming and going in this lobby, placed between desks and shops, bars and specialty restaurants, may accord with the bustling life of New York City, but many a traveler will miss the clear distinction between lobby and lounge areas usually found in Hilton and other international hotels.

Of the lesser problems facing the architect who designs a hotel, the endless hallways, dimly lit and with doors on both sides, have often provoked the designer to exercise his skill and imagination. Hallways can be curved to eliminate the feeling of excessive length (Fig. 21) or divided into sections marked off by door recesses, suspended ceiling panels and changes of lighting (Fig. 27). A system of rectangular room units in a saw-tooth layout can produce a corridor marked by slanting recesses which echo on the interior the jagged rhythm of the façades (hotel in Kuala Lumpur, Fig. 28).

Minor but messy obstacles are the shoes left outside room doors at night. For recent projects, architects have designed shoe safes built into the wardrobe closets and openable from the hallway. Luggage being moved or stored is another and bulkier eyesore. European and United States' methods of handling it differ. While in most U.S. hotels trunks and suitcases pass through the lobby—American guests like to see where their luggage is going—and remain in sight in the rooms so as to be easily accessible, the European trend is to bring in all luggage through a service entrance and service elevators, and to store the bulkier pieces in the wardrobe section of the apartments. In typical hotel apartments built to American standards, the wardrobe and luggage section tends to be small, as many guests will be traveling by air. Large new hotels in Europe, like the Cavalieri Hilton (see page 62) in Rome, have sizable entrance halls for each apartment, closed at night by soundproofed interior doors.

Connecting doors from room to room are found in abundance in new hotels the world over. Their advantage—an increased flexibility in forming suites—will in many cases be no more than theoretical in the eyes of seasoned travelers. Their disadvantages—loss of storage space and lack of privacy, or downright discomfort, due to noise

transmission—are only too familiar. The large numbers of suites provided on the top floors of most projects (Fig. 23) would seem to render at least some of the connecting doors unnecessary.

The main task of hotel designers, however, should be to cater within the limited area of a modern hotel apartment for all those activities which cannot be relegated to the vast public spaces below: reading, writing, intimate conversation, listening and relaxing in private (Fig. 29). Gone are the reading rooms, writing rooms and bridge rooms, the conversation and intimate reception rooms, subtly graded in size and openness, as in the old palace hotels of Ritz's type. All these rooms have been replaced by one large all-purpose lounge fashioned to suit our more amorphous society, and our desire for sociability—and sometimes possessing the sort of majestically-proportioned interior that architects rave about.

The European Ritz tradition survives in places like the Hotel de Mar, Palma (Fig. 30), offering a fair sequence of small and large salons, or Mexico, where the Hotel María Isabel devotes a large section to reception and party rooms of all sizes, in connection with a high proportion of suites, which would seem to show an affinity with North American ideas. It might be added that three of the leading hotels in the world today go back to César Ritz or bear his name—the old Ritz in the Place Vendôme, Paris, the new Ritz Hotel in Lisbon, famous for its service and its antiques and period furniture, and the Grand Hotel in Rome, built by Ritz in 1880, rebuilt today and freshly decorated, which has become the meeting place for Italy's aristocracy and cinema artists.

Quite a number of the old palace hotels have shown a remarkable ability to survive. Renovating a Grand or Palace hotel can be a rewarding task. While rising wages, the need for modern equipment and production-line methods have condemned many an old hotel as functionally impracticable (even the Mount Lavinia Hotel near Colombo, Ceylon, of River Kwai fame, will have to be torn down and replaced), remodeling can sometimes turn the large guest-rooms and vast public spaces of such buildings into most comfortable interiors. The Grand Hotel in Rome, already mentioned, would head any list of renovated hotels. Of the two richly decorated main staircases, one was retained in its original splendor, the other sacrificed to make space for three elevators and two additional apartments on each floor, with baths. In this book there are two examples of renovations and extensions; one in a German Kurpark, where the public rooms lacked space and amenities (see page 96), and the other a resort hotel of world renown near Mont Blanc, expanded and rebuilt entirely from within (see page 94).

Once we leave the sphere of international luxury hotels, those "cathedrals of tourism" (Enzensberger) and "temples of noiseless luxury" (hotel prospectus), whose emphasis on group business, conventions and cost-efficiency techniques makes them cities within cities, we find ourselves among a bewildering diversity of hotel types. Further down the social ladder, one encounters experimental hotels, low-priced in the extreme, like the Europa and Victoria Hotels on the Dutch island of Terschelling, which cater for guests who bring their own bedsheets, make their own beds and take self-service meals. It has already been said that small and medium-sized hotels still hold tremendous opportunities for architecture: they are also a tremendous source of architectural commissions. Hotels like the Stanley in Athens (Fig. 31), furnished entirely by Knoll International, or the Grand Hotel in Cannes (see page 78), which introduced contemporary design to the conservative world of French hostelry, prove that uncompromising designs can be

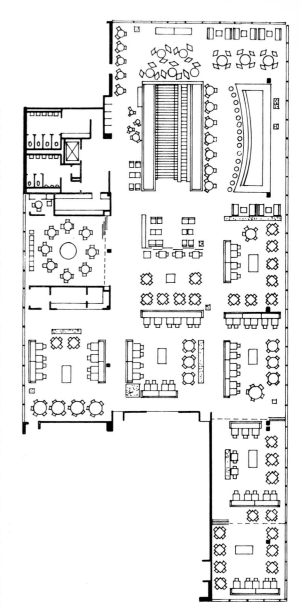

9, 10. Golden Door Restaurant at Kennedy Airport, New York. Plan of interior furnishings and view from the bar over the adjoining sections. Design: Knoll Planning Unit and design department of the Brass-Rail-Restaurant-Group.

9, 10. Golden Door Restaurant am Kennedy Airport, New York. Möblierungsplan und Blick von der Bar auf die anschließenden Sektionen. Planung: Knoll Planning Unit und Entwurfsabteilung der Brass-Rail-Restaurantgruppe.

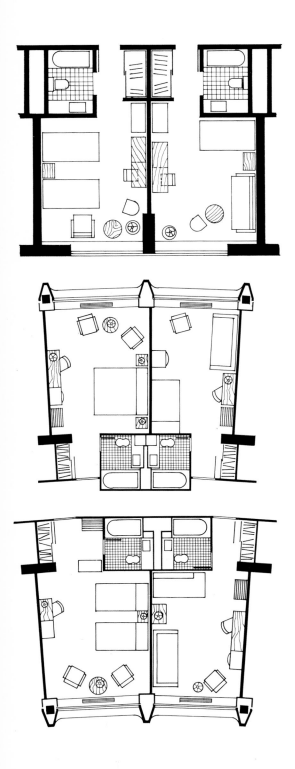

11–13. Standard apartments at the Vienna Intercontinental (above). Architect: Carl Appel; and at the Hilton Hotel, Washington D. C. (center and below), Architect: William B. Tabler.

11–13. Standard-Apartments im Hotel Intercontinental, Wien (oben), Architekt: Carl Appel, und im Hilton-Hotel, Washington, D. C. (Mitte und unten), Architekt: William B. Tabler.

built and run with success. Small hotels like the one at Macchu Picchu, Peru, designed by Schweikher and Elting (Fig. 32), a shallow shelf in surroundings dominated by towering peaks, dug into the rocky slope and constructed of stone quarried on the site, and the Astoria Hotel at Lucerne, Switzerland (Fig. 33), by Theo Hotz, where the reception desk and restaurant are at roof level while the kitchen and service are in the basement, show the wide variety of imaginative ways in which esthetic and functional problems have been tackled.

Residential hotels which cater both for passing travelers and frequent visitors who wish to rent permanent apartments, have come in for a marked revival. The most interesting, architecturally, is Brussels' Hotel Résidence (Figs. 34 and 35), the work of René Stapels, offering 40 small duplex apartments and 5 larger units, mostly two-storeyed, on the top floors. Two recent hotel buildings in Chicago have similar apartments, also with small kitchens, but planned on one level only. Executive House (Figs. 36 and 37), the first major hotel to be built in Chicago in 28 years, has 450 studio rooms and end suites opening onto large balconies set into the façades; since each unit has its separate outside kitchenette, it was possible to finance the 7 million dollar hotel at favorable terms, as an apartment house. Bankers, it seems, have not forgotten the depression of the thirties and its effect on the hotel business. About 80 per cent of the rooms are, however, rented to transients. The Hotel Astor by Bertrand Goldberg (Figs. 38 and 39) has 96 large corner suites, four to each floor, placed on concrete stilts five storeys high, which end in a two-storey podium that houses a bar and 200-seat restaurant operated by Maxim's of Paris. A skating rink has been put on the roof, 30 storeys up.

Motor Hotels

today are very different from the rash of motels brought on by the rapid expansion in car ownership in the United States after the war. Here again the diversity of projects is enormous and the trend is moving away from a limited range of accepted formulas. There are many valid approaches, which may include either such modulations of a well-established personal idiom as Richard Neutra's motor hotels in California (see pages 126–133) and Aris Konstantinidis' Xenia schemes in Greece (see pages 144 to 153), or original but unrepeatable designs like Lundy's motel in Florida (see page 116).

The term motel is seldom used these days, while motor inns, motor lodges and motor hotels abound. The United States has 74 000 hotels and motels with more than ten guest-rooms; of these 27 000 are hotels and 47 000 motels, the two groups having roughly equal shares of the total room capacity. In 1965, 130 000 new motel rooms were completed in the States; motels have shown an increasing tendency to function as inns and recreation centers in the meager environment of suburbia. The division between motels, motor hotels and hotels has, however, become more and more fluid. Parking spaces in motel grounds are no longer automatically placed before the guest-room doors, so long as the basic rule can be kept of giving guests direct access to their rooms, so that they can enter without passing through any formal public areas. Motor hotels may even have tower buildings; Dublin's largest and probably most expensive hotel, the Intercontinental (see page 98), is actually an 8-storey motor hotel, and San Francisco's biggest hostelry, the Hilton (see page 112), has been described as the Motor Pool Hilton. Motels and motor inns have often taken over some of the functions of hotels, providing cocktail loun-

ges, grill restaurants, meeting rooms and wide, landscaped grounds. Motor hotels, while respecting the principle of easy access to the car, will offer larger and superior facilities (sometimes enough for fair-sized conventions), more service and more occasions for tipping. They are usually planned compactly and tend toward multi-storey design. A chain of distinctive motor hotels is being built by the Esso corporation (see page 108) with the idea of promoting their brand name by pleasant accommodation and catering. It is fascinating to pause and consider how a company affiliated to the Rockefeller empire fosters the demand for motor travel in much the same way that the founder of that empire fostered a demand for kerosene when he sold lamps in China.

The pavilion hotel, long known in southern France as the "hotel pavillonaire", or as a bungalow hotel in the tropics, is in many ways an offspring of the motor hotel. A project of this type, with a majority of small single-storey houses, designed by the author in the Var region of the Côte d'Azur (see page 134), shows the essential characteristics: the whole 4 hectare complex is firmly centered on the public rooms in a remodeled nineteenth-century château, in spite of the fact that every unit has a fully-equipped kitchen and more than adequate living space. In a pavilion hotel the apparent density should be kept low. At Sainte-Maxime every dip, fold and swell of the ground was used to tuck houses, cars and humans out of the sight of people who were staying only a few paces away. This project—"Les Tourelles"—one of the few truly contemporary schemes in the region, was not financed by a hotel corporation but built for its members by the German Construction Workers' Union. Similar projects have been sponsored by the same group elsewhere in Germany and Austria. The pavilion hotel under construction at Isny in the Allgäu region of Bavaria (Fig. 40) is a larger version of the Sainte-Maxime project; 150 small, completely furnished houses in loose groups and a "village center" with a library, restaurant, shops, pond and indoor swimming pool, made attractive enough to act as a nucleus to a community whose members will have the tie of belonging to the same trade and the same union. Houses in the scheme will be partly run on a self-service basis with periodical cleaning by chambermaids, while the restaurant will provide both self- and

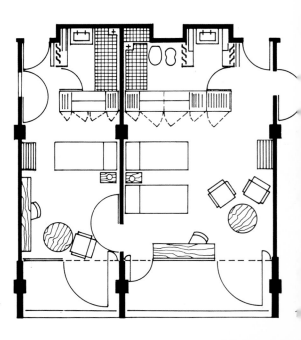

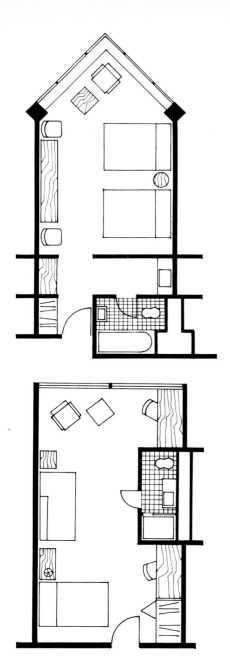

15, 16. Sleeping and sitting areas are defined by position of bathroom (Lynn Charterhouse Hotel) and by projecting angular window bay (Project Civic Center Hotel, Detroit, Mich.).
17, 18. Century Plaza Hotel, Los Angeles, California. Preliminary design. Standard rooms of various sizes. Architects: Minoru Yamasaki and Associates.

15, 16. Trennung von Schlaf- und Wohnbereich durch Umlegen des Badezimmers (Lynn Charterhouse Hotel) und abgewinkelten Fenstersitzplatz (Projekt Civic Center Hotel, Detroit, Mich.).
17, 18. Century Plaza Hotel, Los Angeles, Kalifornien. Vorprojekt. Standardräume in verschiedenen Größen. Architekt: Minoru Yamasaki and Associates.

◁ 14. Plan of a single and double room at the Hotel de France, Conakry. Architects: Lagneau, Weill, Dimitrijevic & Associés.

◁ 14. Grundriß von Einzel- und Doppelzimmer des Hotels de France, Conakry. Architekten: Lagneau, Weill, Dimitrijevic & Associés.

waitress service. Pavilion hotels of this type are a definite step away from the alarming prospect of tomorrow's mass tourism, with its possibilities of vacation cities and "vacation factories" ("usines de vacances" like Royan in France's Gironde region) many times bigger even than today's holiday villages.

It is in the sphere of smaller resort hotels that the challenge is keenest to modern architects to rival the charms of the numerous old castles, villas, medieval inns and villages which have been converted into hotels. The lure of Les Relais de Campagne (Fig. 41), a web of enchanted spots that originated at La Cardinale in the Ardèche region, and has spread over France and the world since the war, or of Germany's Burgen und Schlösser, may be hard to equal, but resort hotels have often been a field in which brilliant architects have excelled. Witness the collection of resort hotels in this volume.

Resort hotels

It is no accident that resort hotels often possess a less artificial atmosphere than most of the international hotels or the monster palaces of Miami Beach. The vacationer of the late sixties may be ready to shed his pretensions and opt for architectural simplicity placed in a natural setting.

The best examples are clean-cut rectangular buildings, with almost no hint of regional style, but having a complete respect for the nature of their site (Hotel de Mar, Palma, see page 190), a sensitive transformation of its character (Corte dei Butteri, see page 154), a harmonious extension of the vegetation and topography (Hotel Hvide Hus, see page 182—a verdant artificial slope climbing an existing hill), or a composition of interwoven architectural and natural elements (Kahala Hilton, see page 196, and Mauna Kea Beach Hotel, see page 203). In some cases, the area round a swimming pool, with its cabins and pavilions, will present an opportunity for exuberant design that does not have to reach right up to the main building or interfere with its architectural character (Hotel Fort Royal, see page 186).

Resort hotels may even house guests of quite different income groups in a single complex of buildings, if the focus of the holiday is entirely upon the beach (Hotel Lakolk, see page 160). In ski hotels, people seem more inclined than usual to get together informally (Prisank, see page 140, and Borgafjäll, Fig. 1): skiers keen on their sport will easily form a group. Guest-rooms in hotels on the beach or in the mountains can often be little more than mere cells to sleep in. Luxury hotels by the sea, on the other hand, whether in Spain (Hotel de Mar) or Hawaii (Kahala Hilton and Mauna Kea Beach), tend to offer very spacious accommodation, allowing their guests to take refuge from the overfull round of society life.

Outlook

So far, there is no sign of any conclusion to the discussion of hotel design in our time. The predominant and necessarily rationalizing nature of the functionalist approach ought to produce more standardized designs, but there seems to be so much uninhibited creativity about, and such an enterprising spirit among developers and architects, that new kinds of hotel, new orders of magnitude and new ideas in town planning come into being every day.

While this book is in the press, a new and lavish establishment will open its gates in St. Tropez: the Byblos (Fig. 42),

in the words of its owner an "anti-hotel", with balconied rooms grouped villagelike around a two-level terrace/plaza shaded by olive and palm trees. At the same time, a 6000-bed hotel is being built in Moscow, and one of the most exclusive of modern hotels, the Mauna Kea Beach (see page 203), built at the astronomical cost of 100 000 dollars per room, is booked for years in advance. While hotels are becoming a major feature of urban renewal projects, from Kuala Lumpur (Fig. 43) to San Francisco's Embarcadero Center—a terraced hotel building with a 16-storey enclosed garden court—the two colossal urban enterprises of our time, Chandigarh and Brasilia, still lack adequate hotel facilities.

In most other parts of the world, hotel construction is going on briskly. Architects in search of more distinctive solutions or new fusions of architecture and interior design, should bear one thing in mind: that a hotel building should be designed to be understood quickly, like a sophisticated advertisement. If it is true that the message of an ad has to be grasped in four seconds, then two days and nights (the average length of stay at a hotel), or a two-hour dinner, should be enough to give an impression, whether lasting or pleasantly fleeting, of an architecture which is in tune with our time and our society.

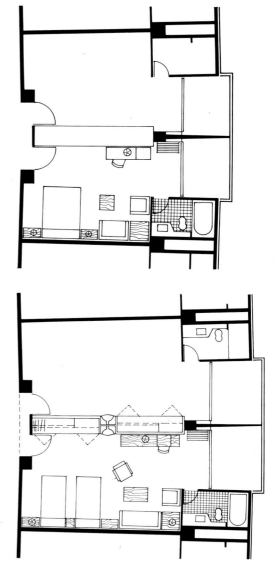

Der Boom

Seit mehr als einem Jahrzehnt erlebt die Welt einen Hotelbau-Boom von bisher unbekannten Dimensionen. Er wurde ausgelöst durch die Entwicklung des Luftverkehrs, durch den Massenandrang amerikanischer Reisender in Europa und anderen Überseeländern, in denen die Hotels überaltert und überfüllt waren. Das Werden neuer Nationen in Asien und Afrika hat eine Vielzahl von Hotelprojekten in Gebieten entstehen lassen, in denen bequeme Hotelunterkünfte bis dahin mehr als knapp gewesen waren. Gefürchtete Außenposten der Diplomatie konnten bald einen Düsenflughafen und ein Luxushotel eines der internationalen Hotelkonzerne aufweisen, und die neuen Anlagen schienen eine weltweite Nachfrage eher anzuregen als sie zu befriedigen – mit dem Ergebnis, daß die Großen Drei der Hotelbranche in der Welt heute von Aruba bis Abidjan und Auckland, von Dacca bis Daressalam, von Port of Spain bis Porticcio und Pago-Pago Hotels betreiben oder im Bau haben. Cervantes' Wort, daß »die Straße besser ist als das Gasthaus«, trifft heute selbst in den fernsten Winkeln der Erde kaum mehr zu.

Obwohl der Boom sich schon als höchst langlebig erwiesen hat, scheint er heute eher noch an Gewicht zu gewinnen. Niedrige Flugpreise und die weiter wachsende (von den USA aus über den Globus verbreitete) Begeisterung für Tagungen großen Stils forcieren zusammen mit dem Wunsch auch weniger bedeutender Städte, ein Prestigehotel zu besitzen, die Entwicklung. Hotelbau und Massentourismus dürften in der Freizeitwelt von morgen neue Höhen erreichen. Wer an der Zukunft der Hotelbranche zweifelt, der sollte sich vor Augen halten, daß an Plätzen wie Kopenhagen, London, Frankfurt, Zürich, Amsterdam, Bangkok, Santiago oder Hamburg das ganze Jahr über nur sehr schwer ein Hotelzimmer zu bekommen ist.

Der bisherige Aufschwung war vorwiegend ein Triumph des amerikanischen Hotels, eines Komforts und Prestiges amerikanischer Art, verbreitet durch die weitgestreuten Schichten der amerikanischen Gesellschaft, die davon angezogen werden. Alle wirklich großen Hotelkonzerne sind im Besitz amerikanischer Gruppen.

Der Boom hat Bauträger und Finanziers, Regierungen und Stadtverwaltungen beschäftigt, Giganten der Industrie wie Alcoa, Luftfahrtunternehmen (die KLM mit ihren Midway Houses war Pionier auf diesem Gebiet, heute gefolgt von PanAm und TWA, die beide internationale Hotelkonzerne besitzen) und Erdölgesellschaften, für die Hotels eine bloße Investition oder auch Teil eines Marketingprogramms sein können. Er hat große Namen wie die Rothschilds, den Aga Khan, die Rockefellerfamilie und selbst den Vatikan auf den Plan gerufen, nur die Architekten blieben, seltsam genug, überwiegend am Rand des Geschehens.

Architektennamen werden in den Pressemitteilungen neuer Hotels kaum erwähnt (nachdem Architekten in unseren Tagen generell wenig Pressewert haben). Sie sind den Hoteldirektoren oft nicht einmal bekannt. Selbst hoch angesehene Namen in der Welt der Architektur werden nie für die Werbung benutzt, während die Lebensläufe eines Hoteldirektors und seiner Familie – seine »dynastischen Verbindungen« – in Hotelprospekten gern bis zum letzten Detail ausgebreitet sind. Hotelkonzerne mögen vielleicht nicht zögern anzudeuten, daß das Hotel von heute distinguierter ist als seine Gäste, aber sie würden niemals zugeben, daß der Architekt von heute einen besseren Geschmack hat als der Durchschnittsgast.

Architekt und Auftraggeber

Wenige unter den großen Architekten haben jemals ein Hotel gebaut. Frank Lloyd Wright entwarf das Imperial Hotel und kam zu neuem Ruhm, als es das Erdbeben von Tokio überstand. Richard Neutra baute mehrere Ferienhotels in Kalifornien (Seite 126 und 130) und entwickelte Pläne für Hilton-Hotels in Brasilien. Arne Jacobsen schließlich schuf für sein heimatliches Kopenhagen ein Hotel ganz aus einem Wurf (Seite 46).

Es ist wahr, daß viele Hotelprojekte von Spezialisten geplant werden, die schnelle Routinearbeit mit zweifelhafter architektonischer Qualität verbinden, und daß die Tätigkeit solcher Routiniers Plätze wie Miami Beach oder

19. T-shaped typical floor plan, Hotel Royal Garden, London. Architects: R. Seifert and Partners.

19. Normalgeschoß in T-Form, Hotel Royal Garden, London. Architekten: R. Seifert and Partners.

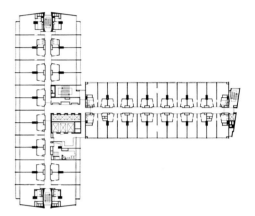

20. Y-shaped typical floor plan. Statler Hilton Hotel, Dallas, Texas. Architect: William B. Tabler.
21. Curved floor plan. Century Plaza Hotel, Los Angeles, Calif. Architects: Minoru Yamasaki and Associates.
22. Double curvature of floor plan. Hilton Hotel, Washington D.C. Architect: William B. Tabler.

20. Normalgeschoß in Y-Form. Statler Hilton Hotel, Dallas, Texas. Architekt: William B. Tabler.
21. Normalgeschoß in Bogenform. Century Plaza Hotel, Los Angeles, Kalifornien. Architekt: Minoru Yamasaki and Associates.
22. Normalgeschoß in Form eines Doppelbogens. Hilton-Hotel, Washington, D. C. Architekt: William B. Tabler.

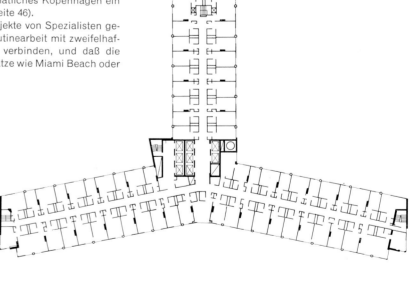

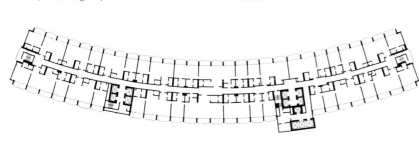

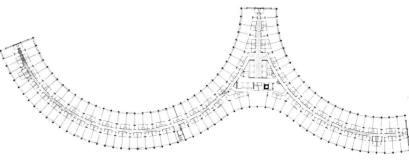

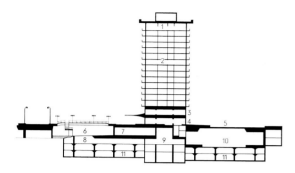

23. Connection of bedroom slab and podium. Century Plaza Hotel, Los Angeles, California. Architects: Minoru Yamasaki and Associates. Key: 1 Penthouse suites, 2 Guest rooms, 3 Mezzanine level, 4 Lobby level, 5 Garden level, 6 Plaza, 7 Plaza level, 8 Convention facilities and meeting rooms, 9 Foyer, 10 Ballroom, 11 Garage.

23. Verbindung von Bettenturm und Breitfußbasis. Century Plaza Hotel, Los Angeles, Kalifornien. Architekt: Minoru Yamasaki and Associates. Legende: 1 Suiten im Dachgeschoß, 2 Gästezimmer, 3 Mezzaningeschoß, 4 Eingangsgeschoß, 5 Gartenniveau, 6 Plaza, 7 Plazageschoß, 8 Geschoß mit Versammlungs- und Konferenzräumen, 9 Foyer, 10 Ballsaal, 11 Tiefgarage.

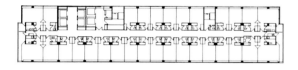

24. Typical floor plan with 30 guest rooms. Hotel Intercontinental, Frankfurt am Main. Architects: O. Apel and H. Beckert, G. Becker, Engineer.

24. Normalgeschoß eines Bettentraktes mit 30 Gästezimmern. Hotel Intercontinental, Frankfurt am Main. Architekten: O. Apel und H. Beckert, G. Becker, Ingenieur.

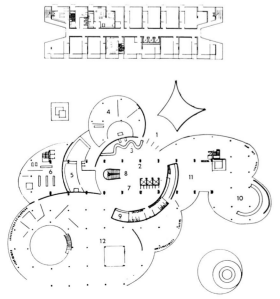

einige mittelmeerische Küstenstriche zu Anhäufungen roher und glatter Klischees gemacht hat. Es ist wahr, daß Hotelentwürfe oft unter demselben Trugschluß leiden, der auch einige US-Botschaftsgebäude in Übersee entstellt: die Verbeugung vor dem einheimischen Genre oder eine dünne Auflage vergangener Glorie. Es ist wahr, daß Hotels eine Art Gesamtkunstwerk sind (nicht ganz im Wagnerischen Sinn), daß die Architektur, wie Wagners Partituren, die Szene tragen sollte, daß sie aber auf weite Strecken von Aktion, Bühnendekoration und Regie übertönt wird.

Sollen wir daraus schließen, daß Hotelprojekte nicht geeignet sind, große Architektur hervorzubringen? Sicherlich nicht. Hervorragende Hotelplanungen sind von Architekten in Mexiko, Spanien und den USA, in Dänemark oder Israel geschaffen worden, und Gio Ponti hat mit seinen Hotels in Sorrent und Rom bewiesen, daß fesselnde individualistische Lösungen verwirklicht werden können. Wenn Hotels selten der puristischen Architektur eine Chance geben, so bieten sie doch Gelegenheit, ein bedeutendes architektonisches Volumen der Stadtsilhouette einzufügen, wohltuende Beziehungen zum Grün und zu größeren Wasserflächen zu schaffen (Hotels am Wasser sind weithin sichtbar und haben eine unverbaubare Aussicht) und das Spiel des Lebens zu organisieren, für Menschen in Muße oder in lebendigem Treiben.

Das sichtbare Dilemma, der Mangel an Rapport zwischen Bauherren und Architekten, bleibt. Das Unbehagen ist auf beiden Seiten. Hoteldirektoren mögen die Architekten als Puristen ansehen, die ihr »kaltes« zeitgemäßes Idiom durchsetzen wollen, statt reichgeschmückte oder glitzernde Interieurs zu bieten, mit dem Hauch von Lebensfreude und Romantik, den man vorzieht – und die Gefahr scheint akuter bei berühmten Architekten, die zu ihren Ansichten stehen. In manchen Fällen kann der Umstand, daß die Planungsgebühren einen erheblichen Teil vom Eigenkapital des Bauträgers beanspruchen, dazu führen, routinierte Planer zu wählen, die sich ihrer Aufgabe schnell entledigen, zu einem Bruchteil der vollen Architektengebühr.

Architekten finden ihrerseits, daß Hoteldirektoren sich zu sehr auf Dekor und Regie verlassen, daß sie ein Übermaß an äußerer Identifizierbarkeit verlangen und damit Silhouetten und Struktur eines Gebäudes beeinträchtigen, daß sie den Architekten die Außenfronten und höchstens die Hotelhalle entwerfen lassen, während sie die »inneren Fassaden« zweifelhaften Dekorateuren überlassen und sich in Kronleuchtern, nachgemachten Antiquitäten und folkloristischen Ausstattungsstücken ausleben. Die Architekten meinen, daß sie zu wenig Kontrolle über den Entwurfsvorgang haben, und daß die meisten Hotels schließlich banale oder übersteigerte Bühnenbilder sind, die man über eine tragende Konstruktion gehängt hat. Sie sollten an ein Wort aus der Zeitschrift

◁ 25. Hotel project in Teheran with free-shaped podium areas and rectangular bedroom block. Architects: M. Foroughi, Ch. Zafar, A. Sadegh and H. Ghiai. Key: 1 Entrance, 2 Lobby, 3 Reception, 4 Administration, 5 Shops, 6 Offices, 7 Lounge, 8 Main stairway, 9 Cloak room, 10 Snack bar, 11 Exhibition area and salon, 12 Dancing.

◁ 25. Entwurf für ein Hotel in Teheran mit frei geformter Basis und blockförmigem Bettenhaus. Architekten: M. Foroughi, Ch. Zafar, A. Sadegh und H. Ghiai. Legende: 1 Eingang, 2 Lobby, 3 Empfang, 4 Verwaltung, 5 Läden, 6 Büros, 7 Lounge, 8 Haupttreppe, 9 Garderobe, 10 Snack-Bar, 11 Ausstellungsbereich und Salon, 12 Dancing.

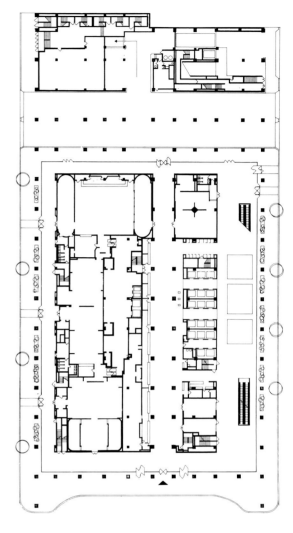

26. Hilton Hotel, New York. Ground floor plan with lobby. Architect: William B. Tabler.
27. Hotel María Isabel, Mexico D. F. Typical floor plan. Architects: José Villagrán García and Juan Sordo Madaleno.

26. Hilton-Hotel, New York. Grundriß des Erdgeschosses mit der Lobby. Architekt: William B. Tabler.
27. Hotel María Isabel, Mexico D. F. Normalgeschoßgrundriß. Architekten: José Villagrán García und Juan Sordo Madaleno.

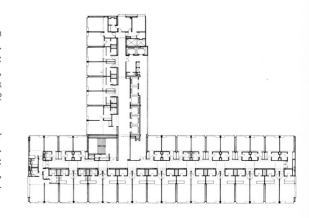

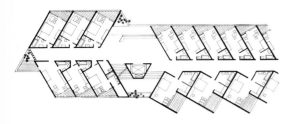

28. Hotel project in Kuala Lumpur. Typical floor plan. Architect: Herbert Weisskamp (Neue Heimat International).

28. Projekt für ein Hotel in Kuala Lumpur. Normalgeschoßgrundriß. Architekt: Herbert Weisskamp (Neue Heimat International).

29. Double room in a Swedish hotel furnished as a living-bedroom.

29. Zweibettzimmer in einem schwedischen Hotel, als Wohn-Schlafraum eingerichtet.

30. Hotel de Mar, Palma de Mallorca. Lounge and restaurant level with intimate niches and salons. Architects: José Antonio Coderch and Manuel Valls; Interior decorators: A. Mila and F. Correa.

30. Hotel de Mar, Palma de Mallorca. Restaurantgeschoß mit intimen Nischen und Salons. Architekten: José Antonio Coderch und Manuel Valls; Innenarchitekten: A. Mila und F. Correa.

»Baumeister« denken: »Puristen und Verteidiger der Moderne um jeden Preis werden im Hotelbau wohl nie ihre Befriedigung finden. Und ein wenig Spiel, etwas Leichtigkeit vergänglicher Ausschmückung können den architektonischen Wert eines Hotels, falls es wirklich gut konzipiert ist, nur selten schmälern.«

Die architektonische Qualität der großen Hotels vom amerikanischen Typus ist mit den Jahren stark verbessert worden, und mehrere Hotelprojekte jüngeren Datums, wie das Tel Aviv Hilton (Seite 20), dürfen als Marksteine neuzeitlichen Bauens in ihren Ländern gelten. Die Architekten sollten ihre Auftraggeber überzeugen, daß ihr Schaffen einen Überschwang der Ideen und der Sinne nicht ausschließt, und Hoteldirektoren sollten sich erinnern, daß kompromißlose Entwürfe aller Richtungen – von Ganzglasgebäuden bis zu skulpturellen Formungen in Sichtbeton – sich als höchst erfolgreiche Lösungen erwiesen haben, in funktioneller wie in wirtschaftlicher Hinsicht.

Begabte Architekten haben den Vorzug, fähig zu sein, das ganze Potential eines Geländes und eines Klimas zu nutzen. Ralph Erskines Borgafjäll Hotel im südlichen Lappland (Abb. 1), mit sehr geringen Kosten gebaut, zeigt, was eine gut durchdachte Planung erreichen kann. »Das Hotel wurde an den Rand einer Kiesgrube gesetzt und zusammen mit dem umgebenden Terrain als gigantische Erdskulptur geformt, in der Hoffnung, zu einer Harmonie mit der Gipfellinie der Berge und mit den Spiralformen windverwehten Schnees zu gelangen. Windbrecher wurden aufgestellt, um den Wind so zu leiten, daß er den Schnee in skulpturellen Formen aushöhlen und aufbauen kann. Die Bodenskulptur, die das Hotel darstellt, bietet zugleich die Übungshänge, die in der nächsten Umgebung fehlen; Abfahrtsläufe beginnen auf dem Dach« (Erskine).

Als Richard Neutra begann, verschiedene Hilton-Hotels in Brasilien zu planen, war seine erste Idee, der neuen Hauptstadt Brasilia etwas zu geben (Abb. 2 und 3), das weithin fehlte: eine Reihe von schattigen Plätzen für das Leben im Freien, darunter ein offener Theatersaal, der sich die Bühne mit dem Ballsaal teilt. Für das geplante Hilton-Hotel in Rio de Janeiro (Abb. 4) begann sein Entwurf mit dem Weg zum Hotel von den Flughäfen Galeão und Santos Dumont. Statt sich in Taxis durch vollgestopfte Straßen und kurvenreiche Küstenpromenaden zu kämpfen, sollten die Gäste auf Motorbooten und Fähren die Bucht überqueren und schnell und spektakulär zur Halbinsel Arpoador gelangen, mit den Stränden von Copacabana und Ipanema zu beiden Seiten und den Tijuca-Bergen, dem Corcovado und dem ganzen Panorama von Rio als Kulisse. Neutra schlug vor, das Hotelprogramm zu erweitern und ein Empfangszentrum für ankommende Touristen unter dem Namen Rio Reception Room zu schaffen.

Architektur gegen Dekoration

Das strittige Gebiet zwischen Auftraggebern und Architekten scheint allerdings selten die Bauplanung zu sein, sondern vielmehr das Niemandsland zwischen neuzeitlicher Architektur und Dekoration. Es liegt auf der Hand, daß sich die Ziele sauberer zeitgemäßer Architektur nicht ohne weiteres für geschlossene Hotelentwürfe anbieten, die zugleich groß aufgemachte oder verspielte Interieurs und ein klar umrissenes und gediegenes Äußeres aufweisen sollen.

Der Architekt kann kapitulieren und sich dem Team der Dekorateure eingliedern. Was dabei herauskommt, zeigt etwa das Century Plaza Hotel in Los Angeles von Yamasaki (Abb. 5 und 6), ein gut geplantes Gebäude von angenehmen, wenngleich überwältigenden inneren Proportionen, das unter einem Übermaß an aufdringlicher Dekoration leidet. Yamasaki sucht »Entzücken, gelassene Lebensfreude und Überraschungen«. Er mag seinem Ziel nahekommen mit seiner »musikerfüllten vertieften Plaza«, aber schwerlich mit seinem »Dekor des Übergangs« – »einer harmonischen Mischung der besten traditionellen und neuzeitlichen Entwürfe«, überladen mit tausend Kronleuchtern und unzähligen handgearbeiteten Kombinationen von Textilien, Stein, Holz, Leder, Metall und keramischen Strukturen. Dem Gast wird vielleicht der »bedeutende Eingang« schmeicheln, geschaffen für die »bedeutende Person«, die er darstellt;

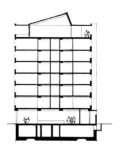

es mag ihm wohltun, »auf dem Weg zum Empfang von einer intimeren Atmosphäre umschlossen zu werden«; er mag es genießen, »ganz und gar von Aufmerksamkeit umgeben zu sein«, von der »totalen Ambiance, aufgebaut auf einer Philosophie, die ganz auf den Gast gerichtet ist«, aber man darf bezweifeln, ob ein so überladenes dekoratives Ganzes eine gültige Antwort sein kann auf das ästhetische Verlangen des reisenden Publikums von heute.

Der Architekt kann dem Raumgestalter einen Teil seiner Domäne überlassen und doch die wesentlichen Akzente im Griff behalten: den Fluß der Volumen, starke oder fein-gegliederte Rhythmen, die farbliche Komposition im Großen, die Sequenzen der Lichtwerte, die Aussichten und das Gefüge der offenen und geschlossenen Räume. Wenn er auf packende, brutalistische Wirkungen, auf gesuchte Formen verzichtet, wenn er seine Tönungen gedämpft oder neutral hält, kann er gut recht den Raumgestalter dahinbringen, aufdringliche Akzente in permanentem Material wegzulassen und statt dessen seinen Einfällen in den Farben, Strukturen und Mustern der Stoffe und Teppiche freien Lauf zu lassen, in Dingen, die auswechselbar sind und allein durch den Umstand ihrer Ersetzbarkeit in einem architektonischen Rahmen weniger verwirrend ins Auge fallen.

Gelegentlich haben Architekten eine schöpferische Phantasie gezeigt, mit der sie an Frische und Übermut ihren Kollegen aus dem Dekorationsfach in nichts nachstanden. Ralph Erskine strich sein Holzgebäude in Borgafjäll in leicht dissonierenden Primärfarben an, um wie eine Lappentracht intensive Farbflächen in die fast farblose Winterlandschaft zu setzen und das Hotel herauszubringen als das, was es ist – ein hölzernes Spielzeug. Gio Ponti machte aus seinem Hotel Parco dei Principi in Sorrent (Abb. 7 und 8) eine Apotheose der keramischen Künste von Salerno, eine Fülle von Mustern in lichtem und tiefem Blau auf Wänden und Böden, ein Echo des Meeres, das unten, hundert Meter tiefer, die Klippen auswäscht.

So wie Architekten es ihrem Gegenpart an Extravaganz gleichtun können, so sind Teams von Raumgestaltern durchaus fähig, architektonische Interieurs zu schaffen, die wohltuend nüchtern oder anspruchsvoll wirken. Ein Beispiel bietet das Golden Door Restaurant im Kennedy Airport in New York (Abb. 9 und 10), gestaltet von der Knoll Planning Unit und der Entwurfsabteilung der Brass Rail-Restaurantgruppe. Der riesige Raum von fast 2000 qm ist in acht Sektionen aufgeteilt, jede von ihnen hat etwa 40 Plätze und wird definiert durch lange Sitzsofas und Pflanzentröge. In einer ruhigen Umgebung neutraler Tönungen (Decke gebrochen weiß, Bezüge in beige, weich getönte Tweedteppiche) werden die Sektionen durch große Deckenkassetten mit Leuchtvouten und durch Kennfarben in Rot, Blau und Beige akzentuiert.

Der warme Effekt von diffuser Allgemeinbeleuchtung aus eingelassenen Deckenleuchten und Lichtvouten kann durch stufenweise schaltbare Widerstände in jeder Sektion variiert werden.

Dämmerige Beleuchtung, Kennzeichen vieler Restaurants in Amerika, könnte von den Entwerfern häufiger dazu benutzt werden, die Aufmerksamkeit von überdekorierten Wänden und überladenem Wandschmuck abzuziehen und das Interesse auf die Tischgedecke, Blumen und Pflanzen zu lenken oder auf die Zubereitung von Spezialgerichten auf den Anrichten der Kellner.

Das Beispiel der drei Intercontinental Hotels in Irland (Seite 98–107) beweist, daß Raumgestalter, denen ein Flair für intime Atmosphäre und den Reiz einfacher Materialien – Holz, Leinen, Tweeds, Kalkstein – zu eigen ist, auch in einem architektonischen Rahmen voller Disziplin und Zurückhaltung hervorragende Ergebnisse erzielen können.

Wo eine solche ideale Zusammenarbeit nicht zu erreichen ist, können Architekten zu strukturellen Formungen auf der Außenseite und im Innern ihres Gebäudes greifen, um durch starke Texturen eine allzu schwungvolle Dekoration zu dämpfen. Die bauliche Struktur als primäres Entwurfselement ist von Edward Killingsworth sehr erfolgreich an seinem Kahala Hilton (Seite 196) angewandt worden und in noch höherem Grad von Skidmore, Owings & Merrill bei ihrem Mauna Kea Beach Hotel (Seite 203), wo das bauliche Gefüge selbst zum führenden dekorativen und raumbildenden Element wird.

Die Rolle des Architekten bei der Gestaltung von Hotels – keine ganz kleine Rolle selbst unter heutigen Verhältnissen –, dürfte in der Zukunft an Bedeutung zunehmen. Mit der Ausbreitung des Booms auf mittelgroße Städte werden mehr und mehr Aufträge an Architekten von regionalem Ruf gehen, und die Aufgabe, ein Hotel einfühlsam in das Bild einer Stadt oder Landschaft einzugliedern, der Wunsch, einen regionalen Charakter anklingen zu lassen und ungezwungene Interieurs zu schaffen, und schließlich das Fehlen von verbindlichen Standardtypen, werden den Weg für eine echte architektonische Aussage ebnen.

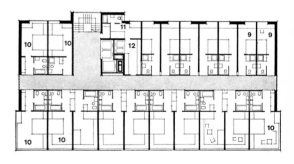

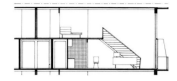

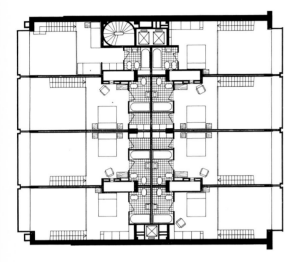

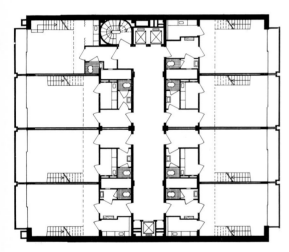

Hoteltypen

Eine Klassifizierung der gegenwärtigen Hoteltypen ist schwer zu geben, da der einzige klar definierte Typ das internationale Luxushotel ist, das durchweg mit dem Namen Hilton oder Intercontinental assoziiert wird. Außerhalb dieses Typs, den man heute selbst an so entlegenen Plätzen wie Kabul, Katmandu und Peshawar findet, werden die Kategorien problematisch, da die Faktoren Funktion, Größe und Einfügung, Kosten und Bauvorschriften die Projekte wesentlich mitformen. Dieses Buch gibt ein Abbild der vielfach differenzierten Hoteltypen und Entwurfsideen, darunter auch einige Projekte, die trotz aller Versuche überhaupt nicht zu klassifizieren waren.

Die internationalen Luxushotels sind gewöhnlich Geschäfts- und Touristenhotels von einer gewissen Größe (500 bis 1200 Zimmer). In den letzten Jahren wurde die Zahl der Räume in einzelnen Fällen gesteigert, bis zu 2150 Zimmern für das New York Hilton, oder auf ein Minimum von 275 Zimmern reduziert, wie bei den Hilton-Hotels in Amsterdam (Seite 42) und Rotterdam, die trotz ihrer mäßigen Größe vollgültige Weltstadthotels sind. Viele internationale Hotels haben heute eine kompakte Größe von 300 bis 400 Räumen. Daneben entwickelten die Hiltongruppe und ihre internationale Konkurrenz ein kleineres Luxushotel, das man oft in Feriengebieten findet und das zwischen 150 und 300 Gastzimmer umfaßt, mit einer unteren Grenze von etwa 100 Gasträumen (Barbados). Die Hilton Inns (Seite 119) – eine Bezeichnung, die man dem geläufigeren Begriff Motor-Hotel vorzieht – haben 150 bis 300 Gastzimmer, während Flughafenhotels (Paris-Orly und Quebec) bei einer Kapazität von 275 Räumen liegen.

Das Luxushotel amerikanischer Prägung, das einen so starken Einfluß auf alle anderen Hoteltypen der Welt ausgeübt hat, zeigt kleine Apartments (der Ausdruck Apartment für ein Hotelzimmer mit Vorraum und Bad wird in diesem Buch durchgehend gebraucht) und große öffentliche Räume: die Gästeapartments mit sparsamen Akzenten kostbarer Materialien, dagegen um so reicher ausgestattete Interieurs in den Hallen, Bars und Restaurants. Dahinter steht die gesunde Theorie, daß jeder kostspielige Akzent in den Gastzimmern Hunderte von Malen wiederholt werden muß, während ein aufwendiger Effekt in der Halle nur einmal vorkommt.

Sehr wenige neue Projekte würden sich als Luxushotel qualifizieren, wollte man für die Raumgröße (einschließlich Badezimmer) den Maßstab des Handbuches »Building, Planning and Design Standards« von Harold Sleeper anlegen:

Minimum 21 qm; Tiefe 5,50 m; Breite 3,80 m
Durchschnitt 26 qm; Tiefe 6,55 m; Breite 4,05 m
Luxusklasse 32 qm; Tiefe 7,15 m; Breite 4,75 m

Der Plan eines Standard-Apartments (Abb. 11–13) zeigt gewöhnlich einen Wandschrank im rechten Winkel zum Hotelflur und eine kurze Badewanne (manchmal weniger als 1,50 m) parallel zum Korridor und zum Gebäude. Mit dieser Anordnung kommt man zu einer minimalen Breite je Apartment, und da jede räumliche Einsparung sich vielfach multipliziert, kann man die größtmögliche Anzahl von Zimmereinheiten in der begrenzten Gesamtlänge des Gebäudes unterbringen.

Wo die Breite des Standard-Apartments keine entscheidende Rolle spielt, lassen sich interessante Lösungen suchen, wie im Hotel de France in Conakry (Abb. 14) und einer Reihe anderer Projekte, die in diesem Band gezeigt sind. Der Wunsch des Gastes, ein Zimmer zu haben, das ein »pied-à-terre« ist statt eines bloßen Schlafraums, der Wunsch nach einer gewissen Trennung von Schlaf-

und Wohnbereich, hat manche Architekten dahin gebracht, die Badezimmer umzulegen (Abb. 16) oder einen abgewinkelten Sitzplatz am Fenster zu schaffen (Abb. 15), der räumlich mehr als bescheiden ist, aber eine weite Sicht öffnet. Die ursprünglichen Pläne für das Century Plaza Hotel von Minoru Yamasaki zeigten für die Standardräume (Abb. 17 und 18) eine Reihe ungewöhnlicher Versionen, von der kleinen zur kleinen mittleren Einheit und von der großen mittleren zur großen Einheit. Die Badezimmer lagen in den Außenfronten und konnten dort die Straßengeräusche und die Belastung der Klimaanlage herabmindern. Die Räume waren abgeteilt durch Schrankwände ohne verbindende Zwischentüren, und durch schalldichte Wandelemente aus Garderobenschrank, Fernsehgerät und Kommodenteilen. Die Gäste sollten nicht nur die Wahl haben zwischen französischen Betten, Doppelbetten oder Tagescouchen, sondern auch zwischen Sitzgruppen aus Sofas oder nur aus Sesseln. Bei der endgültigen Planung fiel jedoch die Entscheidung zugunsten einer konventionellen Lösung.

Der Gesamtplan der Gästeflügel kann geradläufig oder versetzt sein, in L-, T- oder Y-Form (Abb. 19 und 20), ein geschlossenes Geviert (Seite 88) oder eine in einfachem (Abb. 21) oder doppeltem Bogen (Abb. 22) geschwungene Form. Im wesentlichen folgt jedoch jedes internationale Luxushotel einer gleichartigen Funktionsformel. Da ist der vielgeschossige Baukörper mit den Gästezimmern, da sind die öffentlichen Räume (mit den Apartments durch einen vertikalen Schacht verbunden), und da ist ein dritter Sektor, die Serviceräume, streng getrennt von den Sektionen der Gästezimmer und öffentlichen Räume, aber so eingewoben, daß das Bedienungspersonal jeden Raum in den Gästebereichen betreten kann, nur aus einer anderen Richtung. Die vollkommene Bedienung bleibt unsichtbar, doch allgegenwärtig, ganz nach der Art eines modernen Installationssystems. Große Bereiche der Serviceanlagen, besonders die Vorbereitungs- und

34. Hotel Résidence, Bruxelles. Section and floor plans of duplex apartments with upper sleeping level and main living level. Architect: René Stapels.
35. Hotel Résidence, Bruxelles. Exterior elevation with duplex apartments. Architect: René Stapels.

34. Hotel Résidence, Brüssel. Schnitt und Grundrisse von Galeriegeschoß (Schlafbereich) und Hauptgeschoß (Wohnbereich) der Maisonette-Apartments. Architekt: René Stapels.
35. Hotel Residence, Brüssel. Fassadenansicht mit den zweigeschossigen Apartments. Architekt: René Stapels.

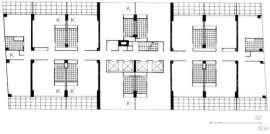

36, 37. Hotel Executive House, Chicago. Exterior view and typical floor plan. K = kitchen. Architects: Milton M. Schwartz & Associates.

36, 37. Hotel Executive House, Chicago. Ansicht und Grundriß eines Normalgeschosses. K = Küche. Architekt: Milton M. Schwartz & Associates.

Kochgruppen im Küchentrakt, haben industriellen Charakter; sie produzieren Halbfertig- und Fertigfabrikate, die bis zur letzten Zutat in der Hauptverwaltung, Tausende von Meilen entfernt, getestet und kalkuliert sind.

Das große Volumen der öffentlichen Räume und der Servicebereiche in Bodennähe macht in jedem Fall eine bedeutende Nutzfläche im unteren Teil nötig, die ein Mehrfaches der Tiefe des Gast-Hochhauses einnimmt. Die breite Basis, häufig der »Pfannkuchen« genannt, hat den Breitfußtyp des Hotels entstehen lassen, mit den besonderen Problemen der Form, die ihm innewohnen (Abb. 23). Der Bettentrakt, eine Reihung gleicher oder ähnlicher Räume, der normalerweise ein Vielfaches der Pflegeeinheit von 15 Räumen je Zimmermädchen enthält, kann leicht als sauber geschnittener Kubus oder als schmaler Turm gestaltet werden (Abb. 24). (Experimente wie das Tamanaco in Caracas mit seinen herabgestuften Giebelenden haben sich als funktionelle Fehllösungen erwiesen, da die Arbeit der Zimmermädchen in verschiedenen Geschossen nicht einwandfrei zu koordinieren ist.)

Das formale Problem stellt sich, wo das Hochhaus auf den flachen Unterbau trifft, wo ein Wald von Stützen die öffentlichen Räume und die Servicebereiche durchdringt. Lösungen dieses Problems gibt es viele, und dieses Buch zeigt eine ganze Reihe davon. Der Hochhaustrakt kann neben die Basis gestellt werden, statt sich auf die Basis zu setzen (Seite 98); die Vielzahl der Stützlasten von den oberen Geschossen kann von Längsträgern aufgenommen werden, die über die volle Höhe eines Zwischengeschosses mit technischen Anlagen gehen (die

übliche Lösung, beispielsweise beim Tel Aviv Hilton, Seite 20); die Auffangkonstruktion kann ein flaches Polster unter dem Hochhaus bilden und sich in die Querwände darüber erstrecken (Cavalieri Hilton in Rom, Seite 62). Die Zahl der Stützen im Hochhaus kann durch konstruktive Maßnahmen stark vermindert werden (Royal Hotel, Kopenhagen, Seite 46; Denver Hilton, Seite 36). In vielen Fällen wird es möglich sein, die Hauptstützen und ihren gleichförmigen Rhythmus recht gut mit der offeneren Anordnung der allgemeinen Publikumsräume in Einklang zu bringen und die Basisgeschosse frei zu entwickeln, wie es ein Hotelentwurf für Teheran von Foroughi, Zafar, Sadegh und Ghiai zeigt (Abb. 25). Das größte unter den in letzter Zeit gebauten Hotels, das New York Hilton, leidet an einem Zuviel an Stützen, die in die Basisgeschosse durchgehen (Abb. 26). Die Haupthalle wird von der Schmalseite her betreten und von schweren Stützen verstellt; sie ist leicht blockiert, wenn größere Gruppen eintreffen, und das Problem gewinnt noch an Gewicht, weil keine anschließenden Loungeräume, sondern nur Innenpromenaden vorhanden sind. (Die Ausdrücke Lobby und Lounge als Bezeichnung der Eingangshalle (Lobby) und der ruhig gelegenen Halle für den Aufenthalt (Lounge) sind übrigens kaum zu übersetzen und hier durchweg in der englischen Form gebraucht). Das ständige Hin und Her in dieser Lobby zwischen Schaltern und Läden, Bars und Spezialitätenrestaurants ist vielleicht abgestimmt auf das pausenlose Getriebe von New York City, doch wird mancher Reisende die deutliche Gliederung in Lobby- und Loungeräume vermissen, die er sonst in internationalen Hotels findet.

Unter den kleineren Problemen, die der Architekt beim Entwurf eines Hotels zu lösen hat, haben die endlosen Flure, zweihüftig angebaut und schlecht beleuchtet, oft Phantasie und Geschick der Entwerfer beschäftigt. Hotelflure können bogenförmig sein, um das Gefühl übertriebener Länge zu vermeiden (Abb. 21), oder in Sektionen unterteilt, die durch Türnischen, abgehängte Deckenflächen und Lichteffekte betont sind (Abb. 27). Ein System rechtwinkliger Räume in sägeförmiger Anordnung kann Flurräume schaffen, die in ihren ausgewinkelten Nischen im Gebäudeinneren den gezahnten Rhythmus der Fassaden widerspiegeln (Abb. 28).

Ein kleines Übel, das viel Unordnung bringt, bilden die Schuhe, die abends auf den Flur gestellt werden. Für Projekte der letzten Jahre haben die Architekten SchuhSafes in den Wandschränken entwickelt, die der Hausdiener vom Flur her öffnen kann. Transport und Unterbringung des Gepäcks, ein anderer unschöner Anblick von gewichtigerer Proportion, werden in den USA und in Europa verschieden gehandhabt. Während große und kleine Koffer in den meisten Hotels Amerikas durch die Lobby gehen (amerikanische Gäste sehen gern, wo ihre Koffer bleiben) und in den Räumen sichtbar sind, so daß man leicht an sie herankommt, ist die Tendenz in Europa eher, alles Gepäck getrennt durch einen Nebeneingang und über die Personalaufzüge zu transportieren, und die größeren Stücke im Garderobenteil des Apartments unterzubringen. In den typischen Hotelapartments nach amerikanischem Standard tendiert der Vorraum für Garderobe und Gepäck zu knapper Anlage, da viele Gäste im Flugzeug mit wenigen Koffern reisen. Große neue Hotels in Europa, wie das Cavalieri Hilton (Seite 62), haben geräumige Vorzimmer für jedes Apartment, die sich nachts durch schalldichte Innentüren schließen lassen. Verbindungstüren von Raum zu Raum sind in der ganzen Welt überreichlich zu finden. Ihr Vorteil einer größeren Flexibilität im Zusammenstellen von Suiten wird in den Augen erfahrener Reisender vielfach nur von theoretischem Wert sein. Ihre Nachteile, ein Verlust an Schrank-

38, 39. Hotel Astor, Chicago. Exterior view and typical floor plan. Architects: Bertrand Goldberg & Associates.

38, 39. Hotel Astor, Chicago, Ill. Ansicht und Grundriß eines Normalgeschosses. Architekt: Bertrand Goldberg & Associates.

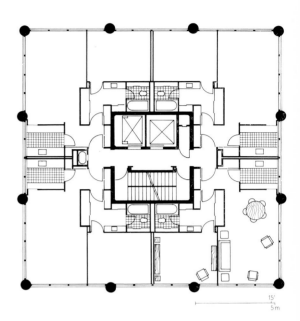

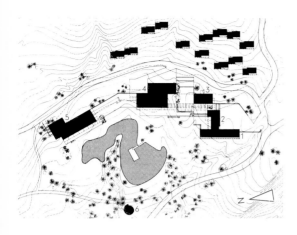

40. Holiday village Maierhöfen-Stockach. Site plan. Architects: Herbert Weisskamp (Neue Heimat International) and Richard Heil. Key: 1 Apartment block, 2 Shops, 3 Administration, 4 Restaurant, 5 Indoor Swimming pool, 6 Chapel.

40. Feriendorf Maierhöfen-Stockach. Lageplan. Architekten: Herbert Weisskamp (Neue Heimat International) und Richard Heil. Legende: 1 Apartmentblock, 2 Ladentrakt, 3 Verwaltung, 4 Restaurant, 5 Schwimmhalle, 6 Kapelle.

raum, ein Mangel an Abgeschlossenheit oder ganz einfach Störungen durch Geräuschübertragung zeigen sich zu oft. Die große Zahl der Suiten, die in den obersten Geschossen der meisten Großprojekte zu finden sind (Abb. 23), dürften eigentlich einen Gutteil der Verbindungstüren überflüssig machen.
Hingegen sollte es die erste Sorge eines Hotelentwerfers sein, in dem beschränkten Rahmen eines modernen Hotelapartments alle jene Tätigkeiten einzuplanen, die man nicht den weiten öffentlichen Räumen zuteilen kann – Lesen, Schreiben, sich vertraulich unterhalten, Musik hören und entspannen (Abb. 29). Dahingegangen sind die Leseräume, Schreibsalons, Spielzimmer, dahingegangen sind die Konversationsräume und die intimen Salons der alten Palasthotels à la Ritz, die sorgfältig in Größe und Offenheit gestaffelt waren – und all das ist ersetzt durch eine große Lounge für alle Zwecke, zugeschnitten auf unsere eher amorphe Gesellschaft, auf unser Verlangen nach Geselligkeit. Dann und wann bieten sie die großen inneren Proportionen, von denen Architekten träumen.
Die Ritztradition, ein Stück europäischen Erbes, lebt weiter in Häusern wie dem Hotel de Mar in Palma (Abb. 30), das eine ansprechende Reihe kleiner und großer Salons bietet, oder in Mexico, wo das Hotel María Isabel große Flächen seinen Empfangs- und Partyräumen aller Größen gewidmet hat, in Verbindung mit den zahlreichen Suiten, die den Gedanken an eine Verwandtschaft mit nordamerikanischen Planungen aufkommen lassen. Als Nebenbemerkung sollte gesagt werden, daß drei der führenden Hotels in der Welt von heute auf César Ritz zurückgehen oder seinen Namen tragen: das alte Ritz an der Place Vendôme in Paris, das neue Ritz in Lissabon, berühmt für seinen Service, seine Antiquitäten und handgearbeitete Stilmöbel, und das Grand Hotel in Rom, von Ritz 1880 gebaut, heute umgestaltet, ein Treffpunkt für die italienische Aristokratie und Filmwelt.
Nicht wenige alte Palasthotels haben eine bemerkenswerte Fähigkeit zu überleben gezeigt. Ein Grand Hotel

oder Palasthotel zu renovieren, kann eine lohnende Aufgabe sein. Wenngleich steigende Löhne, die Notwendigkeit moderner technischer Anlagen und Fließbandmethoden manches alte Hotel funktionell untragbar gemacht haben – selbst das Mount Lavinia Hotel in Colombo, Ceylon, berühmt aus dem Film »Die Brücke am Kwai«, muß abgerissen und durch ein neues ersetzt werden –, kann eine Renovierung die großflächigen Apartments und die weitläufigen Wintergärten und Salons eines solchen Hauses in sehr komfortable Räume verwandeln. Das Grand Hotel in Rom, das gerade erwähnt wurde, dürfte die Liste erfolgreich umgestalteter Hotels anführen. Von den beiden überreich dekorierten Treppenhäusern blieb eines in seiner ursprünglichen Pracht erhalten, während das andere geopfert wurde, um Platz für drei Fahrstühle und zwei zusätzliche Apartments mit Bad in jedem Geschoß zu schaffen. Dieses Buch enthält zwei Beispiele für Renovierung und Erweiterung; das eine, in einem deutschen Kurpark gelegen, brauchte größere und besser gestaltete öffentliche Räume (Seite 96), das andere, ein weltberühmtes Ferienhotel am Montblanc, mußte erweitert und von innen heraus neu erbaut werden (Seite 94).
Wenn wir die Sphäre der internationalen Luxushotels verlassen, die »Tempel eines lautlosen Luxus« (ein Hotelprospekt) die »Kathedralen des Tourismus« (Enzensberger), mit ihrer Betonung auf Gruppengeschäft, Großtagungen und Kostenkontrolltechnik, Häuser, die Städte in der Stadt darstellen, so finden wir eine fast verwirrende Fülle von Hoteltypen. Auf der unteren Sprosse der sozialen Skala gibt es extrem preiswerte Versuchsprojekte wie die Hotels Europa und Victoria auf der holländischen Insel Terschelling, in denen die Gäste eigene Bettwäsche mitbringen, selbst ihre Betten machen und sich bei den Mahlzeiten selbst bedienen. Es wurde schon gesagt, daß kleinere und mittelgroße Hotels noch ein großes Potential an architektonischer Aussage und an Architektenaufträgen haben. Hotels wie das Stanley in Athen (Abb. 31), ganz von Knoll International eingerichtet, und das Grand Hotel de la Croisette in Cannes (Seite 78), das eine zeitgemäße Gestaltung in die reservierten Kreise der französischen Hotelbranche brachte, beweisen, daß kompromißlose Hotels erfolgreich gebaut und betrieben werden können. Kleine Hotels wie das für Machu Picchu von den Architekten Schweikher und Elting geplante Haus (Abb. 32), ein flacher Block in einer Umgebung hochragender Gipfel, der in den Felsenhang eingetieft und aus örtlich gewonnenem Stein gebaut werden soll – oder das Astoria-Hotel in Luzern (Abb. 33) von Theo Hotz, das Empfang und Restaurant im obersten Stock hat und die Küche im Keller, zeigen die ganze Breite schöpferischer Versuche im Ästhetischen wie im Funktionellen.
Wohnhotels für Passanten und für häufig kommende Gäste, die langfristig mieten wollen, sind wieder in den Vordergrund getreten. Das interessanteste in architektonischer Hinsicht ist das Hotel Résidence in Brüssel (Abb. 34 und 35), eine Arbeit des Architekten René Stapels, das 40 Maisonette-Wohnungen und in den obersten Geschossen fünf größere Wohnungen bietet, auch sie zum Teil über zwei Ebenen angelegt. Zwei neuere Hotelprojekte in Chicago haben ähnliche Apartments mit Kleinküchen, jedoch eingeschossig entwickelt. Executive House (Abb. 36 und 37), das erste größere Hotel, das in 28 Jahren in Chicago errichtet wurde, enthält 450 Studio-Apartments und Ecksuiten; alle öffnen sich auf breite Balkons, die in die Fassade gesetzt sind. Da jede Einheit ihre eigene außenliegende Küche hat, konnte das 7-Millionen-Dollar-Hotel zu günstigen Bedingungen als Apartmenthaus finanziert werden. (Die Finanziers haben anscheinend nicht die Wirtschaftskrise der dreißiger Jahre mit ihren Auswirkungen auf die Hotelbranche vergessen.) Etwa

80 Prozent der Räume werden jedoch an Passanten vermietet. Das Hotel Astor (Abb. 38 und 39) von Bertrand Goldberg hat ausschließlich große Ecksuiten, 96 an der Zahl, vier je Geschoß, das Ganze auf Betonstützen von 5 Geschossen Höhe gestellt, verbunden mit einem zweigeschossigen Unterbau, in dem sich eine Bar befindet und ein Restaurant mit 200 Plätzen, das von Maxims in Paris betrieben wird. Ein Eislaufplatz wurde auf das Dach gelegt, 30 Geschosse über dem Boden.

Motor-Hotels

von heute unterscheiden sich sehr wesentlich von den Motels, die in der Nachkriegszeit im Zuge der rapiden Zunahme des Automobilverkehrs überall in den Vereinigten Staaten entstanden. Auch für sie gilt, daß die Verschiedenheit der Projekte sehr groß ist und daß der Trend eindeutig über eine Handvoll anerkannter Formeln hinausgeht. Es gibt viele gültige Ideen, ob es sich um die Ausformung eines gut eingespielten persönlichen Idioms handelt – wie bei Richard Neutras kalifornischen Motor-Hotels (Seite 126–133) oder bei Aris Konstantinidis' Xenia-Projekten in Griechenland (Seite 144–153) – oder um einen fesselnd neuartigen Wurf für eine besondere Situation wie bei Lundys Motel in Florida (Seite 116). Der Ausdruck Motel ist heute selten zu hören, dafür gibt es Motor-Inns, Motor-Lodges und Motor-Hotels in großer

41. Hotel La Cardinale, Baix (Ardèche). Garden Court.
42. Hotel Byblos, Saint Tropez. Overall view of hotel village.

41. Hotel La Cardinale, Baix (Ardèche). Gartenhof.
42. Hotel Byblos, Saint Tropez. Gesamtansicht des Hoteldorfes.

Zahl. Die Vereinigten Staaten haben 74 000 Hotels und Motels mit mehr als 10 Gastzimmern. Von dieser Gesamtzahl sind 27000 Hotels und 47000 Motels, und beide Gruppen teilen sich die gesamte Bettenkapazität etwa zur Hälfte. Im Jahre 1965 wurden in USA 130000 neue Moteleinheiten fertiggestellt, und Motels zeigen eine wachsende Tendenz, als Gasthäuser und Erholungszentren in der mageren Umgebung der Vorstädte zu fungieren. Der Übergang zwischen Motels, Motor-Hotels und Hotels ist dabei immer fließender geworden. Die Parkplätze liegen in Motelanlagen längst nicht mehr automatisch vor den Eingangstüren, doch wird die Grundregel eingehalten, daß der Gast direkt zu seinem Wagen gelangen kann, ohne formelle öffentliche Räume durchqueren zu müssen. Motor-Hotels können sogar als Hochhäuser gebaut werden: Das größte und wahrscheinlich teuerste Hotel in Dublin, das Intercontinental (Seite 98), ist im Grunde ein Motor-Hotel mit achtgeschossigem Bettenhaus, und San Franciscos größten Hotelbau, das Hilton (Seite 112), hat man das Motor-Pool-Hilton genannt. Motels und Motor-Inns haben manche Hotelfunktion übernommen; sie schließen häufig Cocktailbars, Grillrestaurants, Tagungsräume und großangelegte Gartenflächen mit ein. Motor-Hotels respektieren zwar das Prinzip des leichten Zugangs zum Wagen, bieten jedoch gewöhnlich größere, vornehmer gehaltene Räumlichkeiten (manche darunter groß genug für Tagungen von einiger Bedeutung), mehr Service und – mehr Gelegenheiten, Trinkgelder zu geben. Sie werden meist kompakt geplant und tendieren zu mehrgeschossiger Anlage. Eine Kette ausgezeichneter Motor-Hotels wird derzeit von der Esso gebaut (Seite 108) in der Absicht, ihren Markennamen durch gepflegte Unterkünfte und Restaurantbetriebe zu propagieren. Es ist fesselnd, mit einem Seitenblick festzustellen, daß eine Erdölgesellschaft, die an das Rockefellerimperium angeschlossen ist, durch die Förderung des Autoreiseverkehrs in etwa der gleichen Weise einen vermehrten Bedarf an Benzin und Wagenpflege erzeugen will wie einst der Gründer dieses Imperiums, der einen zusätzlichen Bedarf an Petroleum überhaupt erst schuf, indem er billige Lampen in China vertrieb.

Das Pavillonhotel, seit langem im südlichen Frankreich als »Hôtel pavillonaire« oder in den Tropen als Bungalowhotel bekannt, ist in mancher Hinsicht ein Zweig der Gruppe Motor-Hotels. Ein Projekt dieses Typs, mit einer Mehrheit von kleinen eingeschossigen Häusern vom Autor im Gebiet des Var an der französischen Riviera gebaut (Seite 134), zeigt die wesentlichen Züge: Der ganze Komplex von 4 Hektar Fläche ist entschieden auf die öffentlichen Räume in einem renovierten Schloß ausgerichtet, trotz der Tatsache, daß jede Einheit eine voll eingerichtete Küche und mehr als ausreichenden Wohnraum hat. In einem Bungalowhotel sollte die für den einzelnen Gast faßbare Wohndichte niedrig gehalten werden. In Sainte Maxime wurde jedes Gefälle, jede Falte und jede Schwelle des Geländes ausgenutzt, um Gruppen von Wagen, Häusern und Menschen aus dem Blickfeld anderer Gästegruppen zu nehmen, die vielleicht wenige Schritte weiter daheim sind. Das Projekt Les Tourelles, eines der wenigen in der Region, die in echt neuzeitlichem Geiste ausgeführt sind, wurde nicht von einer Hotelgesellschaft finanziert, sondern von der deutschen Industriegewerkschaft Bau-Steine-Erden für ihre Mitglieder gebaut. Ähnliche Projekte werden vom gleichen Auftraggeber an mehreren Plätzen in Deutschland und Österreich realisiert. Die Pläne für einen Bungalowkomplex, der bei Isny im Allgäu erstellt wird (Abb. 40), bringen eine vergrößerte Version des Sainte-Maxime-Projekts: 150 kleine, völlig ausgestattete Häuser in loser Gruppierung und dazu ein »Dorfzentrum« mit Bücherei, Restaurant, Läden, Teich und Schwimmhalle, das attraktiv genug gestaltet ist, in einer »Gemeinde« als Kern zu wirken, die durch berufliche und gewerkschaftliche Bande zusammengehört. Die Anlage wird teilweise im Self-Service für die Häuser betrieben, mit Reinigung durch das Personal in regelmäßigen Abständen, während die Mahlzeiten im Restaurant von Kellnerinnen oder mit Selbstbedienung serviert werden können. Bungalowhotels dieser Art sind ein Schritt abseits der erschreckenden Perspektiven des Massentourismus von morgen, der da propagiert wird mit der Idee von »Ferienstädten« und »Ferienfabriken« (»Usines de vacances« wie Royan im Gironde-Gebiet), die an Größe heutige Feriendörfer weit übertreffen.

Der Wettbewerb zwischen moderner Hotelarchitektur und alten Plätzen, den zahlreichen Schlössern, Villen, mittelalterlichen Gasthöfen und Dörfern, die zu Hotels umgestaltet sind und mit deren Charme die moderne Gestaltung rivalisiert, wird am stärksten in der Sphäre der kleineren Reise- und Ferienhotels spürbar. Der Reiz der »Relais de Campagne« (Abb. 41) in Frankreich (einer Kette zauberhafter Plätze, die sich seit dem Kriege über ganz Frankreich und die Welt verbreitet hat, ausgehend von »La Cardinale« im Bezirk Ardèche) und der deutschen »Hotels in Burgen und Schlössern« ist schwer auszustechen, doch sind gerade Ferienhotels oft ein Feld gewesen, auf dem begabte Architekten sich hervortun konnten. Der Beweis ist die Auswahl von Ferienhotels in diesem Band.

Ferienhotels

Es ist kein Zufall, daß viele neue Ferienhotels in Eindruck und Atmosphäre weniger gekünstelt erscheinen als die meisten der internationalen Hotels oder als die Monsterpaläste von Miami Beach. Vielleicht, daß der Feriengast der späten sechziger Jahre den Anspruch auf repräsentativen Dekor daheim läßt, daß er den Reiz baulicher Einfachheit, einer sicheren Einfügung in den landschaftlichen Rahmen mehr und mehr empfindet.

Die besten Beispiele zeigen eine rechtwinklig klare oder kristalline Architektur fast ohne Anklänge an regionale Formen, zeigen eine absolute Schonung (Hotel de Mar, Palma, Seite 190) oder behutsame Umgestaltung der landschaftlichen Substanz (Corte dei Butteri, Seite 154), eine harmonische Steigerung der Vegetation und Topographie (Hotel Hvide Hus, Seite 182, ein gebauter grüner Hang auf einem gewachsenen Hügel) oder eng verwobene Kompositionen aus Baukunst und Gartenkunst (Kahala Hilton, Seite 196, und Mauna Kea Beach Hotel, Seite 203). In manchen Fällen gibt das Schwimmbad mit seinen Badehütten und Pavillons die Gelegenheit, dekorativen Überschwang auszuspielen, ohne die architektonische Sphäre des Hauptbaues zu berühren oder zu durchdringen (Fort Royal, Seite 186).

Ferienhotels können sogar Gäste recht verschiedener Einkommensgruppen in einem Komplex zusammenbringen, wenn das Ferienerlebnis ganz auf den Strand (Hotel Lakolk, Seite 160) oder die Berge bezogen ist. In Skihotels zeigt sich mehr als anderswo der Drang zum geselligen Zusammenrücken (Hotel Prisank, Seite 140, und Borgafjäll, Abb. 1): Skifahrer bilden schnell eine Zunft. Für Hotels an der See und im Schnee können die Gasträume oft zu bloßen Schlafzellen werden. Luxushäuser am Meer dagegen, ob in Spanien (Hotel de Mar) oder in Hawaii (Kahala Hilton und Mauna Kea Beach) tendieren zu großzügiger räumlicher Anlage in den Apartments, wo Leute von Welt ihren privaten Rahmen jenseits des Getriebes großer Geselligkeit finden.

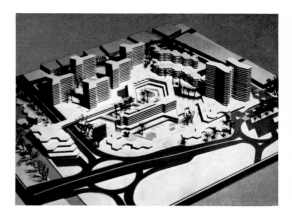

43. High street redevelopment project Kuala Lumpur. Architect: Herbert Weisskamp (Neue Heimat International).

43. Vorentwurf für das Sanierungsgebiet High Street, Kuala Lumpur. Architekt: Herbert Weisskamp (Neue Heimat International).

Ausblick

Das Thema Hotel als Bauaufgabe unserer Tage ist noch lange nicht zu Ende diskutiert. Das Primat der Funktionsabläufe und der Zwang zum Rationalisieren müßten eigentlich typisierend wirken, doch scheinen so viel freie Phantasie der Bauherren und der Architekten, so viel unternehmerische Initiative im Spiel zu sein, daß jeden Tag neue Kategorien, neue Größenordnungen und neue städtebauliche Zusammenhänge von sich reden machen. Während dieses Buch publiziert wird, empfängt in St. Tropez eine neue Karawanserei ihre Gäste: das Byblos-Hotel (Abb. 42), ein »Anti-Hotel« nach den Worten seines Besitzers, mit Räumen und Balkonen, die im Schatten von Olivenbäumen und Palmen eine Dorfatmosphäre um eine zweigeschossig angelegte Plaza-Terrasse schaffen. Zur gleichen Zeit entsteht in Moskau ein Hotel mit 6000 Betten, und eines der exklusivsten unter den modernen Ferienhotels, das Mauna Kea Beach Hotel (Seite 203), das mit dem astronomischen Aufwand von 100000 Dollars je Raum gebaut wurde, ist auf Jahre voraus gebucht. Während Hotels ein wesentlicher Faktor in Sanierungsprojekten von Kuala Lumpur (Abb. 43) bis zu San Franciscos Embarcadero Center werden (zu dem ein Hotel in Form einer Stufenpyramide mit einem 16geschossigen geschlossenen Gartenhof gehören wird), haben übrigens die beiden kolossalen städtebaulichen Unternehmungen unserer Zeit, Chandigarh und Brasilia, nur ungenügende Hotelunterkünfte.

In anderen Teilen der Welt geht der Hotelbau weiter im Zeitraffertempo vor sich. Die Architekten sollten auf der Suche nach klareren Lösungen, nach einer neuen Einheit von Architektur und Dekoration in architektonischem Rahmen, ein Faktum nicht übersehen: daß Hotelarchitektur dazu bestimmt ist, schnell erfaßt zu werden, wie eine Werbeanzeige für den gehobenen Anspruch. Wenn es wahr ist, daß die »Botschaft« einer Anzeige in vier Sekunden aufgenommen werden muß, dann sollten zwei Tage und zwei Nächte (die durchschnittliche Aufenthaltsdauer eines Gastes im Hotel) oder ein Diner von zwei Stunden genügen, einen bleibenden oder einen reizvoll flüchtigen Eindruck zu hinterlassen von einer Architektur, die abgestimmt ist auf unsere Zeit und unsere gesellschaftliche Struktur.

Hilton Hotel, Tel-Aviv

Architects: Y. Rechter, M. Zarhy; M. Peri, engineer

This luxury hotel was opened in 1965, and occupies an open site by the sea, in the center of Independence Park, which is gradually being turned into a green promenade along the shore. The architects did not wish to give the hotel any gardens or terrace areas of its own: the building and its terraces are therefore either oriented towards the sea, or enclosed and inward-turning. The site, a shallow mound overlooking the sandy beach, is skilfully molded. The garage, the parking area and delivery court are below ground level: activities centered on the swimming pool and sheltered snack bar terrace are concentrated in a sunken area opening to the sea, so that there can be no disturbance to the peace of the park. Built at the center of a vast belt of greenery, the hotel asserts itself by its massiveness and the strong regular modeling of its guest-room slab; this modeling is directly derived from the structure of the slab, which has its long axis at a right angle to its low base and to the beach. All rooms, therefore, have an equally good view of the sea, the park and the city: none are troubled by street noises or by the hot western sun. The fronts of the balconies are turned to face slantwise towards the sea: the saw-tooth façades emphasize the orientation towards the surf and beach.

The aesthetic problems of the junction of the tower to the podium are solved convincingly. The guest-room tower grows neatly and naturally from the massive base, which is elongated and has a straight roofline to complement the serrated surfaces of the tower. An essential element contributing to this happy solution is the intermediate floor under the guest-room tower; it houses a variety of plant, collects the loads of the tower and transmits them to a few piers on the lounge and restaurant floors. The longitudinal beams of this mechanical services floor are of reinforced concrete, heavy enough to have a sculptured character, and more than 4m deep.

The spatial arrangement takes the form of a long lobby, extended by a quiet bay adjoining the open, glazed patio, which also admits daylight to the intimate cocktail bar. The guest is naturally led towards the elevators. The large lounge is pleasantly secluded, and connects with the entrance via the shopping arcades. A spiral staircase leads down to further shops, the night club and the restaurants. The rooms for dining and entertaining are partly below ground level in the mound that covers most of the site; they are kept fairly dark, but have terraces facing the sea.

The snack bar to the northwest serves the characteristically rich Israeli breakfast from the buffet, and also serves the café-terrace. The swimming pool below, sunk further into the site but separated from the public beach, is surrounded by changing cabins on two sides; on the east there is a series of pool-side apartments.

The ballroom is raised above the swimming pool level, occupying part of the main floor of the podium. Access to it is through a large foyer from the end of the lobby, or from its own entrance on the street front. Wide doors open to the glazed foyer and the sea. Both hotel guests and ballroom visitors arrive and alight in a quiet area: cars at once drive away out of sight, descending a ramp to the sunken parking space and the underground garage. A large perforated slab with fountains and a reflecting sheet of water hides the ramp, turning the driveway into a cool quiet spot. The lofty guest-room tower has a convex end wall on the entrance side. It offers the minimum obstruction of the view towards the sea; the wall at the seaward end is concave. The free and sculptural treatment of its concrete work will give this building a formative influence in Israel, which is still in search of an architectural idiom of its own

Hilton-Hotel, Tel-Aviv

Architekten: Y. Rechter, M. Zarhy; M. Peri, Ingenieur

Das jüngste unter den Luxushotels von Tel-Aviv wurde 1965 eröffnet. Es liegt völlig frei am Meer inmitten des Independence Park. Die Architekten verzichteten darauf, dem Hotel eigene Gärten oder ausgreifende Terrassen zu geben; ihr Bau ist im wesentlichen nach innen und zum Meer hin orientiert. Das Gelände, eine flache Schwelle über dem Sandstrand, wurde geschickt modelliert: Tiefgarage, Parkplatz und Lieferhof sind in das Terrain eingearbeitet; das Leben und Treiben um Schwimmbad und Caféterrasse spielt sich in einer tiefgezogenen Senke zum Meer ab.

Die plastisch gegliederten Betonmassen sind aus der Konstruktion und dem architektonischen Rhythmus geformt. Die skulpturale Form geht eng mit der Funktion des Bettenhauses zusammen, das quer zum Flachtrakt und zum Ufer steht. Alle Räume haben gleich gute Sicht auf Meer, Park und Stadt. Die Balkone wurden schräg zur See orientiert, der Sägeschnitt der Fronten betont die Beziehung zu Sand und Wellen.

Die formalen Probleme, die sich aus der Verbindung des Hochhaustraktes mit der Breitfußanlage ergeben, sind überzeugend gelöst. Das Bettenhaus wächst klar und zwanglos aus der massiven Basis, die flachgestreckt mit völlig glatter Dachlinie die plastische Bewegung des Hochhauskörpers unterstreicht. Zu der glücklichen Lösung trägt wesentlich ein Zwischengeschoß unter dem Bettenhaus bei, das die Vielzahl der technischen Anlagen aufnimmt, die Stützenlasten des Hochhausblocks sammelt und auf ganz wenige Pfeiler der Empfangs- und Restaurantgeschosse überträgt. Die Längsträger in diesem Geschoß sind in massigem Stahlbeton vier Meter hoch dimensioniert und skulpturell durchgeformt.

Die räumliche Organisation entwickelt sich zwanglos von der gestreckten Eingangshalle aus. Sie wird visuell erweitert durch eine ruhige Bucht am offenen, verglasten Patio, der auch der intimen kleinen Bar Licht gibt. Die groß zugeschnittene Lounge liegt wohltuend abgesondert, mit dem Eingang übereck durch die Ladengruppe verbunden. Eine Wendeltreppe führt nach unten zu weiteren Läden, zum Night-Club und zu den Restaurants. Die Speise- und Gesellschaftsräume liegen in der Geländeschwelle, sind dunkel gehalten, haben aber ihre Terrasse zum Meer.

Die Snackbar nach Nordwesten serviert das reichhaltige israelische Frühstück vom Buffet und bedient die Caféterrasse. Das Schwimmbad darunter, tiefer in das Gelände eingelassen, doch getrennt vom öffentlichen Strand, ist an zwei Seiten von Kabinen umgeben, am Ostrand ist eine Reihe von Gäste-Apartments untergebracht. Der Ballsaal liegt erhöht über dem Schwimmbad, im oberen Hauptgeschoß des Flachtraktes; er wird vom Ende der Hotelhalle über ein üppiges Foyer erreicht oder von einer eigenen Vorfahrt auf der Eingangseite. Weite Türen öffnen sich zum vollverglasten Foyer und zum Meer. Für Hotelgäste und Ballbesucher eine ruhig einladende Vorfahrt: Wagen halten an und verschwinden sogleich über eine Rampe nach unten zum Parkplatz und zur Tiefgarage. Eine breite durchbrochene Stegplatte mit Fontänen und spiegelndem Wasser verdeckt die Rampe, läßt das Vorfeld als kühl gestaltete Plaza erscheinen. Das hochragende Bettenhaus hat auf der Eingangsseite einen konvex geformten Giebel. Er stellt sich dem Blick zum Meer so wenig wie möglich entgegen, während der Seegiebel sich konkav zum Wasser auftut.

Die schöpferisch skulpturelle Ausformung seiner Betonarchitektur macht dieses Hotel zu einem wegweisenden Bau, in einem Land, das im Bauen noch seinen eigenen Ausdruck sucht.

1. The convex wall at the eastern end. The regularly-spaced main columns are carried through from the entrance drive across the lounge area to the west terrace.
2. The west side; a concave wall opening towards the sea.
3. The entrance drive. Inverted pyramids of concrete transfer the wall loads of the guest-room tower to the heavy longitudinal beams.

1. Der konvexe Ostgiebel. Der Rhythmus der Hauptstützen geht von der Anfahrt über die Halle zur Westterrasse.
2. Der Westgiebel, dessen konkave Linie sich zum Meer öffnet.
3. Die Vorfahrt. Betonkeile übertragen die Wandlasten des Bettentraktes auf die mächtigen Längsträger.

Key to section: 1 Roof restaurant, 2 Offices in the services floor, 3 Shops, 4 Lobby, 5 Main kitchen, 6 Storage and mechanical floor, 7 Ballroom, 8 Garage.
Key to plan of entrance level: 1 Lounge, 2 Bar, 3 Shops, 4 Lobby, 5 Reception, administration, 6 Private dining rooms, 7 West terrace, 8 Childrens' playground, 9 Ballroom foyer, 10 Ballroom, 11 Ballroom servery, 12 Storage, 13 Main entrance, 14 Access, 15 Patio, 16 Tennis courts, 17 Passage to parking garage.
Key to plan of restaurant level: 1 Café-terrace, 2 Snack bar, 3 Café, 4 Lower lobby, 5 Night club, 6 Restaurant, 7 Restaurant terrace, 8 Bar, 9 Shops, 10 Main kitchen, 11 Employees' dining room, 12 Truck loading, 13 Delivery entrance, 14 Women's changing space, 15 Garage, 16 Up ramp to main entrance, 17 Men's changing space, 18 Terrace guest rooms, 19 Changing cabins for swimming pool, 20 Parking area.

Legende zum Schnitt: 1 Dachrestaurant, 2 Büros im Zwischengeschoß, 3 Läden, 4 Lobby, 5 Hauptküche, 6 Lager und technisches Geschoß, 7 Ballsaal, 8 Tiefgarage.
Legende zum Grundriß Eingangsgeschoß: 1 Lounge, 2 Bar, 3 Läden, 4 Lobby, 5 Empfang, Verwaltung, 6 Räume für private Veranstaltungen, 7 Westterrasse, 8 Kinderspielplatz, 9 Foyer Ballsaal, 10 Ballsaal, 11 Anrichte Ballsaal, 12 Lager, 13 Haupteingang, 14 Anfahrt, 15 Patio, 16 Tennisplätze, 17 Durchgang zur Tiefgarage.
Legende zum Grundriß Restaurantgeschoß: 1 Caféterrasse, 2 Snackbar, 3 Café, 4 Untere Lobby, 5 Night-Club, 6 Restaurant, 7 Restaurantterrasse, 8 Bar, 9 Läden, 10 Hauptküche, 11 Personalkantine, 12 Laderampe, 13 Wirtschaftseingang, 14 Umkleideraum Frauen, 15 Tiefgarage, 16 Ausfahrtrampe zum Haupteingang, 17 Umkleideraum Männer, 18 Terrassenzimmer, 19 Umkleidekabinen für das Schwimmbad, 20 Parkplatz.

Ritual rules are strictly observed, as they are in all hotels in Israel. The restaurants and kitchens are separated for meat dishes and milk products, – this results in especially large kitchen areas compared with the size of the restaurants

Wie in allen Hotels Israels werden die rituellen Speisevorschriften streng eingehalten. Die Restaurants und die Küchen sind für Fleisch- und Milchspeisen getrennt, das erklärt die besonders großen Küchenflächen im Verhältnis zu den Restaurants.

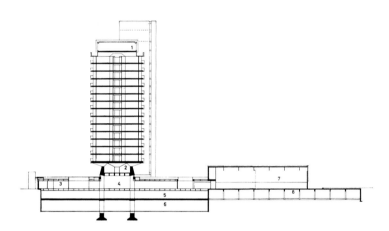

Section from north to south / Schnitt in Nord-Süd-Richtung.

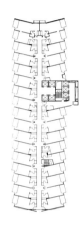

Plan, typical floor / Grundriß Normalgeschoß.

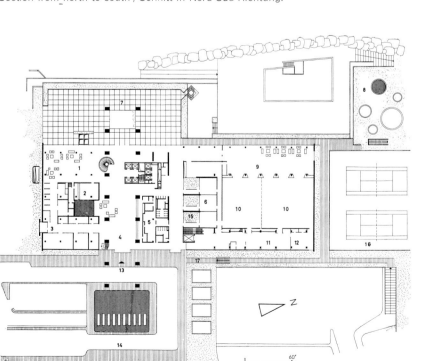

Plan, entrance level / Grundriß Eingangsgeschoß.

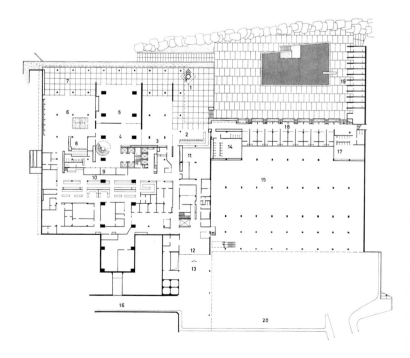

Plan, restaurant level / Grundriß Restaurantgeschoß.

4. View from the north, showing the seaward-facing dining and entertaining rooms in the podium, and the recessed pool and café-terrace.
5. The south elevation, shielded by balconies from the glaring summer sun.

4. Blick von Norden auf die zum Meer orientierten Speise- und Gesellschaftsräume mit der zurückgesetzten Schwimmbad- und Caféterrasse.
5. Die Südfront, durch Balkone gegen die steile Sommersonne geschützt.

6, 7. The façades and end walls are not the only strongly-modeled surfaces: the underside of the slab has deeply-profiled panels of exposed concrete, which form the ceiling of the lobby. A large pale cube is suspended above the entrance.

6, 7. Die plastischen Werte beschränken sich nicht auf die Fronten und Giebel. Auch die Unterseite des Bettenhauses zeigt tiefe Kassetten in Sichtbeton; sie bildet die Decke der Hotelhalle darunter. Ein heller Kubus ist über die Türfront gehängt.

8. The lounge. Dark-stained wood ceilings, glass walls on the seaward side.
9. Spiral stair between the upper lobby and the restaurants.
10. The ballroom foyer.

8. Die Lounge. Dunkel getönte Holzdecke, weit geöffnete Glaswand zum Meer.
9. Wendeltreppe zwischen der oberen Hotelhalle und den Restaurants.
10. Foyer des Ballsaales.

Hotel Intercontinental, Frankfurt-on-Main

Architects: O. Apel and H. Beckert; G. Becker, engineer

The hotel was built in 1964 on the site of the former de Bary Park, facing the Main promenade known as the Nizza. With more than 500 guest-rooms, three restaurants and bars, and seven shops, it is a US-type luxury hotel, and cost 10 million dollars to build and furnish. It is not, however, a convention hotel of American type (as a trade fair center, Frankfurt already has adequate convention and conference facilities), though the main ballroom, holding 650, does offer movie projection and simultaneous translation systems. As a hotel for executives, trade fair visitors and foreign tourists, the Intercontinental has very large lounges and public rooms, but apartments are of rather modest size. Most of the clients are businessmen who use their rooms only for sleeping: the bedrooms were therefore rationalized and kept compact, like the bathrooms. All public rooms are air-conditioned, as is the 20th floor with the Presidential Suite. The typical apartment floors can be connected with a central air-conditioning system later on. Bathrooms are mechanically ventilated.

The podium building occupies the entire depth of the site, but can be entered only from the north side. It was decided not to allow any vehicles (except fire engines) to enter from the riverside drive; cars reach the entrance by the one-way street to the north, and drive onto the down-ramp of the basement garage. When they leave, the up-ramp at the northwest corner of the site leads them back to the entrance or directly into the oneway traffic outside. The basement garage can accommodate 165 cars and fills the entire space under the three-lane access drive and the public street. The garage is connected with the lobby by a separate stairway, which continues in a spiral to the upper floor ballroom. Next to the garages in the basement are the staff rooms, workshops (joiner, painter, upholsterer, printer, electrician, plumber), the laundry and the mechanical services plant controled by the resident engineer.

Vertical circulation inside is by four guest elevators, each for 18 persons, two service elevators to all floors, and two service and emergency stairways connected with each other by fireproof corridors. Fire ladders at the end of the tower floors (with exits at the fourth and tenth floors) serve as emergency connections from floor to floor in case of smoke. The only noticeable part of this system of vertical connections is the group of guest elevators. One pair of elevators is finished in pale green onyx, a high-

light in a lobby which has costly finishes throughout—travertine floor, paneling of Andaman padouk, boutiques inside frameless cubes of glass, Wengé and Oregon pine. The lobby is long, and for a specific reason: the walk from the entrance to the elevators, past the hall porter's desk, the reception and the cashier's counter, discourages undesirable visitors. Several main columns in the lounge, supporting the guest-room floors, are either incorporated in the elevator stack or placed where they do not offer any obstruction; they articulate the lounge into a series of intimate areas containing two groups of seats, and another area with a circle of chairs surrounding the fire.

The bar and restaurant face the river Main and have a floating terrace projecting to the south. These quiet, carefully-designed spaces would benefit from some connection with the riverside promenade: the idea is under consideration for the future.

The Dell'Arte restaurant, designed by the architects, has glass cases as room dividers: they contain dolls in theatrical costumes. Dark walls of Andaman padouk, natural-colored curtains, Saarinen chairs, benches of dark brown leather and the large disc of an Italian crystal chandelier combine to produce a genuinely modern

1. The hotel from the river Main. Narrow bands of gray limestone facing; the massive sweep of the roof is interrupted by the roof terrace.

1. Das Hotel von der Mainseite. Muschelkalkfassade, schmal gebändert; Dachterrasse eingeschnitten in den massiven Zug des Dachrandes.

interior. The blue tones of ceiling, seat covers and carpets were subsequently changed to a deep red, the glow of which was kinder to women's evening make-up than the colder blue had been. The Brasserie, mainly a daytime restaurant, uses different timbers for its décor. The walls are finished in large flush panels of makore, and room dividers are built up from massive blocks of Oregon pine, tied together with wooden fillets.

The main kitchen of the hotel has hot and cold kitchen and patisserie sections arranged in a U-shape around the service area, with a separate beverage counter and dishwashing sections for china, silverware and pots and pans. All cooking apparatus is concentrated in compact units. The brasserie kitchen is entirely separate, next to the staff kitchen. The adjoining staff dining room is almost as large in area as the brasserie restaurant. A service and delivery court is placed to the east of the building, at ground level but out of sight of visitors.

A few statistics: floor area of the podium building is 74×61 m, of the guest-room slab 74×16,40 m, enclosed space 125 000 m³. The slab is 60 m tall, not including a few small structures on the roof. The podium and guest-room slab are not rigidly separated but carefully combined. An intermediate floor for structure and service machinery was not required. There are only 10 sets of columns for 18 sets of apartments on each face of the building—normally two guest-rooms per bay—and it was easy to fit these columns into the lounge, as also into the kitchen and service rooms. The lobby, restaurants and ballroom are in the two-storey podium where they are clear of the high-rise structure and so they only require a few comparatively slim columns. The ballroom is in the core of the building and constructed without interior columns. It is reached by two spiral staircases from the lobby and from the ballroom entrance. Its kitchen also caters for the private dining rooms on the south side. Further rooms on the first floor accommodate the hairdresser and barber shops, the medical rooms and the hotel management. The General Manager lives in a suite just above the offices, on the lowest of the guest-room floors.

The columns of the tall slab, 7,50 m apart, are removed from the corners of the building and the floor slabs are cantilevered at the ends. This makes it possible to have larger rooms and suites at the ends, on the same floor as the standard apartments. The luxury suite on the 20th floor has an area of 160 m². Each typical floor has 30 apartments, corresponding exactly to the working capacity of two chambermaids. Apartments can be let as single or double rooms. Beds and daybeds are arranged in several fashions, but double beds are rare. Every floor has staff WCs, plus a linen store and a shoeshine room.

A further room for private receptions, a supper club, and a bar with a cocktail lounge and roof terrace, are at roof level. The tall structure on the roof houses the elevator machinery and the cooling equipment.

The overall appearance of the building is quiet but distinguished. Gray Kirchheim limestone has been used as cladding for the structures on the roof, round the access areas, and along the continuous ribbons of the façades; there are a few touches of white at the ends of the building.

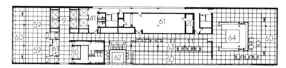

Plan, 21st floor / Grundriß 21. Obergeschoß.

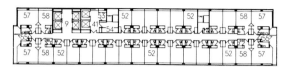

Plan, 4th to 19th floor / Grundriß 4.–19. Obergeschoß.

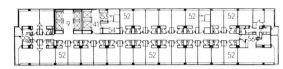

Plan, 3rd floor, with manager's suite / Grundriß 3. Obergeschoß mit Managersuite.

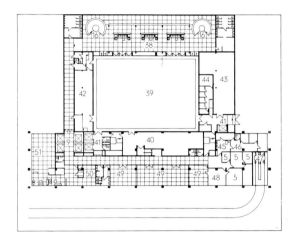

Plan, Mezzanine / Grundriß Mezzanin.

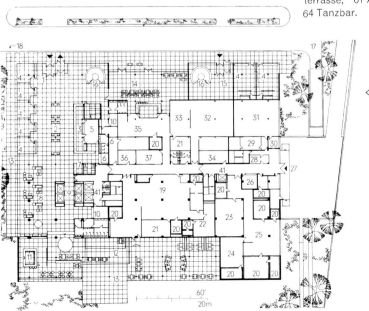

Plan, ground floor / Grundriß Erdgeschoß.

Key to plans: 1 Main entrance, 2 Lobby, 3 Front desk, 4 Shops, 5 Office, 6 Telephone exchange, 7 Periodicals, 8 Lounge, 9 Passenger elevators, 10 Coats, 11 Bar, 12 Dining room, 13 Terrace, 14 Café, 15 Entrance ballroom, 16 Stairway to ballroom, 17 Down-ramp to garage, 18 Up-ramp from garage, 19 Main kitchen, 20 Refrigeration rooms, 21 Dish-washing area, 22 Bakery, 23 Food storage, 24 Beverage storage, 25 Food preparation, 26 Delivery, 27 Service court with truck ramp, 28 Control, 29 Staff office, 30 Cash office, 31 Bookkeeping, 32 Employees' dining room, 33 Employees' kitchen, 34 Food and beverage manager, 35 Coffee kitchen, 36 Luggage, 37 Room service, 38 Ballroom foyer, 39 Ballroom, 40 Ballroom kitchen, 41 Service elevators, 42 Storage, 43 Fan room, 44 Film projection and translation booths, 45 Waiting room, 46 Doctor's surgery, 47 Fire ladder, 48 Manager, 49 Private dining rooms, 50 Barber's shop, 51 Hairdresser, 52 Guest-room, 53 Linen storage, 54 Mechanical plant, 55 Emergency stairway, 56 Manager's suite, 57 Living room of suite, 58 Bedroom of suite, 59 Private dining room, 60 Roof terrace, 61 Servery, 62 Bar, 63 Restaurant lounge, 64 Supper club.

Legende zu den Plänen: 1 Haupteingang, 2 Lobby, 3 Empfang, 4 Läden, 5 Büro, 6 Telephonzentrale, 7 Zeitschriften, 8 Lounge, 9 Personenaufzüge, 10 Garderobe, 11 Bar, 12 Speisesaal, 13 Terrasse, 14 Café, 15 Eingang Ballsaal, 16 Treppe zum Ballsaal, 17 Einfahrt zur Tiefgarage, 18 Ausfahrt aus der Tiefgarage, 19 Hauptküche, 20 Kühlräume, 21 Spülküche, 22 Bäckerei, 23 Lebensmittellager, 24 Getränkelager, 25 Lebensmittelvorbereitung, 26 Warenannahme, 27 Wirtschaftshof mit Laderampe, 28 Kontrolle, 29 Personalbüro, 30 Kasse, 31 Buchhaltung, 32 Personalspeiseraum, 33 Personalküche, 34 Lebensmittel- und Getränkechef, 35 Kaffeeküche, 36 Gepäck, 37 Etagenservice, 38 Foyer Ballsaal, 39 Ballsaal, 40 Ballsaalküche, 41 Personalaufzüge, 42 Lagerraum, 43 Ventilatorraum, 44 Film- und Simultanübersetzerkabinen, 45 Warteraum, 46 Praxis Hotelarzt, 47 Feuerleiter, 48 Manager, 49 Speiseräume für private Veranstaltungen, 50 Frisiersalon Herren, 51 Frisiersalon Damen, 52 Gastzimmer, 53 Wäscheraum, 54 Installation, 55 Nottreppe, 56 Managersuite, 57 Suite Wohnraum, 58 Suite Schlafraum, 59 Speiseraum für private Veranstaltungen, 60 Dachterrasse, 61 Anrichte, 62 Bar, 63 Restaurant-Lounge, 64 Tanzbar.

Section see page 29 / Schnitt siehe Seite 29.

Hotel Intercontinental, Frankfurt am Main

Architekten: O. Apel und H. Beckert; G. Becker, Ingenieur

Das Hotel wurde 1964 an der Main-Promenade des »Nizza« auf dem Gelände des de Bary'schen Parks errichtet, ein großes Luxushotel amerikanischer Prägung mit über 500 Zimmern, drei Restaurants und Bars, sieben Läden und Gesamtkosten von 40 Millionen Mark. Ein Kongreßhotel im amerikanischen Zuschnitt ist es nicht (die Messestadt Frankfurt hat genug Tagungsstätten), wenn auch im Ballsaal für 650 Personen Film- und Simultan-Anlagen eingebaut sind. Als Haus für Manager, Messebesucher und ausländische Touristen hat das Intercontinental weitflächige Hallen und Empfangsräume und recht kleine Apartments. Die Geschäftswelt stellt den größten Teil der Clientèle. Die meisten Gäste suchen ihren Raum nur zum Schlafen auf; er kann, wie die Bäder, knapp und streng rationell entwickelt werden. Alle öffentlichen Räume sind klimatisiert, dazu das 20. Geschoß mit der Präsidentensuite. Die normalen Apartmentgeschosse können später an eine zentrale Klimaanlage angeschlossen werden. Die Bäder sind mechanisch belüftet.

Die Breitfußanlage nimmt die ganze Tiefe des Blocks ein, kann aber nur auf der nördlichen Seite erreicht werden. Jede Anbindung an den Verkehr der Uferstraße, außer für die Feuerwehr, war ausgeschlossen. Wagen kommen über die nördliche Einbahnstraße zum Eingang, fahren dann weiter zur Abfahrtsrampe der unterirdischen Garage. Von der Ausfahrtsrampe an der Nordwestecke des Geländes gelangt man wieder zur Vorfahrt oder direkt in den Einbahnverkehr. Die Tiefgarage kann 165 Wagen aufnehmen und füllt den ganzen Raum unter der dreispurigen Vorfahrt und der öffentlichen Verkehrsstraße aus. Eine Treppenhalle verbindet sie mit dem Empfang und einer Wendeltreppe zum Ballsaal im Obergeschoß. Neben den Garagen liegen im Kellergeschoß die Personalräume, Werkstätten (Schreiner, Maler, Polsterer, Drucker, Elektriker, Installateur), die Wäscherei und die technischen Anlagen.

Der innere Verkehr in der Vertikalen geht über vier Aufzüge für Gäste (je 18 Personen), zwei Aufzüge für Personal und Lasten durch alle Geschosse, und zwei Personal- und Fluchttreppen, untereinander durch feuerfeste Gänge verbunden. Feuerleitern am Ende der Hochhausflure (mit Austritten im 4. und 10. Geschoß) dienen als Notweg von Flur zu Flur bei Verqualmung. Von diesem System vertikaler Verbindungen wird für den Gast nur die Fahrstuhlgruppe sichtbar. Der halbe Block mit

zwei Fahrschächten ist ganz in hellgrünem Onyx verkleidet, Glanzlicht einer in jedem Teil aufwendig gestalteten Halle – Boden aus Travertin, Andaman-Padouk-Holz, Boutiques als rahmenlose Würfel aus Glas, Wengé und Oregon Pine. Die Lobby ist langgezogen aus bestimmtem Grund. Der Weg vorbei an Portierloge, Empfang und Kasse wirkt für nicht ganz erwünschte Personen als psychologische Sperre zwischen Eingang und Fahrstuhl. In der Lounge kommen einige Hauptstützen aus den Wohngeschossen herunter, gehen teils im Fahrstuhlblock auf und stören nirgends. Im Gegenteil, sie gliedern die Lounge in intime Bereiche von je zwei Sitzgruppen und eine Kaminrunde. Zur Mainseite nach Süden liegen die Bar und Restauranträume mit vorspringender Terrasse.

Für das Restaurant »Dell'Arte« entwarfen die Architekten als Raumteiler Glaskästen mit plastischen Figurinen aus Bühnenbildern. Dunkle Wände aus Andaman-Padouk, naturfarbene Vorhänge, Saarinen-Sessel, Bänke in dunkelbraunem Leder, das große Rund eines flächigen Kristallüsters aus Italien schufen ein zeitgemäßes Interieur. Das Tagesrestaurant auf der Nordseite (»Brasserie«) ist buchstäblich »aus anderem Holz geschnitzt«. Die Wandverkleidung aus Macoré bleibt flächig, doch sind die Raumteiler aus massiven Holzblöcken von Oregon Pine, mit Gratleisten zusammengesteckt.

Die Hauptküche des Hotels zeigt in U-förmiger Anordnung die kalte, warme und Caféküche um den Kellnergang mit abgeteilter Getränkeausgabe und Geschirr-, Silber- und Topfspüle. Alle Kochanlagen sind in Blöcken zusammengefaßt. Die Brasserieküche liegt abgesetzt neben der Personalküche. Anschließend der Speisesaal der Angestellten, in der Fläche fast so groß wie die Brasserie. Der Wirtschaftshof geht nach Osten zu ebener Erde, aber aus dem Blick genommen.

Das Gebäude in Zahlen: Grundfläche des Breitfußes 74×61 m, des Bettenblocks 74×16,40 m, umbauter Raum 125 000 cbm. Das Hochhaus ist ohne Dachaufbau 60 m hoch. Flachtrakt und Turmhaus sind nicht scharf geschieden, sondern geschickt verbunden. Ein statisch-technisches Zwischengeschoß war nicht nötig. Auf die 18 Apartmentbreiten des Hochhauses kommen nur 10 Stützenreihen – immer zwei Räume auf jeden tragenden Rahmen – und die konnten in der Lounge, in der Küche und den Nebenräumen leicht eingeordnet werden. Lobby, Restaurants und Ballsaal liegen in dem

zweigeschossigen Flachtrakt nicht unter dem Bettenblock und kommen mit wenigen, leichteren Stützen aus. Der Ballsaal ist stützenfrei im Innern des Gebäudes gelegen. Er wird von zwei Wendeltreppen aus der Lobby und vom Sondereingang erreicht. Seine Küche versorgt zugleich die Speiseräume für private Veranstaltungen auf der Südseite. Im ersten Obergeschoß liegen die Frisiersalons, Arzträume und die Direktion. Der Manager bewohnt eine Suite darüber im untersten Zimmergeschoß. Die Stützen des Hochhauses im Abstand von rund 7,50 m sind von den Ecken zurückgesetzt, die Giebel kragen aus. Damit entstehen an den Enden größere Räume und, gekoppelt mit dem nächsten Apartment, großflächige Suiten. Die Luxussuite im 20. Obergeschoß mißt 160 qm. Jedes Normalgeschoß hat 30 Gäste-Apartments, das entspricht für den Service genau der Arbeit von zwei Zimmermädchen. Die Räume können mit einem oder mit zwei Betten vermietet werden. Betten und Tagescouchen wurden in mehreren Variationen angeordnet, französische Betten sind selten. Auf jeder Etage finden sich Personaltoiletten, Wäsche- und Schuhputzkammer.

Im Dachgeschoß sind ein weiterer Raum für private Empfänge, eine Bar und Cocktail-Lounge mit Dachterrasse und eine Tanzbar untergebracht. Der aufgesetzte hohe Kubus nimmt die Aufzugsmaschinerie und das Rückkühlwerk auf.

Die Gesamterscheinung ist gediegen-neutral. Die Fassaden in umlaufender Bandstruktur mit den sauber geschnittenen, gestreckten Kuben der Dachzone und der Vorfahrt sind mit grauem Kirchheimer Muschelkalk verkleidet, hinzu kommen wenige weiße Akzente an den Giebeln.

2. A broad and canopied sidewalk, and three-lane access (or parking) drive. The deep lobby can be seen through the glass walls.
3. The lobby, with cashier's desk, reception and hall porter. Travertine floor, islands of carpet, and clean lines. A little gaiety appears in the folded light fitting.

2. Vordach über breitem Gehweg, drei eigene Fahr- und Parkspuren. Durch Glaswände Blick in die Halle.
3. Die Eingangshalle mit Kasse, Empfang und Portierloge. Travertinboden, Teppichinseln. Lineare Klarheit, ein spielerischer Effekt im modellierten Lichtband.

4. The lounge and the long vista of the lobby. To the right is the elevator stack, clad in green onyx, washed with soft light.
5. Details of the perfume boutique: hexagons of glass and Wengé wood, and round bull's-eye display windows.
6. The lounge fireplace, not a display item but hidden away in a quiet backwater of the lobby.

4. Die Lounge und die langgestreckte Perspektive der Lobby. Rechts der Fahrstuhlblock in grünem Onyx, leicht angeleuchtet.
5. Details der Parfümerie, Rhomben aus Glas und Wengé-holz im Wechsel, runde Schauluken.
6. Kamingruppe in der Lounge, nicht Schaustück im großen Blickfeld, sondern ruhige Bucht abseits vom Treiben in der Halle.

Cross section / Querschnitt.

7. The restaurant lounge and roof terrace, and access to the supper club.
8. The brasserie. Solid sculptured grids of Oregon pine used as room dividers. Spherical wicker lamps; warm-toned walls and flooring.
9. Interior of the Silhouette bar and dancing and supper club at roof level, with its ceiling of gilt rings.
10. The south restaurant has a view of the Nizza promenade. Ceilings are patterned with thin boards. Chairs are by Saarinen, made by Knoll.
11. Corridor on the 21st floor. Suspended ceiling of plywood pyramids.
12. The 21st floor roof terrace. High beams in gray and white, and a view of the river and Frankfurt cathedral.

7. Restaurant-Lounge mit Dachterrasse, Durchgang zur Tanzbar.
8. Die »Brasserie«. Blockhafte Skulpturen aus Oregon Pine als Raumteiler. Kugellampen aus Korbgeflecht, warme Töne der Wände und Böden.
9. Blick in die Tanzbar »Silhouette« im Dachgeschoß. Decke aus vergoldeten Ringen.
10. Das Südrestaurant mit Blick auf die Parkpromenade des »Nizza«. Decken in dünnen Brettern strukturiert, Saarinen-Sessel von Knoll.
11. Gang im 21. Obergeschoß. Deckenverkleidung aus abgehängten Sperrholzpyramiden.
12. Die Dachterrasse im 21. Geschoß. Hohe Balken grau und weiß. Blick auf den Main und den Frankfurter Dom.

Hilton Hotel, Portland, Oregon

Architects: Skidmore, Owings & Merrill

A downtown convention hotel with 500 rooms: an intricate brief, and a difficult one to accommodate in a single city block.

The two basic functions of sleep in quiet secluded rooms and business activities in the public spaces, are clearly expressed in the overall form—a 22-storey tower with large bands of windows, and a strong, solid-looking podium with hardly any openings in its walls. These walls enclose a large complex of lounges, bars, restaurants, banqueting rooms, and exhibition areas, as well as the services and garages. On all sides, this podium goes down far below ground level. The large ballroom (900 m²), though above garages, is still below street level. On its roof is the main entrance, an open court with arcades on both sides, which leads into the lobby. Surprisingly, the roof canopy at the street entrance ends in a closed wall—doors are arranged symmetrically on each side. The court with its reflection pool overlooked by the glass wall of the speciality restaurant, is intimate and secluded. Two further entrances and lobbies, to the hotel and the ballroom, are on the rear (Broadway) side; a separate bar serves this area.

The plaza level is an unusual feature. It includes a formal roof garden with a swimming pool, a private club in the guest-room slab, with large cocktail lounge, dining room, and a dancing space, and the Junior Ballroom, a free-standing pavilion, glazed on all sides, seating 340 for dinner or 480 for lectures. The architects have used this plaza, raised a few meters above street level, as a major feature of the design. The plaza widens the corridor street and gives it variety and relief; both hotel guests and the tenants of adjoining buildings are able to enjoy a view of its attractive landscaping.

At the ends of all 18 typical floors are variable suites formed by combining 2 or 3 standard apartments (with bedrooms of 16 and 19 m²). The suites on the 19th floor are not simply combinations of smaller units, but cover a much larger area. The corner windows, free of structural members, have wide views at this high level.

The structure of the tower is clearly expressed on the exteriors. The columns protrude increasingly from the façades as the loads increase and cross-sections broaden towards the base. They carry part of the increasing moments from lateral loads, and relate the structure of the tower to its base. The lightweight concrete of the columns is bush-hammered to produce a rich surface resembling that of the podium walls, which are clad in precast panels with specially selected aggregate.

1. The tower is clearly distinguished from the podium. The glass-walled pavilion on the plaza is the junior ballroom.
2. Strong columns, narrow horizontals of concrete. A screen wall of travertine shields the entrance court.
3. Rear of the tower; the podium has hardly any openings. The planting on the plaza is formal.

1. Der Turm ist klar abgesetzt von der Basis. Auf der Plaza ein Glaspavillon: der kleine Ballsaal.
2. Starke Stützen, schmale Brüstungen. Eine Wandfläche in Travertin schirmt den Innenhof ab.
3. Die Rückseite des Turms. Basis fast ohne Öffnungen, darüber die streng geometrischen Pflanzenbeete der kleineren Plaza.

Hilton-Hotel, Portland, Oregon

Architekten: Skidmore, Owings & Merrill

Ein City- und Kongreßhotel mit 500 Gastzimmern; ein Raumprogramm, das die Architekten mit Mühe auf dem Grundstück in der Größe eines ganzen Straßenblocks unterbringen konnten.

Die Grundfunktionen – Übernachtungen in ruhiger, abgeschlossener Lage und gesellschaftlich-geschäftliches Leben in den öffentlichen Räumen – sind in der baulichen Gesamtform klar herausgestellt: durch den 22-geschossigen Turm, in breiten Bändern verglast, und durch den Sockelbau mit seinen fast ungebrochenen Mauern, die einen weitläufigen Komplex von Hallen, Bars, Restaurants, Bankettsälen und Ausstellungsflächen umschließen, dazu noch die Serviceräume und Garagen. Diese Basis geht auf allen Seiten bis tief unter die Straßenebene. Der große Ballsaal (fast 900 qm) liegt über den Garagen, aber noch im Erdreich. Auf seiner Decke führt der Haupteingang, ein offener Zierhof mit Arkaden, in die Halle. Ein überraschender Effekt: Das Vordach der Anfahrt hat hinter sich eine geschlossene Wandfläche. Die Eingänge liegen symmetrisch zu beiden Seiten. Der Hof mit seinem Wasserbecken und der Glasfront des Spezialitätenrestaurants bleibt intim geschlossen. Auf der Rückseite (Broadway) liegen zwei weitere Eingänge und Lobbies, zum Hotel und zum Ballsaal, mit ihrer eigenen Bar. Ungewöhnlich ist das Plazageschoß, ein streng formal angelegter Dachgarten mit Schwimmbad, im Innern ein Privatclub – großräumige Bar, Speiseraum, Tanzfläche – und, als herausgesetzter Pavillon, ringsum verglast, der kleine Ballsaal für 340 Personen zum Dinner oder 480 zu Vorträgen. Die Architekten machten aus der Plaza wenige Meter über der Straße ein wesentliches Moment der Gestaltung. Die Plaza erweitert den Straßenkorridor und gibt ihm Relief; sie bietet den Gästen wie den Mietern der umliegenden Gebäude einen gärtnerisch gepflegten Anblick.

In allen 18 Normalgeschossen finden sich an den Giebelenden variable Suiten aus zwei oder drei Standard-Apartments (Schlafräume zwischen 16 und 19 qm), im 19. Wohngeschoß dagegen weiträumige Suiten, die nicht einfach aus kleineren Einheiten addiert sind. Die stützenfreien Ecken bieten hier besonders offene Ausblicke.

Die statische Struktur des Turmbaues ist auf der Außenseite klar abzulesen. Die freiliegenden Stützen treten mit wachsenden Lasten und wachsendem Querschnitt plastisch stärker aus der Fassade und verbreitern sich im untersten Teil auch seitlich. Sie können einen Teil der zunehmenden Momente aus Seitenkräften aufnehmen und machen das Aufsetzen der Turmlasten auf die solide Basis des Unterbaues sinnfällig. Der Leichtbeton der Stützen ist gestockt und der steinartigen Oberfläche der Basiswände in Vorsatzbeton angenähert.

4. The entrance court and lobby beneath the plaza level.
Columns are broadened at the base.
5. Spiral stair in the lobby.

4. Eingangshof und Halle unter dem Plazageschoß.
Breit aufgesetzte Stützenfüße.
5. Rundtreppe der Empfangshalle.

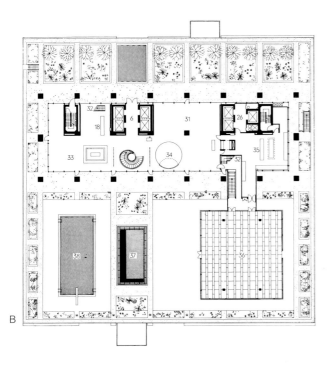

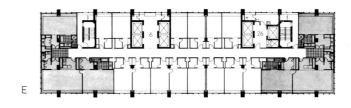

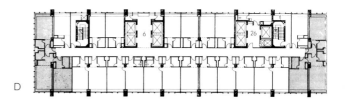

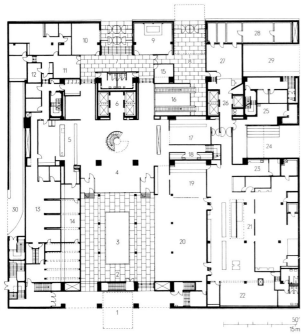

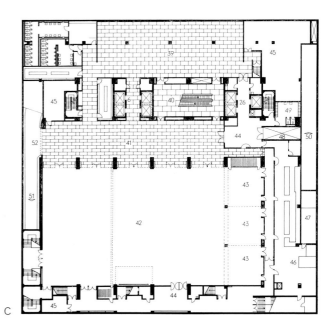

50'
15m

A Plan, entrance floor / Grundriß Erdgeschoß.

B Plan, plaza level / Grundriß Plazageschoß.

C Plan, ballroom level / Grundriß Untergeschoß mit Ball-saal.

D Plan, typical guest room level / Grundriß Gästezimmer-Normalgeschoß.

E Plan, guest room level with special suites (22th floor) / Grundriß 22. Geschoß mit Spezialsuiten.

Key to plans: 1 Canopy at the main entrance from Sixth Street, 2 Entrance court, 3 Reflection pool, 4 Main lobby, 5 Front desk, 6 Passenger elevators, 7 Broadway lobby, 8 Ballroom lobby, 9 Bar, 10 Drugstore, 11 Reception, 12 Manager, 13 Accounting, 14 Storage, 15 Florist, 16 Escalators to ballroom level, 17 Café, 18 Coats, 19 Cocktail lounge, 20 Speciality restaurant, 21 Main kitchen, 22 Dishwashing area, 23 Room service, 24 Unloading bay,

25 Canned food storage, 26 Service elevators, 27 Food storage, 28 Refrigeration rooms, 29 Ramp in, 30 Ramp out, 31 Dining room, 32 Up to mezzanine toilets, 33 Bar, 34 Dance floor, 35 Service kitchen, 36 Junior ballroom, 37 Void over entrance court, 38 Swimming pool, 39 Exhibition foyer, 40 Escalator lobby, 41 Foyer, 42 Ballroom: Capacities (foyer included)—for lectures 2221 persons, for dining 1552 persons, 43 Private dining room, 44 Service corridor, 45 Ballroom storage, 46 Service kitchen, 47 Fan room, 48 Access, 49 Staff lockers and WCs, 50 Ramp up, 51 Ramp down, 52 Access door.

Legende zu den Plänen: 1 Vordach über der Hauptvor-fahrt an der Sixth Street, 2 Eingangshof, 3 Wasserbecken, 4 Haupthalle, 5 Empfang, 6 Gästeaufzüge, 7 Broadway-Lobby, 8 Ballsaal-Lobby, 9 Bar, 10 Drugstore, 11 Ver-waltung, 12 Manager, 13 Buchhaltung, 14 Abstellraum, 15 Blumenladen, 16 Rolltreppe zum tieferliegenden Ball-

saalgeschoß, 17 Café, 18 Garderobe, 19 Cocktail-Lounge, 20 Spezialitätenrestaurant, 21 Hauptküche, 22 Spülküche, 23 Zimmerservice, 24 Lastwagenanfahrt, 25 Lagerraum, 26 Aufzüge für Personal, 27 Lagerraum für Lebensmittel, 28 Kühlräume, 29 Einfahrtrampe zur Tiefgarage, 30 Aus-fahrtrampe von der Tiefgarage, 31 Speisesaal, 32 Treppe zu den Toiletten im Mezzaningeschoß, 33 Bar, 34 Tanz-fläche, 35 Anrichte und Servierküche, 36 Kleiner Ball-saal, 37 Luftraum Eingangshof, 38 Schwimmbecken, 39 Foyer für Ausstellungen, 40 Lobby mit Rolltreppen zum Eingangsgeschoß und zur Tiefgarage, 41 Foyer, 42 Ball-saal, Fassungsvermögen (mit Foyer) bei Versammlungen 2221 Personen, bei Banketten 1552 Personen, 43 Raum für private Veranstaltungen, 44 Kellnergang, 45 Zum Ballsaal gehöriger Lagerraum, 46 Bankettküche und An-richte, 47 Ventilatorraum, 48 Fahrstuhl für Lieferwagen, 49 Personal-Kleiderablagen und WC, 50 Auffahrtrampe, 51 Abfahrtrampe, 52 Behelfszufahrt zum Ballsaal.

6. Large corner suite on the top floor.
7. The club restaurant and plaza terrace. Structural members are exposed lightweight concrete, bush-hammered.

6. Große Ecksuite im obersten Turmgeschoß.
7. Club-Restaurant mit Terrasse zur Plaza. Tragwerk freiliegend, in gestocktem Leichtbeton.

Hilton Hotel, Denver, Colorado

Architects: I. M. Pei & Partners
Design: Araldo A. Cossutta

This hotel fills an entire city block and is connected by pedestrian bridge to a department store, planned and built at the same time and covering another full city block. The pedestrian bridge, enclosed by a transparent plastic vault, also serves as a roof canopy for the entrances of both buildings.

The hotel site was large enough for the guest-room slab and the lower block containing the public rooms to be placed side by side. The long and tall slab—21 floors with 918 guest apartments—called for a large volume and variety of service areas below ground level. There are four basement floors. The three lower levels are garages which extend across the full width of the hotel and department store sites and can be used from both sides. All elevators for guests and staff go right down to the lowest basement level. Above the garages is the concourse level with an attached mezzanine, both still below ground level. It houses the garage ramps, staff rooms and cafeterias for the hotel and the department store, as well as, in the east wing, television studios with a visitors' gallery.

At ground floor level are the driveways, separated for car-borne guests and for taxis and delivery vans, three entrances for guests (those to the north and south are marked by small plazas), an entrance for the television and office section and another at the unloading court, for staff. At ground level there are ample shopping facilities for guests, but only a small lobby to the hotel. This serves to heighten the impact of the main reception area on the next floor, covering the entire length of the slab structure—about 120 m. There are two bars and a cocktail lounge at the ends. The main lounge and assembly area are two-storeyed throughout, without galleries or mezzanines, divided only where the free-flowing space narrows between the pedestrian bridge and the elevators. The assembly area can be screened off for exhibitions, acting as an extension to the ballroom when the latter is used for trade fairs. The columns of the tall guest-room slab all continue down to the basement floors. As they are in scale with the very large volume of the long lounge, they are far from being a disturbing element, but impart rhythm and scale.

The ballroom is large enough for 1000 dinner guests or 750 dancing couples. It has a separate banquet kitchen and is in the core of the building, screened from outside noises. The main restaurant, however, opens its tall glass wall to the north-east. Above the main floor are a mezzanine level—6 rooms for private receptions, the hotel administration and rentable office space—a mechanical services floor with stairs leading to a terrace garden three and a half storeys above street level, and an office floor with an unbroken area of 2000 m².

The guest-room slab starts at this level with the first of 17 typical floors. Columns are some distance behind the façades, spaced at 8,90 m. They define pairs of apartments on both sides of the building, four apartments per bay, built to four different plans. On the east side the ceiling span is halved by the main partition, but one of the apartments is less deep than the other and sacrifices some of its area to the bathroom of the neighbouring unit. On the west side the span is unequally divided, giving four window bays to one apartment and six to the other, but both bathrooms borrow space from the larger unit. The entrances to the apartments are varied in plan, as are the bedrooms. The hotel thus offers some diversity of spaces; a choice of different accommodation for regular visitors.

The architects chose tall narrow windows which are almost flush on the inside, but have deep jambs on the exterior, giving a close rhythm and rich modeling to the façades. The great precision of the details is achieved not by sharp rectangular profiles, but, almost paradoxically, by the use of beveled jambs and sills. The building as a whole is a full scale experiment in precast stone. Terrazzo and precast stone units, treated with silicone, polished, chiseled or richly profiled, cover the building and its interiors.

1. The hotel from the south. In the foreground is the ballroom wing with a large office space on its upper floor.
2. The glazed pedestrian bridge and entrance canopy crosses from the department store to the hotel, ending in a recessed porch. The lobby area and services floor have cladding with a deep and intricate pattern.

1. Das Hotel von Süden. Im Vordergrund das Gebäude des Ballsaals mit einem Großraumbüro im obersten Geschoß.
2. Die gläserne Fußgängerpassage, gleichzeitig Vordach, führt vom Warenhaus ins Hotel. Sie endet in einer Mauernische. Ein tief perforiertes Muster kleinerer Waben im Bereich der Halle und des technischen Geschosses.

Hilton-Hotel, Denver, Colorado

Architekten: I. M. Pei & Partners
Entwurf: Araldo A. Cossutta

Das Hotel füllt ein ganzes Straßengeviert und ist durch eine Fußgängerbrücke mit einem Warenhaus, ebenfalls in Blockgröße und in einem Zuge mitgeplant, verbunden. Die gewölbte, verglaste Fußgängerpassage ist zugleich Vordach über der Anfahrt zu beiden Gebäuden.

Das ziemlich große Gelände erlaubte es, die Hochhausscheibe und den Block der öffentlichen Räume nebeneinander zu setzen. Das langgezogene Hochhaus – 21 Geschosse mit 918 Apartments – macht eine Vielzahl von Räumen unter Geländehöhe nötig. Es gibt vier Kellergeschosse. Die untersten drei ziehen sich als Garagen unter die gesamte Fläche des Hotels und des Warenhauses und können von beiden Seiten benutzt werden. Alle Fahrstühle für Gäste und Personal führen bis zur untersten Kellersohle. Über den Garagen folgt der Concourse Level mit einem angehängten Zwischengeschoß, immer noch im Bereich der Keller. Hier sind die vier Wagenrampen, Personalräume, Cafeterias für Hotel und Warenhaus und, im Ostteil, Fernsehstudios mit Besuchergalerie untergebracht.

Im Erdgeschoß sind die Ein- und Ausfahrten getrennt für Gäste und für Taxis und Lieferwagen; drei Eingänge für Gäste, im Norden und Süden betont durch kleine Plazas, ein Eingang für die Fernseh- und Büroräume und ein weiterer Zugang für Angestellte am Lieferhof.

Hotelgäste finden im Erdgeschoß ganze Ladengruppen, aber eine knappe Eingangslobby. Um so größer wirkt auf der nächsten Ebene, dem Hauptgeschoß, die Sequenz der Empfangsräume über die volle Länge des Hochhauses (rund 120 m). Zwei Bars und eine Cocktail-Lounge an den Enden, die große Halle – Lounge und Versammlungsbereich – durchgehend zweigeschossig, ohne Galerien, nur unterteilt durch den Engpaß zwischen Fußgängerbrücke und Fahrstühlen. Hier kann der Versammlungs-

bereich für Ausstellungen abgeschirmt und der Ballsaal im östlichen Teil für Warenschauen ergänzt werden. In dem langgestreckten Volumen können die Stützen des Hochhauses, die alle bis unten durchgeführt werden, nicht stören – im Gegenteil, sie geben dem Raum Rhythmus und Gliederung.

Der Ballsaal bietet Platz für 1000 Dinnergäste oder 750 Tanzpaare. Er hat seine getrennte Bankettküche und liegt akustisch abgeschirmt im Gebäudeinnern. Das Hauptrestaurant dagegen öffnet sich in einer hohen Glaswand nach Nordosten. Es folgen: ein Mezzaningeschoß, sechs Räume für private Empfänge, die fensterlose Hotelverwaltung und vermietete Büroflächen; ein technisches Geschoß mit Treppen zum Terrassengarten, 3½ Stockwerke über Straßenniveau; ein Bürogeschoß von 2000 qm in einer zusammenhängenden Fläche.

Auf diesem Niveau setzt der Bettenblock mit dem ersten von 17 Normalgeschossen an. Die Stützen stehen weit hinter der Fassade im Abstand von 8,90 m. Sie formen Gruppen von je zwei Apartments auf beiden Seiten heraus, die vier verschiedene Formate haben. Auf der Ostseite teilt die Zwischenwand das Stützenfeld mittig, aber das eine Apartment wird weniger tief und gibt etwas Raum für das Bad des Nachbarn ab. Auf der Westseite ist die Feldbreite im Verhältnis 4 zu 6 Fensterachsen geteilt, dafür gehen beide Bäder zu Lasten des quergelegten Zimmers. Wie die Räume so sind auch die Eingangslösungen der Apartments variiert; man kommt damit ganz verschiedenen Raumvorstellungen entgegen und bietet häufigen Gästen Abwechslung.

Die Architekten wählten für die Fenster ein flaches Hochformat, das innen flächig gereiht ist und nach außen stark profiliert. Die Fassaden wirken durch den feinen Rhythmus und den plastisch tiefen Raster. Der präzise

Eindruck der Details wird nicht durch rechteckig scharfkantige Profile erreicht, sondern – was fast paradox klingt – durch abgeschrägte Laibungen. Der Bau als Ganzes ist ein großer Wurf in Kunststein. Vorsatzbeton mit Silikonzuschlag, poliert, ziseliert, kassettiert, bestimmt die Flächen außen und im Innern.

Site plan / Lageplan.

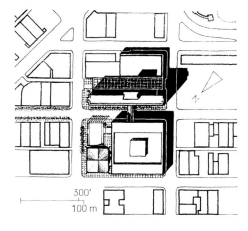

3. View from the north. In the right foreground are the department store and its low extension building.

3. Ansicht von Norden. Vorn rechts das Warenhaus und sein niedriger Erweiterungsbau.

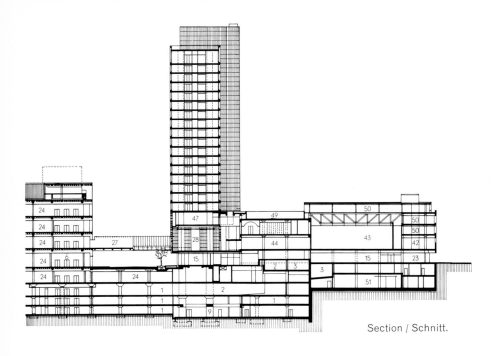
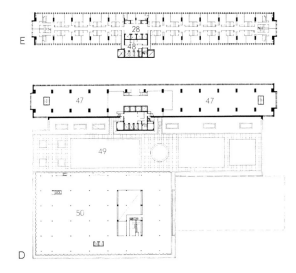

Section / Schnitt.

E

D

A Plan, 3rd basement level / Grundriß 3. Untergeschoß.
B Plan, ground floor / Grundriß Erdgeschoß.
C Plan, main floor / Grundriß Hauptgeschoß.
D Plan, terrace level / Grundriß Terrassengeschoß.
E Plan, typical floor / Grundriß Normalgeschoß.

Key to plans: 1 Parking garage, 2 Ramp in, 3 Ramp out, 4 Ramp down, 5 Stair, 6 Department store elevators, 7 Passengers unloading, 8 Motor lobby, 9 Mechanical services, 10 Boiler room, 11 Laundry receiving, 12 Fan room, 13 Main hotel entrance, 14 Escalators, 15 Rentable area, 16 North-south arcade, 17 East-west arcade with rentable area, 18 Speciality restaurant, 19 Staff entrance, 20 Truck loading, 21 Car lift, 22 Taxi entrance, 23 Office and TV studio entrance, 24 Department store, 25 Ex-

tension building, 26 Skating rink, 27 Bridge, 28 Elevator lobby, 29 Lounge, 30 Cocktail lounge, 31 Assembly area, 32 Bar, 33 Registration, 34 Gourmet room, 35 Main dining room, 36 Main kitchen, 37 Room service, 38 Dishwashing area, 39 Refrigeration rooms, 40 Storage, 41 Banquet kitchen, 42 Bakery, 43 Ballroom, 44 Exhibition area, 45 Coats, 46 Roof of extension building, 47 Mechanical services floor, 48 Service, 49 Terrace gardens, 50 Rentable office space, 51 TV studio.

Legende zu den Plänen: 1 Tiefgarage, 2 Einfahrtrampe, 3 Ausfahrtrampe, 4 Abfahrtrampe, 5 Treppe, 6 Aufzüge zum Warenhaus, 7 Vorfahrt für Hotelgäste, 8 Lobby Parkgeschoß, 9 Technische Räume, 10 Boilerraum, 11 Wäschereiannahme, 12 Lüftungsaggregate, 13 Hauptein-

gang Hotel, 14 Rolltreppe, 15 Vermietbare Ladenfläche, 16 Nord-Süd-Arkade, 17 Ost-West-Arkade, 18 Spezialitätenrestaurant, 19 Angestellteneingang, 20 Ladezone, 21 Aufzug für Lieferwagen, 22 Taxivorfahrt, 23 Eingang Fernseh- und Büroräume, 24 Warenhaus, 25 Erweiterungsbau, 26 Eis- und Rollschuhbahn, 27 Brücke, 28 Aufzugsvorhalle, 29 Halle, 30 Cocktail-Lounge, 31 Versammlungszone, 32 Bar, 33 Anmeldung, 34 Kleiner Speisesaal, 35 Großer Speisesaal, 36 Hauptküche, 37 Zimmerservice, 38 Spülküche, 39 Kühlräume, 40 Lagerraum, 41 Bankettküche, 42 Bäckerei, 43 Ballsaal, 44 Ausstellungsbereich, 45 Garderobe, 46 Dach Erweiterungsgebäude, 47 Technisches Zwischengeschoß, 48 Service, 49 Gartenterrasse, 50 Vermietbare Bürofläche, 51 Fersehstudio.

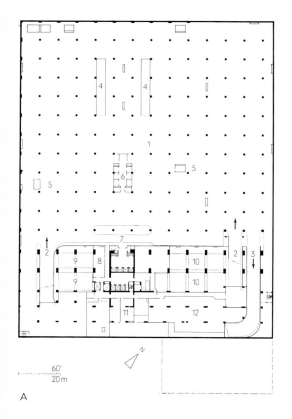

60'
20 m

A

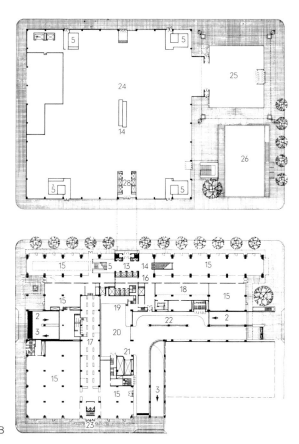

B

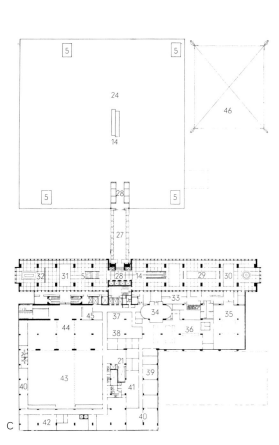

C

4. The lounge. A variety of monochrome effects. The concrete grid of the exterior is repeated inside.
5. The lounge, two storeys high for its whole length, has no major view of the spaces below. All columns of the slab structure go down to the basement. The grid pattern of the cast stone façade is veiled by light curtains.

4. Die Halle. Vielfalt monochromer Wirkungen. Das Betongitter der Fassade ist auf der Innenseite wiederholt.
5. Die Halle ist von Giebel zu Giebel zweigeschossig, ohne große Durchblicke nach unten. Alle Stützen aus dem Hochhaus sind nach unten durchgeführt. Der Wabenraster der Fassade ist verschleiert durch leichte Vorhänge.

6. A massive rectangular porch swallows the light transparent bridge and narrows the long lobby. Cast stone of a variety of textures, smooth flooring, a chiseled ceiling.

7. The open space of the lounge seen through the concrete grid of the inner perimeter (gallery above the front desk).

8. The lounge. The decorative ceiling extends into the side bays to counteract the powerfully linear character of the lounge space. Easy chairs of the same simple shape are also used in the bar and apartments.

9. The bar. Flooring, ceilings, and perforated façades are all part of a unified whole. A tall space filled with light. There is no hint of regional décor.

6. Ein massiver Block nimmt die luftige Glasbrücke auf und bildet einen Engpaß in der langen Halle. Kunststein in vielen Texturen, glatter Boden, ziselierte Decke.

7. Der Luftraum der Halle, gesehen durch den Betonraster der Innenseite (Galerie über dem Empfang).

8. Halle. Die dekorative Decke greift aus in die Seitenbuchten: Gegentendenz zur einseitigen Längsentwicklung des Volumens. Die gleiche schlichte Sesselform kehrt wieder in der Bar und in den Apartments.

9. Die Bar. Kontinuität der Böden, der Decken und durchbrochenen Fassaden. Ein hoher durchlichteter Raum. Nicht ein einziger Anklang von regionalem Dekor.

10. An apartment, sober in character. Narrow windows with very low sills.

11. The glass wall of the restaurant, facing northeast, flush and polished, contrasts with the richly coffered façade of cast stone sections.

10. Ein Apartment mit sachlicher Note. Schmale Fenster, fast ohne Brüstung.

11. Nach Nordosten die Glaswand des Hauptrestaurants: flächig-spiegelnd eingefügt in die vielfältig kassettierte Fassade aus Kunststeinteilen.

Hilton Hotel, Amsterdam

Architects: H. A. Maaskant, F. W. Vlaming and H. Salm

just over a dozen single rooms that can be opened to a suite as living rooms. All standard apartments have connecting doors to make them into suites when needed. The top (eleventh) floor has two luxury suites of three rooms and a kitchen, and a party room for 50 persons, with a panoramic view. 15 different color schemes were used in decorating the guest-rooms. They are carefully co-ordinated from room to room, to harmonize colors when rooms are opened to form suites.

To revert to technical data: the guest-room slab is of egg-crate construction, and since no concrete beams were needed, it was possible to reduce the floor-to-floor height: a concrete frame building would have had one storey less for the same overall height. The space between crosswalls was filled with partly prefabricated façade elements. Every two weeks another floor was added to the structure. The structural and mechanical services level is less deep than the guest-room floors above. It collects the wall loads from above onto heavy reinforced concrete beams (1,33 m by 3,00 m) and transmits them to the ground floor columns (1,00 m by 1,30 m) spaced at 8 m. This services floor houses the air-conditioning plant for the public rooms at ground floor level, and the ventilation machinery for the apartments (fresh air is blown into the guest-rooms and drawn back through vents in the bathrooms), plus the switchboard apparatus, accumulators, and quantities of pipes and ducts.

The hotel has an enclosed area of 5 530 m² at ground floor level and a total floor area of 23 300 m²; it was designed in 1959 and finished three years later. The cost of the structure was 2,36 million dollars with 1 million dollars added for installations. The total expenditure for the site, construction work, furniture, accessories, fees and financing costs was 5,5 million dollars.

This hotel, sited between the Apollolaan and the Noorder Amstel Kanaal, is described by the owners as a tourist, luxury and smaller convention hotel. It opened in 1962 and is in a fashionable residential district not far from the heart of the city. The building is symmetrical in general form and is designed as the terminal feature of a major axial street—Minervalaan. The hotel presents a slightly concave façade to the broad square before it; its rear elevation roughly accords with the curve of the canal. The architects, however, were anxious to avoid absolute symmetry in the main south front. On that façade, therefore, the principal staircase is marked by unglazed cladding, is off center and rises well above the roofline. The podium containing the public rooms is entirely asymmetrical. The hotel is a neat and well-balanced piece of architecture, but its outline is a little lacking in vitality. The building forms a very shallow V-shape in plan and is close to the canal, thus leaving space for a large tree-shaded parking area on the entrance side. Guests in the apartments on the north have a near view of the quiet sheet of water: and pay more for their rooms than those on the south side. The canal was widened to accommodate a landing stage; guests can descend a few steps from the lounge to reach the sightseeing boats, and can return from the city the same way. This approach to the hotel is in the true Dutch vein and gives pleasure to every tourist.

The Amsterdam Hilton was the first Hilton Hotel not to be designed by US architects, but by a local team. The Hilton management laid down certain requirements: the public rooms had to be large and numerous. They were decorated by the Hilton design team, with the exception of the lobby-lounge area. Architects have criticized the

folksy décor and eclectic details, as well as the weakness of the transition between the coffee bar and the restaurant. The Half Moon Bar, named after the ship that took Henry Hudson to New York in 1609, has a nautical décor in imitation of a ship's cabin: but the entire 80-ton vessel, with its bowsprit, would fit easily into the cocktail lounge. Olive green, melon yellow and plum were used as 'culinary colors'.

The Dutch architects have put glazed-in gardens containing tropical plants on each side of the entrance—a gesture to the Dutch love of everything green and growing—and an ever-changing display of rare plants is sent by Hilton hotels all over the world. The lobby and lounge were designed as one integrated unit, with a suspended copper chimney and round its fireplace a large circular flame-colored rug (13 m across), woven from wools of 24 colors from charcoal to orange.

The architects also designed the 275 apartments, with a total of 500 beds; and did so with great care. In the words of H. Salm: "A hotel organisation gets most of its revenue from the guest-rooms. This means that there have to be as many rooms as possible. The trend is toward smaller units, but with a maximum of comfort. Furniture has to be built-in or placed along the walls, in order to provide some open space in the shrinking rooms." A full size mock-up of a typical apartment with its adjoining corridor was put up on the site and tested to the last detail for furniture, fittings and pipe and conduit systems. (There are large service ducts, accessible from the corridor.) Almost two-thirds of the apartments are of 'studio' type with one bed and a daybed, and one in five has twin beds. In addition the hotel offers a dozen larger alcove rooms, where twin beds are placed in an alcove screened by curtains, and

1. The hotel at the intersection of two boulevards, flanked by road bridges. A convex façade faces the canal: the podium has a freer form.

2. South elevation. A sculptural handling of the corners: suites vary in plan, having balconies facing south, or outwards if on the end walls.

Hilton-Hotel, Amsterdam

Architekten: H. A. Maaskant, F. W. Vlaming und H. Salm

Das Haus zwischen Apollolaan und Noorder Amstel-Kanaal wird von seinen Erbauern als Touristen-, Luxus- und kleineres Kongreßhotel bezeichnet. Es steht seit 1962 in einem vornehmen Wohnviertel am Rande der City. Der Hauptbau ist als Zielpunkt einer großen städtebaulichen Achse (Minervalaan) symmetrisch angelegt und zu seinem weiten Vorplatz konkav geknickt. Er folgt damit in etwa dem bogenförmigen Lauf des Kanals. Eine Symmetrie der Platzwand umgingen die Architekten aber bewußt. Das Haupttreppenhaus ist in der Südfassade als geschlossener Block von der Achse abgerückt und betont hoch über Dach geführt. Die Basis mit den Publikumsräumen weicht der Symmetrie völlig aus. Es entsteht eine Architektur, die sauber und gekonnt ist, jedoch mehr großen Atem brauchte. Der Bau in seiner flachen V-Form wurde dicht an den Kanal gestellt. Damit blieb vor dem Eingang ein großer umgrünter Parkplatz; die Gäste in den Nordzimmern bekamen einen besseren Blick auf die ruhige Wasserfläche (sie zahlen mehr für ihre Zimmer als auf der Südseite). Ein Bootshafen erweitert die Gracht. Gäste können aus der Lounge über eine Freitreppe das Motorschiff für Rundfahrten erreichen und auf dem selben Weg heimkehren. Diese Anfahrt ist sehr holländisch, eine Freude für jeden Touristen.

Das Amsterdamer Haus war übrigens das erste Hilton-Hotel, das nicht von amerikanischen Architekten gebaut wurde, sondern von einheimischen. Die Hilton-Gruppe machte bestimmte Auflagen. Die Gesellschaftsräume sind zahlreich und groß angelegt; sie wurden, bis auf den Empfang und die Halle, von hoteleigenen Entwerfern gestaltet. Folkloristischer Dekor und historisierende Anklänge, der etwas akzentlose Übergang zwischen Café, Snackbar und Tagesrestaurant sind in Architektenkreisen kritisiert worden. (Die Half-Moon-Bar, ge-

nannt nach dem Schiff, das Henry Hudson nach New York trug, ist wie die Kabine dieses Schiffes »nautisch« dekoriert, nur – der 80-Tonnen-Segler von 1609 würde in seiner ganzen Länge mit Bugspriet bequem in den Barraum passen. Olivgrün, Melonengelb und Pflaumenblau werden als »kulinarische« Farben gewertet.)

Die holländischen Architekten legten zu beiden Seiten des Eingangs Glashäuser mit tropischen Gewächsen – eine Reverenz an die Vorliebe der Holländer für alles Grünende und Blühende und eine immer wechselnde Schau seltener Pflanzen, übersandt von Hilton-Hotels in aller Welt. Sie entwarfen eine kombinierte Lobby-Lounge, einen schwebenden Kupferkamin über der großen Kreisfläche (13 m) eines flammend rot wirkenden Wollteppichs, gewebt aus 24 Farben von Anthrazit bis Orange. Sie entwarfen schließlich die 275 Apartments mit ihren 500 Betten, und sie taten ganze Arbeit. H. Salm schreibt dazu: »Für eine Hotelorganisation kommt das meiste Geld aus den Zimmern, also muß man so viele Zimmer wie möglich machen. Der Trend geht zu kleineren Einheiten, aber mit einem Höchstmaß an Komfort. Die Möbel müssen eingebaut oder an den Wänden aufgestellt werden, um Platz zu schaffen in den kleiner werdenden Räumen.« Ein Modell des typischen Apartments mit einem Stück Flur wurde in voller Größe auf dem Baugelände erstellt und in allen Einzelheiten der Möblierung, Installation und Leitungsführung erprobt. (Die Leitungsschächte sind von den Fluren zugänglich.)

Fast zwei Drittel aller Apartments vertreten den Studiotyp, ein Fünftel hat Doppelbetten. Daneben gibt es ein Dutzend breitere Alkovenzimmer – die Doppelbetten stehen in Nischen mit Vorhängen – und ein gutes Dutzend Einzelzimmer, die auch als Wohnräume einer Suite verwendet werden können. Die Standard-Apartments haben

sämtlich Zwischentüren im Vorraum, um weitere Suiten zu bilden. Im obersten, elften Geschoß sind zwei Luxussuiten (aus drei Räumen mit Küche) und ein panoramischer Empfangsraum für 50 Personen untergebracht. In den Apartments kommen 15 verschiedene Farbstellungen vor. Sie sind in der Reihung der Zimmer sorgfältig koordiniert; die Farben harmonieren, wenn Räume zu Suiten zusammengelegt werden.

Das Bettenhaus wurde als Schottenbau ausgeführt. Unterzüge fielen weg, es konnte an Raumhöhe gespart werden. Ein Skelettbau hätte bei gleicher Höhe ein Geschoß weniger gehabt. Zwischen die Schotten wurden die teilfabrizierten Elemente der Fassaden eingehängt. Alle zwei Wochen entstand ein Geschoß im Rohbau. Das statisch-technische Zwischengeschoß ist schmaler als das Bettenhaus. Es sammelt die Wandlasten von oben in massiven Betonträgern von 1,33 auf 3,00 m und überträgt sie auf Stützen des Erdgeschosses (1 m auf 1,30 m) im Abstand von 8 m. Im Zwischengeschoß liegen Klimageräte für das Erdgeschoß, Lüftungsanlagen für die Apartments – Luft wird in die Wohnschlafzimmer eingeblasen, in den Bädern abgesaugt – Akkuraum, Telefonzentrale und Bündel von Rohrleitungen.

Das Hotel mit seinen 5530 qm Grundfläche, 23300 qm Geschoßfläche, wurde 1959 entworfen, drei Jahre später fertiggestellt. Rohbaukosten 9,5 Millionen DM, Installationen gut 4 Millionen DM. Gesamtaufwand für Grundstück, Bau, Möbel, Ausstattungen, Honorare und Finanzierung 22 Millionen DM.

1. Das Hotel am Schnitt zweier Boulevards, flankiert von Straßenbrücken. Konvexe Fassade zur Gracht, freie Geometrie des Flachbaues.
2. Vorfahrt und Südfassade. Plastisch variierte Gebäudeecken: die Ecksuiten wechseln im Zuschnitt; ihre Balkone gehen nach Süden oder zum Giebel.

3. The glazed-in gardens at the entrance: exotic plants from all round the world, a welcome in the Dutch vein. Steps before a hotel can be an invitation, as well as an obstacle.
4. News stand beside the lobby. Reception desk in the background.

3. Die Glashäuser zu beiden Seiten des Eingangs mit exotischen Pflanzen aus aller Welt: ein Willkomm nach holländischer Art. Stufen vor einem Hotel können eine Einladung sein oder ein Hindernis.
4. Zeitschriftenstand neben der Eingangshalle. Im Hintergrund der Empfang.

Plan, typical floor / Grundriß Normalgeschoß.

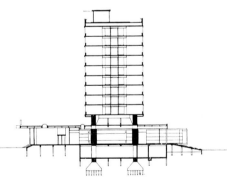

Cross section / Querschnitt.

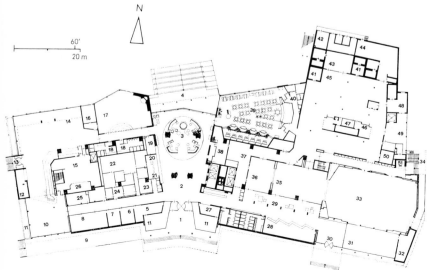

Plan, floor ground / Grundriß Erdgeschoß.

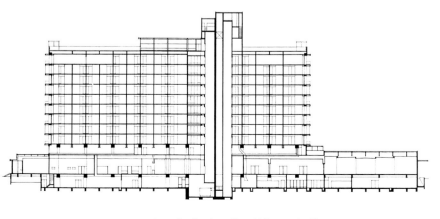

Longitudinal section / Längsschnitt.

5. The lobby-lounge. Logs burning under a copper chimney. The flaming red rug is not a focal point but a quiet enclave.

6. A south apartment with a view of the city. Furniture from Dutch workshops. The daybeds can be extended to serve as double beds.

7, 8. A studio unit. A writing desk and baggage rack, a built-in radio and storage unit are all against the walls to leave open space in a small room.

5. Die Lobby-Lounge. Ein Holzfeuer im kupfernen Kamin. Der feuerrote Teppich nicht Drehscheibe, sondern ruhiges Rund.

6. Ein Apartment der Südseite mit Stadtblick. Möbel aus holländischen Werkstätten. Die Tagescouchen können als Doppelbett ausgezogen werden.

7, 8. Studio-Einheit. Schreibtisch und Kofferbank, eingebautes Radio und Bettkasten rücken an den Wänden zusammen, um auf kleinem Raum Platz zu lassen.

Key to ground floor plan: 1 Main entrance, 2 Lobby, 3 Lounge with fireplace, 4 Terrace, 5 Flower shop, 6 Jeweller, 7 American Express, 8 Hairdressing salon, 9 Terrace, 10 Patisserie, 11 Plant boxes, 12 Coats, 13 Entrance to grill room, 14 Grill room, 15 Kitchen for grill room, 16 Office, 17 Bar, 18 W.C., 19 Cashier, 20 Reception, 21 Porter, 22 Financial department, 23 Telephone exchange, 24 Managing staff, 25 Barber shop, 26 Beverage counter, 27 KLM, 28 Coats, 29 Lounge, 30 Entrance ballroom, 31 Foyer, 32 Storage, 33 Ballroom, 34 Employee's entrance, 35 Large dining room, 36 Small dining room, 37 Room service, 38 Coats, 39 Restaurant with bandstand, 40 Artists' room, 41 Refrigeration rooms, 42 Transformer, 43 Butcher, 44 Bakery, 45 Main kitchen, 46 Beverage counter, 47 Chief cook, 48 Garbage, 49 Goods reception, 50 Silverware, 51 Ice freezer.
Key to typical floor plan: 1 Lift lobby, 2 Service, 3 Bathroom, 4 Bedroom (studio type), 5 Suite, 6 Suite (variant).

Legende zum Erdgeschoßgrundriß: 1 Haupteingang, 2 Eingangshalle, 3 Halle mit Kamin, 4 Terrasse, 5 Blumenladen, 6 Juwelier, 7 American Express, 8 Damenfriseur, 9 Terrasse, 10 Patisserie, 11 Gewächshäuser, 12 Garderobe, 13 Eingang Grillroom, 14 Grillroom, 15 Grillküche, 16 Büro, 17 Bar, 18 WC, 19 Kasse, 20 Empfang, 21 Portier, 22 Buchhaltung, 23 Telephonzentrale, 24 Direktion, 25 Herrenfriseur, 26 Getränkeausgabe, 27 KLM, 28 Garderobe, 29 Lounge, 30 Eingang Ballsaal, 31 Foyer, 32 Lagerraum, 33 Ballsaal, 34 Personaleingang, 35 Großer Speisesaal, 36 Kleiner Speisesaal, 37 Zimmerservice, 38 Garderobe, 39 Restaurant mit Musikpodium, 40 Künstlerzimmer, 41 Kühlräume, 42 Transformator, 43 Metzgerei, 44 Bäckerei, 45 Hauptküche, 46 Getränkeausgabe, 47 Küchenchef, 48 Abfall, 49 Warenannahme, 50 Silber, 51 Eisherstellung.
Legende zum Normalgeschoßgrundriß: 1 Vorraum Aufzug, 2 Service, 3 Bad, 4 Zimmer (Studiotyp), 5 Ecksuite, 6 Ecksuite (Variante).

SAS Hotel Royal, Copenhagen

Architect: Arne Jacobsen

This luxury hotel and airline terminal for the Scandinavian Airlines System was conceived as a unified whole: Arne Jacobsen was commissioned to design in his own office the building and all its furniture and accessories, down to the lighting fittings, cutlery, glasses and tableware. The result was, architecturally and functionally, a most successful hotel, providing Scandinavian comfort.

The narrow site on the Vesterbrogade had to accommodate a large hotel with 275 rooms (475 beds) as well as the air terminal, which alone took up half the area. To allow space for parking and for access lanes for the airport buses, the architects decided to build over the railroad tracks to the west. The hotel therefore had to be a tall building, as Jacobsen would have wished in any case, because of the noise from the surrounding streets. Restrictions imposed by the city authorities limited the volume of the building and limited its maximum height at 70 m. Jacobsen evolved a low two-storey block containing the air terminal and the reception and restaurant areas of the hotel, and above the low block, a high building of twenty storeys. Because of its proportions, the tall slab has a close resemblance to a tower: hardly the most economical shape for the guest-room floors, but the building regulations had to be obeyed. The appearance of the slab was kept as light as possible, so that it would not dominate its neighbors around the nearby Tivoli gardens. The hotel's curtain walls are smooth, an almost uninterrupted reflecting surface, in colour a light gray-green.

The tower rests on two longitudinal walls and five cross-walls of reinforced concrete. The longitudinal walls with their heavy loads are supported at the third and fourth floor levels (where there are rooms for service machinery, the administration, and the staff cafeteria) by longitudinal beams which are two full storeys deep. The beams, with the six heavy columns in the lobby-lounge area and basement, form rigid frames. This disposition of longitudinal and cross-walls keeps the corners of the building free from structural members: the bands of windows extend uninterruptedly along all four sides.

Once inside these non-commital walls, the guest finds himself in quiet, dimly-lit interiors — the rooms are soundless and softly carpeted. The muted effect is by no means lifeless, however. The grain of woods and the figuring of marble stand out under soft lights, and the upholstered chairs by Jacobsen (the Egg and the Swan models) almost startle by the distinctiveness of their shapes.

Deep in the 400 m² lobby is a spiral stair leading to the restaurant and two-storey winter garden, which has a large rooflight. Orchids grow all the year round in heated glass boxes on two sides of the room. The glass ceiling of the winter garden, 8 m high, is the only source of natural light for the lobby-lounge area, other than the glass walls of the entrance. The snack bar also gets its daylight from the winter garden.

The guest apartments, all air-conditioned, are distributed over 17 of the 22 storeys. The corridors are agreeably short, but even so Jacobsen has enlivened them by putting striplights over the slightly recessed doors. Guestrooms have wall-to-wall windows. Continuous paneling 0,90 m high, of Wengé wood, adds a touch of warmth. The bedside tables, drawers, desk and dressing table are all cantilevered from the paneling and can be moved laterally, like the light fittings. Colors in the rooms are confined to shades of gray-green and blue, intended to recall the tints of the waters of the Sound, and recurring in curtains, bedsheets, carpets, blankets, towels, ashtrays, telephones—even on the stationery.

The two-storey podium containing the lobby and terminal has a relatively dark gray-green exterior, to make it seem a more solid base for the paler gray-green tower.

1. The tall slab; a light gray-green surface with continuous bands of windows.

1. Der Turmbau. Lichte graugrüne Hülle, umlaufende Fensterbänder.

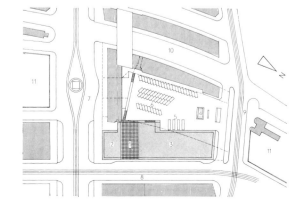

Site plan. Key: 1 Hotel, 2 Restaurant, 3 Air terminal, 4 Gas station, 5 SAS buses, 6 Parking, 7 Vesterbrogade, 8 Hammerichsgade, 9 Vesterport, 10 Vester Farimagsgade, 11 Railway.

Lageplan. Legende: 1 Hotel, 2 Restaurant, 3 Air-Terminal, 4 Tankstelle, 5 SAS-Autobusse, 6 Parkplätze, 7 Vesterbrogade, 8 Hammerichsgade, 9 An der Vesterport, 10 Vester Farimagsgade, 11 Bahngeleise.

SAS-Hotel Royal, Kopenhagen

Architekt: Arne Jacobsen

Die Fluggesellschaft SAS plante in der Innenstadt von Kopenhagen ein Hotel für höchste Ansprüche und ein Air-Terminal. Arne Jacobsen wollte eine Anlage aus einem Guß schaffen. Er wurde beauftragt, den Bau mit allen Einrichtungen bis hin zu den Möbeln, Lampen, Bestecken, Gläsern und Geschirren im eigenen Atelier zu entwerfen. Das Ergebnis war ein gestalterisch und funktionell höchst erfolgreiches Hotel, das echten skandinavischen Wohnkomfort spiegelt.

Auf dem knappen Gelände an der Vesterbrogade war außer einem großen Hotel mit 275 Zimmern (475 Betten) das Air-Terminal unterzubringen, das allein das halbe Grundstück einnahm. Um Parkplätze und Zufahrten für die Flughafen-Busse zu gewinnen, mußte das Bahngelände nach Westen überbaut werden. Für das Hotel blieb nur eine Hochhauslösung, die Arne Jacobsen in jedem Fall wollte, wegen des Straßenlärms von allen Seiten. Auflagen der Stadtverwaltung beschränkten das Bauvolumen und legten eine maximale Bauhöhe von 70 Metern fest. Jacobsen formte einen niedrigen zweigeschossigen Block aus dem Air-Terminal und dem Empfangs- und Restaurantteil des Hotels und ein Hochhaus von zwanzig Geschossen darüber. Es gewinnt durch seine geringe Länge eine packende turmartige Form, die naturgemäß nicht die wirtschaftlichste Lösung für die Wohngeschosse darstellt. Hier waren die Vorschriften im Wege. Jacobsen hielt das Hochhaus so leicht wie möglich, damit es nicht die umgebenden Gebäude optisch erdrückte. Er schuf eine glatte Vorhangfassade, eine fast ungebrochene, spiegelnde, graugrüne Haut. Die Hochhausgeschosse ruhen auf zwei Längswänden und fünf Querschotten aus Stahlbeton. Die stark belasteten Längswände werden im dritten und vierten Stockwerk – hier liegen technische Räume, die Verwaltung und die Kantine des Personals – von Längsträgern in der vollen Höhe der beiden Geschosse aufgefangen. Die Träger bilden mit den sechs mächtigen Stützen durch Halle und Keller steife Rahmen. Das konstruktive Konzept aus Längswänden und Schotten hält die Gebäudeecken von jeder Konstruktion frei, die Fensterbänder laufen ungebrochen über die vier Fassaden.

Im Innern der bewußt neutralen Hülle findet der Gast eine ruhige dämmerige Atmosphäre, in weich ausgelegten, lautlosen Räumen. Der gedämpfte Effekt wirkt nicht einen Augenblick tot. Holzmaserungen und Marmormuster treten in mattem Licht hervor, die Polstermöbel aus Jacobsens Hand überraschen durch stark variierte Grundformen wie »Ei« und »Schwan«. In der Tiefe der Halle von 400 qm liegen die Wendeltreppe zum Restaurant und der zweistöckige Wintergarten. Orchideen wachsen das ganze Jahr in temperierten Glasgehäusen an den Längsseiten.

Für die Gastzimmer, die alle klimatisiert sind, stehen siebzehn der zweiundzwanzig Stockwerke zur Verfügung. Die Korridore sind angenehm kurz, trotzdem hat Jacobsen sie durch Lichtstreifen über den leicht zurückgesetzten Türen belebt. Die Zimmer öffnen sich in Fenstern von Wand zu Wand. Umlaufende Holzpaneele in Wengéholz, neunzig Zentimeter hoch, geben ein geborgenes Gefühl. Die Nachttische, Schubladen-, Schreib- und Toilettenelemente werden in die Täfelung eingehängt und lassen sich, wie die Wandleuchten, seitlich verschieben. Farblich sind die Räume auf graugrüne und blaue Töne abgestellt. Sie sollen die Farbnuancen des Öresunds anklingen lassen und kehren wieder in Vorhängen und Bezügen, in Teppichen, Decken und Handtüchern, in Aschbechern und Telephonen – selbst auf dem Briefpapier. Im Gegensatz zum Hotelturm mit seinem lichten Graugrün ist der zweigeschossige flache Trakt als Basis in einem dunkleren graugrünen Ton gehalten.

A Longitudinal section. Key: 1 Machinery floor, 2 Suites, 3 Typical guest-room floor, 4 Office floor, 5 Services floor, 6 Restaurant, 7 Lounge, 8 Bar, 9 Shops, 10 Lobby, 11 Winter garden, 12 Snack bar, 13 Storage, 14 Garage, 15 Bar, 16 Air terminal, 17 Tourist office, 18 Canteen.
B Plan, typical guest-room floor. Key: 1 Single room, 2 Double room, 3 Convertible room, 4 Service room, 5 Service elevators, 6 Passenger elevators, 7 Ventilation ducts, 8 Stairs.

A Längsschnitt. Legende: 1 Installationsgeschoß, 2 Suiten, 3 Normalgeschoß Gästezimmer, 4 Bürogeschoß, 5 Installationsgeschoß, 6 Restaurant, 7 Lounge, 8 Bar, 9 Läden, 10 Lobby, 11 Wintergarten, 12 Snackbar, 13 Lagerräume, 14 Tiefgarage, 15 Bar, 16 Air-Terminal, 17 Reisebüro, 18 Kantine.
B Normalgeschoß Gästezimmer. Legende: 1 Einbettzimmer, 2 Zweibettzimmer, 3 Wandelbares Zimmer (Wohn- oder Schlafraum), 4 Serviceraum, 5 Serviceaufzüge, 6 Gästeaufzüge, 7 Ventilationskanal, 8 Treppe.

A

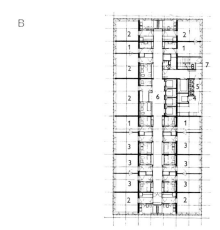

B

C Plan, ground floor. Key: 1 Hotel entrance, 2 Lobby, 3 Front desk, 4 Telephone exchange, 5 Elevators, 6 Stairs to 2nd floor, 7 Winter garden, 8 Snack bar, 9 Shops, 10 Newsstands, bookstalls, 11 Pastries, 12 Ramp in, 13 Goods reception, 14 Luggage, 15 Snack bar kitchen, 16 Stairs to the toilets, 17 Stairs to the bar, 18 Air terminal, 19 Bank, 20 Porch, 21 Bus station, 22 Luggage, 23 Service, 24 Offices, 25 Tourist office, 26 European bookings, 27 Overseas bookings, 28 Inland bookings, 29 Cashier, 30 Car-hire, 31 Stairs to offices.

C Grundriß Erdgeschoß. Legende: 1 Hoteleingang, 2 Lobby, 3 Empfang, 4 Telephonzentrale, 5 Aufzüge, 6 Treppe zum ersten Obergeschoß, 7 Wintergarten, 8 Snackbar, 9 Läden, 10 Kioske, 11 Konditorei, 12 Einfahrt Tiefgarage, 13 Warenannahme, 14 Gepäckkorridor, 15 Küche der Snackbar, 16 Treppe zu den Toiletten, 17 Treppe zur Bar, 18 Air-Terminal, 19 Bank, 20 Windfang, 21 Autobushaltestelle, 22 Gepäck, 23 Kundendienst, 24 Büroräume, 25 Reisebüro, 26 Europa-Expedition, 27 Übersee-Expedition, 28 Inland-Expedition, 29 Kasse, 30 Autoverleih, 31 Treppe zu den Büros.

C

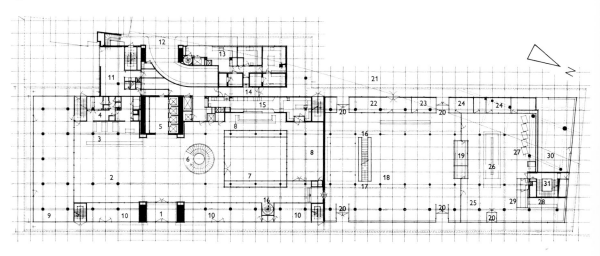

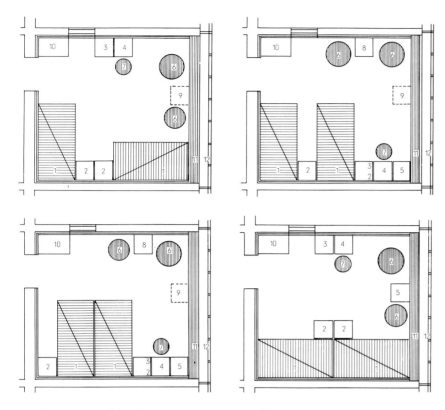

Furniture variants of double rooms. Key: 1 Bed, 2 Bedside table, 3 Radio, 4 Make-up table, 5 Drawer unit, 6 Lounge chair, 7 Easy chair, 8 Table, 9 Writing table, 10 Luggage bench, 11 Air conditioner, 12 Window.

Möblierungsvarianten der Doppelzimmer. Legende: 1 Bett, 2 Nachttisch, 3 Radio, 4 Frisiertisch, 5 Schubkasten, 6 Ruhesessel, 7 Leichter Sessel, 8 Tisch, 9 Schreibplatte, 10 Kofferbank, 11 Klimaanlage, 12 Fenster.

2. The lobby. Flooring of gray Norwegian marble, and occasional rugs. Beyond is the winter garden.
3. Restaurant lounge: walls are of black Italian marble.
4. The elevator lobby on the first floor level.
5. Guest apartment. Wall-to wall window, partitions and air-conditioner sheathed in Wengé wood. Sliding lamp for bedside table and writing desk.
6. Egg and Swan chairs in an apartment.
7. Make-up table lit from within, and cantilevered from the wall paneling.

2. Die Halle. Boden aus grauem norwegischem Marmor, Teppich-Inseln. In der Tiefe der Wintergarten. Seine Glasdecke 8 m hoch gelegen, ist neben der Eingangsfront die einzige Lichtquelle für Hotelhalle und Snackbar.
3. Restaurant-Lounge. Wände in schwarzem italienischem Marmor.
4. Die Fahrstuhlhalle im Restaurantgeschoß.
5. Gastzimmer. Fenster in voller Breite. Wände und Klimaanlage in Wengéholz verkleidet. Gleitende Lampe für Nachttisch und Schreibplatte.
6. Ei- und Schwanensessel in einem Apartment.
7. Frisiertisch von innen beleuchtet, in die Wandverkleidung eingehängt.

8. The narrow glass-walled space of the winter garden, which rises through two storeys.
9. Snack-bar on the ground floor level.
10. Hotel glasses by Jacobsen, elegant but sturdy enough to stand up to dish-washing equipment.
11. The restaurant on the second floor: a low dark ceiling above well-lit tables.
12. The restaurant lounge. Rosewood, green fabrics and carpeting. The ceiling is stained dark gray-green.

8. Die »Glasräume« des Wintergartens, schmal über zwei Geschosse.
9. Die Snackbar im Erdgeschoß.
10. Hotelgläser von Jacobsen, gut geformt, doch robust genug für Spülmaschinen.
11. Restaurant im Obergeschoß. Niedere dunkle Decke über der gut beleuchteten Tischebene.
12. Restaurant-Lounge. Wandverkleidung aus Palisanderholz, grüne Bezüge und Spannteppich, dunkel getönte Decke in Graugrün.

Hotel María Isabel, Mexico, D. F.

Architects: José Villagrán, García and Juan Sordo Madaleno; Assistant: Agustín Caso Bercht

1. The hotel and office building from the south. In the foreground the Independence Statue.

1. Hotel und Geschäftsgebäude von Süden. Vorn rechts die Unabhängigkeitssäule.

Site plan with hotel and office building. Under the raised plaza are ramps to the garage.

Lageplan mit Hotel und Geschäftsgebäude. Unter der neugeschaffenen Plaza die Zufahrtsrampen zur Tiefgarage.

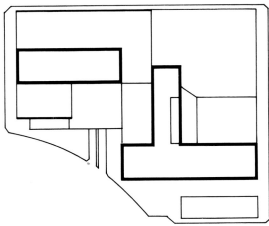

The leading luxury hotel of the Mexican capital is on the Paseo de la Reforma, at the spot where the avenue with its rich greenery widens to form a square almost 200 m across, with the Independence Monument at its centre. The architects have related their hotel and the adjoining office building closely to the square, adding a minor element in the form of a raised hotel plaza. Since the hotel is basically T-shaped, not all of its guest-rooms face the Paseo, and the defect of interminable corridors has been avoided. The architects have designed a pure glass cube 19 storeys high, in a city normally noted for more massive buildings. The glassy surface conceals a diversity of interiors: the wide lobbies and lounges, the broad and gently ascending stairways all show rich color schemes. Walls are of white marble, wood trellises under the ceilings are stained a matt black, floors are covered with textured carpets of deep red. Some Mexican onyx is used, light in color and cut thin, and some stainless steel.

The expansiveness of the lobby and lounge obviously contribute to the enjoyment of visitors. Arriving guests drive to a sunken patio with their luggage: their suitcases are immediately taken out of sight, to reappear in their rooms. Residents alight from their taxis at the Paseo entrance, from which they descend a few steps to the lobby. Pedestrians can also reach the lounges, bars and restaurant from the plaza screened by the main building. The owners wanted a hotel of European type. The apartments are larger than those of typical luxury hotels in the United States, and a European designer was commissioned to furnish the numerous suites.

The basic module of 8 m is shown on the plan by sound-proof double walls. The ends of the partitions, recessed slightly from the glazing line, dictate the rhythm of the façades. Apartments on the 12 typical floors are each 4 m wide. Single apartments in the main building and doubles in the northwest wing follow the layout widely used in the United States: their closets are at a right angle to the corridor, bath tubs are parallel with it. The double apartments have built-in washbasins in niches outside their bathrooms. In the Paseo rooms, which are about 9 m deep, a closet is used as a room divider. It screens off a comfortable dressing area with a washbasin. Guests can choose among apartments with a variety of color schemes, though strong primary colors have been shunned. The corridors are most skilfully designed. Their width is varied by niches on both sides; changes in ceiling height and lighting have also been made use of. The entrances to the apartments are staggered on plan, so that a blank wall faces each door.

In keeping with its reputation of being one of the hubs of social life in Mexico, the María Isabel offers a wide choice of ballrooms, salons and party rooms. The great Salón de Fiestas is at ground level projecting to the northwest from the tall slab of the main wing. Other public rooms are on the top floors, close to the suites.

The hotel convinces by its unity of expression. Remaining parts of the podium are put out of sight in screened areas. The many functions of a big hotel: restaurants, mechanical services, apartments, suites, swimming pool and patio—all are shrouded behind huge sheets of glass and can only be traced in the pattern of mullions on the mirror-like façade.

Hotel María Isabel, Mexico, D. F.

Architekten: José Villagrán, García und Juan Sordo Madaleno; Mitarbeiter: Agustín Caso Bercht

Das führende Luxushotel der Hauptstadt steht am Paseo de la Reforma, dort wo die Prachtstraße mit ihrem vielen Grün sich um das Unabhängigkeitsdenkmal zu einem Platz von fast zweihundert Metern ausdehnt. Die Architekten bezogen ihr Hotel und ein Bürogebäude, das daneben entstand, ganz auf diese Platzgestaltung und setzten ihr in kleinerem Maßstab den Akzent einer erhöhten Plaza entgegen. Das Grundschema des Hotels ist ein Winkelbau, der nicht die ganze Masse des Bettenblocks von 440 Zimmern zum Paseo zeigt und schon durch diese Grundanlage endlose Hotelflure vermeidet. Das Gebäude wurde als völlig verglaster Kubus von 19 Geschossen entworfen, eine reine Glasarchitektur in einer Stadt, die eher zu massiveren Bauten neigt. Die spiegelnde Hülle des Baues birgt einen Kontrast. Die weiten Hallen des Inneren, die flach ansteigenden, fürstlich breiten Aufgänge sind in starken Farbakkorden gehalten: Wände in weißem Marmor, matt schwarz gebeizte Balkenroste unter den Decken, Böden ausgelegt mit kassettenhaft gemusterten Teppichen in einfarbig tiefrotem Ton. Dazu wenige Akzente von dünn geschnittenem, hellem mexikanischem Onyx und Edelstahl. Der räumliche Aufwand der Empfangsgeschosse dient wirklich dem Komfort des Gastes. Neuankommende mit Gepäck fahren beim Untergeschoß in einem vertieften Patio vor, die Koffer gehen sofort einen getrennten Weg und werden erst im Gastzimmer wieder gesehen. Wer schon im Hotel wohnt und im Taxi vorfährt, nimmt den Eingang am Paseo, der über ein paar Stufen abwärts in die Halle führt. Fußgänger erreichen Hallen, Bars und Restaurant außerdem von der hochgelegten Plaza im geschützten Winkel des Hauptbaues.

Die Auftraggeber wünschten ein Hotel europäischer Prägung. Die Apartments sind größer als in den typischen Luxushotels der USA; für die zahlreichen Suiten wurde ein Innenarchitekt aus Europa geholt.

Ein Grundraster von 8 m ist im Plan durch schalldämmende Doppelwände markiert; die Mauerenden, gegen die Außenfläche etwas zurückgesetzt, bestimmen den Ablauf der Fassaden. Die Apartments der zwölf Normal-

geschosse nehmen je 4 m Breite ein. Die Einzelräume im Hauptbau und die Zweibett-Apartments im Nordwestflügel folgen dem amerikanisch-rationellen Modus (Schränke quer, Badewannen parallel zum Flur), haben aber für die Doppelzimmer eingebaute Waschbecken in einer Nische vor dem Bad. In den Apartments zum Paseo, die über 9 m tief sind, dient eine Schrankwand als Raumteiler. Es entsteht eine bequeme Ankleideecke mit Waschbecken. Der Gast kann in den Apartments unter einer Reihe von Farbgebungen wählen, starke Primärfarben sind aber vermieden. Besonders geschickt wurden die Flure gelöst: in der Breite wechselnd, links und rechts mit verschieden tiefen Nischen, die Decken durch abgehängte Streifen und Lichteffekte unterteilt. Die Eingänge zu den Apartments versetzen sich gegeneinander, jeder Tür liegt eine Wandfläche gegenüber.

Seinem Ruf entsprechend, einer der Mittelpunkte des Gesellschaftslebens in Mexico zu sein, bietet das María Isabel eine ganze Anzahl von Ballsälen, Salons und Partyräumen. Der große Salón de Fiestas liegt zu ebener Erde, herausgesetzt, nach Nordwesten, aus der aufgehenden Masse des Haupttraktes. Andere Festräume sind in den obersten Geschossen nahe den Suiten untergebracht.

Das Hotel überzeugt durch seinen geschlossenen Ausdruck. Was vom Breitfuß bleibt, ist auf der Abseite in Nebenzonen gelegt. Die vielen Funktionen eines Großhotels – Restaurants, statisches Geschoß, Apartments, mechanische Anlagen, Suiten, Schwimmbad und Patio auf dem Dach – gehen optisch hinter der Glasfläche auf, zeigen sich nur in der Sprossenteilung der spiegelnden Fassade.

2. The main wing facing the Paseo. The functions of a hotel complex are expressed in the precise patterns of a glass façade.
3. The T-shaped building seen from southwest. Steps lead to the raised plaza.

2. Der Hauptflügel zum Paseo. Die Funktionen eines Hotelkomplexes aufgezeichnet in den präzisen Teilungen einer Glasfassade.
3. Der Winkelbau von Südwesten. Aufgang zur höher gelegten Plaza.

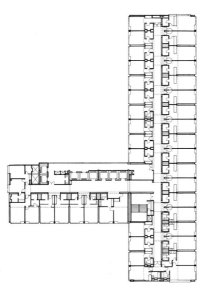

Plan, typical floor / Grundriß Normalgeschoß.

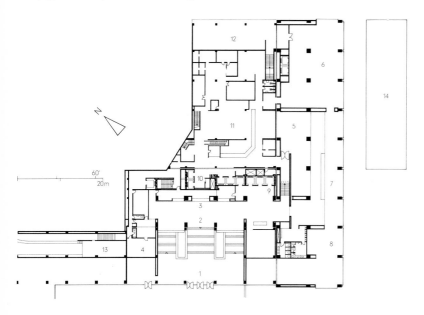

Plan, lobby level / Grundriß Empfangsgeschoß.

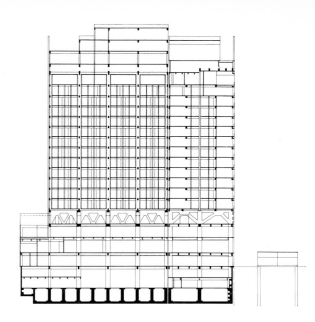

Section north-west/south-east/Schnitt Nordwest/Südost.

Key to plan: 1 Entrance from Plaza, 2 Lobby, 3 Front desk, 4 Manager and secretary, 5 Main dining room, 6 Specialties' restaurant, 7 Lounge, 8 Bar, 9 Passenger elevators, 10 Service elevators, 11 Kitchen, 12 Dining room, 13 Service court, 14 Shops' pavilion.

Legende zum Grundriß: 1 Eingang Plaza, 2 Lobby, 3 Empfang, 4 Direktion und Sekretariat, 5 Großer Speisesaal, 6 Spezialitätenrestaurant, 7 Lounge, 8 Bar, 9 Gästeaufzüge, 10 Personalaufzüge, 11 Küche, 12 Salon, 13 Wirtschaftshof, 14 Ladenpavillon.

4, 5. Living room of a corner suite, and a twin-bedded apartment. Spacious rooms with unpretentious clean-lined furniture.

4, 5. Wohnraum einer Ecksuite und ein Twinbett-Apartment. Großzügige Raumwirkung; klare, einfache Möbel.

6. The upper lounge overlooking the Paseo. All emphasis is on the strongly-patterned ceiling.
7. Information desks and shops in the lower lobby.
8. The main stairway, invitingly broad. Light sources are large, and of low intensity.
9. White marble, deep red carpeting, light-colored onyx, cut thin to diffuse the lighting.

6. Obere Halle zum Paseo. Alle Akzente in der stark gegliederten Decke.
7. Informationsstände und Läden in der unteren Lobby.
8. Die einladende Breite der Haupttreppe. Flächig verteilte Lichtquellen.
9. Weißer Marmor, tiefroter Teppich, heller Onyx, dünn geschnitten, für diffuse Beleuchtung.

Royal Garden Hotel, London

Architects: R. Seifert and Partners

One of the most recent luxury hotels in London—opened in 1965—the Royal Garden is fortunately situated. It is within easy reach of the West End and is not far from the West London Air Terminal, and near fashionable shopping streets and the exhibition centers of Earl's Court and Olympia. The hotel is magnificently sited on the edge of Kensington Palace Gardens. With town planning permission for a building of not more than 38 m high, it was necessary to adopt a T-shaped plan which gave only some of the rooms a view of the park to the east. This unrivaled prospect of Kensington Gardens and Hyde Park is shared by most of the double rooms and suites—all of which have private balconies—and by the hotel's principal restaurants—the Garden Room and the Royal Roof.

The low height of only 38 m imposed by the authorities, forced four of the fifteen storeys down under ground. The two lowest basements house over 300 cars and are accessible from spiral ramps. The second basement accommodates a number of administrative offices, the staff lockers and storage rooms, and the boiler house. On the uppermost basement level are the staff dining room, the Banquet Hall and the Maze Coffee House. All basement levels can be reached by lorries from the ramps to the car park.

Access to the hotel is from an elevated drive on the south, Kensington High Street, elevation. The main ground floor houses the foyer and its annexed facilities, the kitchen complex and the main restaurant and lounge with a huge wall of windows facing east towards the park. The public spaces of this floor are supplemented on the lower ground floor level by the Bulldog Bar and Chophouse, which has separate access from the main street. The entrance foyer connects with another foyer serving the Banquet Hall below and thus with a car park lift. The mezzanine level is occupied by conference rooms and private dining rooms, the administration offices, and, largely, by voids above the foyer and restaurant areas.

The ten floors total over 500 bedrooms. Each typical floor contains 28 single and 18 double rooms, plus 4 corner suites. While chambermaids take care of 14 single units each in the west wing, the number of rooms serviced drops to 11 per maid for the doubles and suites.

The double rooms offer a choice of double beds, twin beds or daybeds. The suites are individually furnished and each bears the name of one of England's stately homes. It is here that the dilemma emerges of modern building exteriors and contemporary lounge areas in combination with interior decorator's furnishings in a far from contemporary vein. There are "cornices, ceilings, architraves and cupboards enriched with decorative plasterwork and lacquered ormolu to complement the period furniture." The Penthouse Suites are the culmination, both in terms of spacious comfort—drawing rooms of up to 15 m long—and of a bewildering amalgam of modern and period design.

In contrast with the neat openness of the main foyer and the Garden Room Lounge, the four restaurants try to combine modern elements with traditional overtones. The Maze Coffee House, open 24 hours, is shaped to suggest the maze in a Tudor garden. The Bulldog Bar and Chophouse, with its oyster bar and open charcoal grill, is paneled in dark walnut and has engraved mirrors depicting bull and bear baiting, but the wished-for pub atmosphere is not truly apparent. The Garden Room takes up the contemporary theme established in the foyer and lounge areas, but adds the feature of a painted barrel vault ceiling. These rooms seem more in character with the Royal Borough of Kensington than with the idiom of modern design.

Technically, the Royal Garden is one of the most advanced hotels in the world today. The reception has a transistorized electronic room reservation data system and electronic equipment to locate staff at any time. The meeting and conference rooms also offer perfect technical facilities. The Banquet Hall or Palace Suite, seating 600 guests for dinner, or a convention of 1000 delegates, can be divided into two rooms by hydraulically lowering a soundproof curtain from the ceiling. For special exhibitions there is direct access from the car park ramps, wide enough for outsize equipment like caravans and combine harvesters, and the floor loading of 425 kg per m² allows exhibits as heavy as printing machinery to be shown. Besides film projection, a public address system with 30 microphone points, and full theatrical lighting controls for the stage, there is short-wave broadcasting for simultaneous translation and closed circuit television relayed to the bedrooms for the use of resting guests. All these impressive technical features are operated by a resident engineer from a master control room. A fully-equipped press gallery with translators' booths runs the full length of the room at an upper level.

The Balmoral Suite on the mezzanine floor has reversible wall panels which reveal different surfaces on their other side. Tan leather or orange silk are used to create changing color schemes, or the panels can be removed to reveal continuous cork surfaces for pin-up displays. On the first bedroom floor there are 28 rooms whose walls can be removed to form intercommunicating suites of up to five rooms. The Syndicate Suites are suitable for smaller dinners, meetings or press receptions and can be used in conjunction with large conferences.

The construction of the building is based on a reinforced concrete frame with a double cantilever forming the ten bedroom floors. Traffic noise from Kensington High Street is dealt with by double windows on the south elevation, with a 15 cm gap between inner and outer sliding panels.

Exterior facings are white marble and mosaic, with some black granite on the canopy and Bardiglio Fiorito marble on the flank walls of the entrance. Both end walls of the east wing are clad in fluted stainless steel. Windows have silver anodized aluminum frames; the glass infill panels below sill height are framed in gold anodized aluminium.

1. The building seen from the south-east. Contrast of balconied east wing and curtain-walled west wing with aluminium trim. End wall faced in fluted stainless steel panels.
2. The main entrance and canopy. White marble columns, polished black granite on canopy slab. Lift in right corner connects with the basement car parks.

1. Das Gebäude von Südosten gesehen. Gegensatz zwischen dem Ostflügel mit seinen Balkonen und der Glasfassade des Westflügels mit Aluminiumrahmen. Giebelwand mit gerippten Edelstahlplatten verkleidet.
2. Haupteingang und Vordach. Weiße Marmorsäulen, geschliffener schwarzer Granit an den Stirnflächen des Vordachs. Der Fahrstuhl in der rechten Ecke verbindet mit den unterirdischen Parkgeschossen.

Hotel Royal Garden, London

Architekten: R. Seifert and Partners

Als eines der neuesten Luxushotels von London hat das Royal Garden eine besonders günstige Lage in der City. Es ist vom Westend und von Chelsea leicht zu erreichen und liegt nahe dem West London Air Terminal, den vornehmen Einkaufsstraßen der Stadt und den Ausstellungszentren von Earl's Court und Olympia. Das Hotelgebäude wurde in besonders schöner Umgebung am Rande der Kensington Palace Gardens erstellt. Da die Bauvorschriften nur eine Gebäudehöhe bis zu 38 m zuließen, mußte ein Plan in T-Form entwickelt werden, so daß nicht alle Räume nach Osten auf den Park gehen. Teil an dieser einmalig schönen Aussicht auf die Kensington Gardens und den Hyde Park haben die meisten Doppelzimmer und Suiten – durchweg mit Balkonen – und die Hauptrestaurants des Hauses (Garden Room und Royal Roof).

Die vorgeschriebene Gebäudehöhe von nur 38 m zwang dazu, vier der fünfzehn Geschosse unter Geländehöhe anzulegen. Die beiden untersten Kellergeschosse haben Garagen für 300 Wagen und werden über Wendelrampen erreicht. Das zweite Kellergeschoß von oben nimmt einen Teil der Verwaltungsräume auf, die Personal- und Lagerräume und die Heizanlage. Im obersten Kellergeschoß liegt der Speiseraum des Personals, der Festsaal und das Maze Coffee House. Alle Kellerebenen können mit Lastwagen über die Garagenrampen erreicht werden.

Die Zufahrt zum Hotel liegt an einer überhöht angelegten Fahrbahn auf der Südseite (Kensington High Street). Die öffentlichen Räume des Erdgeschosses (Main Ground Floor) – die Hotelhalle und damit zusammenhängende Funktionen, der Küchenkomplex, das Hauptrestaurant und die Lounge, beide mit einer riesigen Glaswand nach Osten zum Park geöffnet – werden im unteren Erdgeschoß (Lower Ground Floor) durch die Bulldog Bar and Chophouse mit eigenem Zugang von der Hauptstraße ergänzt. Die Eingangshalle des Chophouse ist mit dem Foyer des Festsaals auf der unteren Ebene und mit den Fahrstühlen zur Garage verbunden. Das Mezzaningeschoß wird von Tagungs- und privaten Gesellschaftsräumen und dem Verwaltungstrakt eingenommen; weiter von den Lufträumen im oberen Bereich der Hotelhalle und des Restaurants.

Die zehn Obergeschosse mit etwa 500 Gästezimmern haben jeweils 28 Einzel- und 18 Doppelzimmer (sämtliche mit Bädern), dazu je 4 Ecksuiten. Während die Zimmermädchen im Westflügel je 14 Einzelzimmer besorgen, sinkt die Zahl der Räume je Zimmermädchen für die Doppelzimmer und Suiten auf elf.

Die Doppelzimmer sind nach Wahl mit französischen Betten, Doppelbetten oder Tagescouchen ausgestattet. Die Suiten sind individuell gestaltet und jede von ihnen trägt den Namen eines der Stately Homes von England. Hier tritt das Dilemma zwischen moderner Gestaltung in den Außenfronten und öffentlichen Räumen und einer ganz und gar nicht zeitgemäßen Raumgestaltung zutage. In den Suiten findet man »Gesimse, Decken, Architrave und Schränke mit dekorativen Stuckarbeiten und Blattgold verziert, welche die antiken Möbel ergänzen«. Die Penthouse Suites zeigen ein Höchstmaß an räumlichem Komfort – Wohnräume mehr als 15 m lang – und gleichzeitig ein verwirrendes Amalgam von moderner und historisierender Raumgestaltung.

Im Gegensatz zu der klaren, offenen Architektur der Haupteingangshalle und der Garden Room Lounge, versuchte man in den vier Restaurants, moderne Elemente und traditionelle Obertöne zu vereinen. Das Maze Coffee House, das 24 Stunden täglich geöffnet ist, soll in seiner Anlage einen Irrgarten aus der Tudor-Zeit suggerieren. Die Bulldog Bar and Chophouse mit Austernbar und offenem Holzkohlengrill ist in dunkler Walnuß getäfelt und hat ge-

(Fortsetzung Seite 58)

(Fortsetzung von Seite 57)
schliffene Spiegelmotive, die Bären- und Bullenhatzen zeigen; die gewünschte Pub-Atmosphäre wird aber nicht wirklich erreicht. Der Garden Room nimmt die zeitgemäße Gestaltung der Eingangshalle und der großen Lounge auf, fügt aber mit der gemalten gewölbten Deckenschale ein neues Element hinzu. Diese Räume scheinen mehr mit dem Charakter des Royal District of Kensington im Einklang zu stehen als mit dem formalen Ausdruck unserer Zeit.

Technisch ist das Royal Garden heute eines der fortschrittlichsten Hotels in der Welt. Der Empfang hat ein volltransistoriertes »Room-Status-System« und elektronische Anlagen, um die Bewegungen des Personals zu verfolgen. Auch die Versammlungs- und Konferenzräume sind technisch vollkommen ausgestattet. Der Festsaal (Banquet Hall oder Palace Suite), mit Platz für 600 Gäste zum Diner oder 1000 Konferenzteilnehmer, kann in zwei Räume geteilt werden, indem man einen schalldichten Vorhang von der Decke hydraulisch herunterläßt. Für besondere Ausstellungen ist eine direkte Zufahrt von den Garagenrampen gegeben, breit genug für übergroße Ausstellungsstücke wie Wohnwagen oder Mähdrescher; der Fußboden kann Lasten bis 425 kg/qm aufnehmen, so daß selbst schwere Ausrüstungen wie Druckereimaschinen gezeigt werden können. Außer Filmprojektion, einer Lautsprecheranlage mit 30 Mikrophonauslässen und einer voll regulierbaren Bühnenbeleuchtung gibt es Kurzwellenübertragung zur Simultanübersetzung und ein internes Fernsehsystem, das den Ablauf einer Tagung in die einzelnen Gästezimmer überträgt. Alle diese eindrucksvollen technischen Anlagen werden durch einen hauseigenen Ingenieur von einem Kontrollraum aus gesteuert. Eine voll ausgestattete Pressegalerie mit Übersetzerzellen nimmt im oberen Bereich eine ganze Wand des Festsaals ein.

Die Balmoral Suite im Mezzaningeschoß bietet Raum für 130 bis 170 Personen; sie hat umkehrbare Wandflächen, die auf beiden Seiten verschiedene Materialien zeigen. Leder in Beige oder orangerote Seide werden genutzt, um wechselnde Farbeindrücke zu geben; die Panels können auch ganz entfernt werden, um durchgehende Korkflächen zum Anheften von Übersichten und graphischen Objekten freizulegen. Im ersten Schlafraumgeschoß liegen 28 Räume, deren Wände herauszunehmen sind, um durchgehende Suiten in der Größe von bis zu fünf Räumen zu schaffen. Diese Syndicate Suites sind für kleinere Diners, Konferenzen und Presseempfänge geeignet und können auch in Verbindung mit großen Kongressen gebraucht werden.

Das konstruktive System des Gebäudes basiert auf einem Stahlbetonskelett mit doppelten Kragplatten in den zehn Schlafgeschossen. Das Problem des Verkehrslärms von Kensington High Street wurde gelöst, indem auf der Südseite Doppelfenster mit 15 cm Abstand zwischen den inneren und äußeren Schiebefenstern ausgeführt wurden.

Die Außenflächen sind in weißem Marmor und Mosaik gehalten, mit schwarzem geschliffenem Granit am Vordach und Bardiglio-Fiorito-Marmor an den Seitenwänden der Vorfahrt. Beide Giebelwände des Ostflügels wurden mit gerippten Edelstahlplatten verkleidet. Die Fenster haben Rahmen aus silbereloxiertem Aluminium, die gläsernen Brüstungsplatten sind in goldeloxierten Aluminiumrahmen gefaßt.

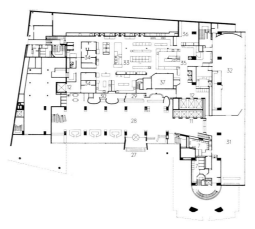

Plan, upper ground floor / Grundriß Erdgeschoß, oberes Niveau.

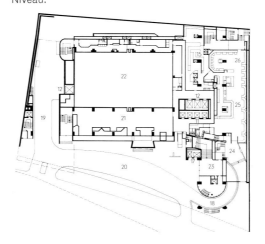

Plan, lower ground floor / Grundriß Erdgeschoß, unteres Niveau.

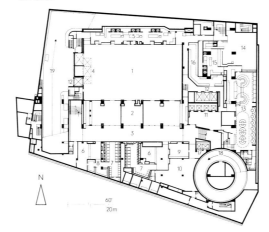

Plan, first basement floor / Grundriß erstes Untergeschoß.

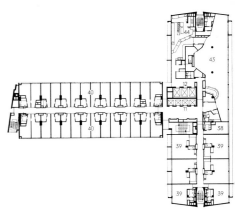

Plan, 13th floor / Grundriß 13. Obergeschoß.

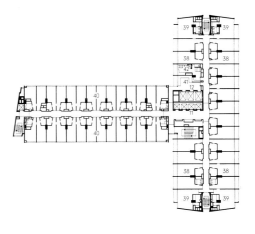

Plan, typical floor (5th to 12 th floor) / Grundriß Normalgeschoß (5.–12. Obergeschoß).

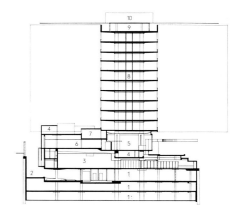

Section / Schnitt.

Key to plans: 1 Ballroom, 2 Reception ballroom, 3 Ballroom foyer, 4 Stage, 5 Service area, 6 Coats, 7 W.C.s, 8 Powder room, 9 Barber shop, 10 Beauty shop, 11 Passenger lifts, 12 Service lifts, 13 Maze Coffee House, 14 Staff dining room, 15 Service, 16 Wine storage, 17 Car park lifts, 18 Entrance ramp to car park levels, 19 Exit ramp, 20 Entrance drive, 21 Ventilation plant, 22 Void above ballroom, 23 Foyer and staircase of ballroom, 24 Foyer of bar, 25 Bar, 26 Grill room, 27 Hotel entrance, 28 Lobby, 29 Front desk, 30 Cashier, 31 Lounge and bar, 32 Restaurant, 33 Main kitchen, 34 Storage and refrigeration rooms, 35 Service area, 36 Pastry, 37 Telephone switchboard, 38 Double bedroom, 39 Suite, 40 Single bedroom, 41 Floor service, 42 Linen, 43 Roof restaurant, 44 Kitchen of roof restaurant.

Legende zu den Plänen: 1 Ballsaal, 2 Empfang für Ballgäste, 3 Ballsaalfoyer, 4 Bühne, 5 Servicebereich, 6 Garderobe, 7 Toiletten, 8 Schminkraum, 9 Friseur, 10 Schönheitssalon, 11 Gästefahrstühle, 12 Personalfahrstühle, 13 Maze Coffee House, 14 Personalspeiseraum, 15 Anrichte, 16 Weinlager, 17 Aufzüge zu den Parkgeschossen, 18 Einfahrtrampe, 19 Ausfahrtrampe, 20 Vorfahrt, 21 Ventilatoren, 22 Luftraum über Ballsaal, 23 Treppenhaus des Ballsaals, 24 Foyer der Bar, 25 Bar, 26 Grillraum, 27 Hoteleingang, 28 Lobby, 29 Empfang, 30 Kasse, 31 Lounge mit Bar, 32 Restaurant, 33 Hauptküche, 34 Lager- und Kühlräume, 35 Anrichte und Servicebereich, 36 Bäckerei, 37 Telephonvermittlung, 38 Doppelzimmer, 39 Suite, 40 Einzelzimmer, 41 Etagenservice, 42 Wäsche, 43 Dachrestaurant, 44 Küche Dachrestaurant.

Section. Key: 1 Car park basement, 2 Exit ramp, 3 Ballroom, 4 Ventilation plant, 5 Lobby, 6 Main kitchen, 7 Administration, 8 Guest-room slab, 9 Water storage, 10 Lift motor room.

Schnitt. Legende: 1 Parkgeschosse der Tiefgarage, 2 Ausfahrtrampe, 3 Ballsaal, 4 Ventilatorenraum, 5 Lobby, 6 Hauptküche, 7 Verwaltung, 8 Bettenblock, 9 Wasserbehälter, 10 Aufzugsmaschinenraum.

3. The entrance foyer, a tall unbroken space of contemporary design. Precise polished materials—stone, metal, mirror strips, dark wood. Small windows above the mural give a view from the administrative area on the mezzanine level.
4. The tall space of the main foyer; quiet bays by the windows marked by island carpets.
5. The Garden Room Lounge Bar overlooking Kensington Gardens.

3. Die Eingangshalle, ein hoher durchgehender Raum in neuzeitlichem Gewande. Polierte Präzision in den Materialien: Stein, Metall, Spiegelstreifen, dunkles Holz. Kleine Fenster über dem Wandgemälde erlauben Einblick von den Verwaltungsräumen im Mezzaningeschoß.
4. Die große Eingangshalle. Ruhige Buchten an der Fensterfront, unterstrichen durch Teppichinseln.
5. Die Garden Room Lounge Bar mit Blick auf die Kensington Gardens.

6. The Garden Room Restaurant, a re-statement of the neat interiors of the foyer and lounge with the added feature of a painted vaulted ceiling. On the right are the trees of Kensington Gardens.

7. The Royal Roof Restaurant, a late-night spot for theatergoers, overlooking Kensington Gardens and the London scene.

8. The banquet hall arranged for a large dinner party.

9. The Palace Suite (main banquet hall) set up for a convention. Removable red carpeting in a room designed to display exhibits of considerable size and weight. A complete range of technical facilities.

10. The Balmoral Suite at the mezzanine level. Reversible wall panels of tan leather and orange silk hiding a cork wall facing to pin up charts and graphic displays.

11. Maze Coffee House: an example of the interpenetration of contemporary and period design elements.

12.–15. Sitting-room and bedroom interiors blend contemporary and traditional elements, sliding glass doors and decorative plaster work.

6. Das Garden Room Restaurant, eine thematische Fortsetzung der klaren Raumgestaltung in den Hotelhallen mit einem zusätzlichen Akzent in der gemalten, flachgewölbten Decke. Zur Rechten die Bäume der Kensington Gardens.

7. Das Royal Roof Restaurant, ein Platz für Theaterbesucher in den späten Abendstunden; Blick auf die Kensington Gardens und London von der Höhe des Gästezimmerblocks.

8. Der Festsaal, hergerichtet für ein großes Diner.

9. Die Palace Suite (Festsaal), für eine Konferenz hergerichtet. Der Raum kann Ausstellungsstücke von bedeutendem Umfang und Gewicht aufnehmen, der rote Teppich ist abnehmbar. Ein vollständiges System technischer Einrichtungen.

10. Die Balmoral Suite im Mezzaningeschoß. Drehbare Wandverkleidungen, mit beigem Leder und orangeroter Seide bespannt; dahinter Korkplatten zum Aufhängen von Tabellen und graphischen Übersichten.

11. Das Maze Coffee House als Beispiel für das Nebeneinander moderner und historisierender Elemente.

12–15. In den Wohn- und Schlafräumen vermischen sich Elemente zeitgemäßer und traditioneller Raumgestaltung, Schiebewände aus Glas und dekorative Stuckarbeiten.

1

Hotel Cavalieri Hilton, Rome

Architects: Ugo Luccichenti, Emilio Pifferi, Alberto Ressa

round the swimming pool. A glass-walled atrium, containing a Japanese maple, euphorbia and four grindstones from the old coral mills of Leghorn, illuminates the core of the lounge. There are four smaller patios placed before the doors of the private dining rooms. The first is designed as a 16th-century Italian garden, with clipped hedges and begonias, the second as a desert garden, and the other two are planted with pampas grasses and waterside plants. These four different gardens on a site of a few square meters are seen from above as open rectangles of greenery in the broad and long mosaic terrace—pastel-colored in gray, beige and brown—of the entrance level.

The broad podium of lower floors—broad in section even compared with the considerable depth of the guest-room slab—is visible only in certain views from the swimming pool area; from most other points it remains hidden in the ground. The six guest-room floors are separated from the basement by a slim intermediate floor only half a storey high, which is not deep enough to collect the loads from the upper columns. The supporting structure therefore extends through to the lowest guest-room floor, where it is housed in the main partitions. It reduces the number of columns per frame from six on the standard upper floors to two in the podium.

The structural engineers, P. L. Nervi among them, designed six different structural systems, two based on steel and four on reinforced concrete. The steel structures were excluded as too costly; of the reinforced concrete schemes, however, the architects chose not the most economical structural solution, but the one offering the least obstruction to plumbing and electrical services. The tall slab, with six guest-room floors, has exterior

(Continued page 64)

Rome, for visitors from all parts of the world, is the city of seven hills and numberless monuments, so it is appropriate that this recent luxury hotel should be built on a hill, the Monte Mario, and have all Rome's monuments at its feet.

The Hilton is easily reached from Fiumicino Airport and is well placed for major highway connections like the Autostrada del Sole and the Via Aurelia. The fifteen minutes' car journey to the city is not a major disadvantage. There are hourly bus connections with Roma Termini and Via Veneto and the hotel is a city in itself: it might well be called Hilton City. Its usable floor area of 56000 m² equals one seventh of the area of the Vatican City. This new recipe for a Roman hotel was immediately accepted by foreign visitors; Italian travelers, used to smaller city hotels, took a little more time to find their way to Monte Mario.

The Cavalieri Hilton occupies a 6 hectare site in a fashionable residential area near the observatory of Monte Mario. The view is one of the most beautiful imaginable. The Vatican and the dome of St. Peter's form one side of the view and the panorama of the city unrolls as if on a wide screen. To the south-east the Alban Hills rise above the haze and to the east one can see the Abruzzi.

Of the three sections which comprise a modern hotel—guest-room block, public rooms and service areas—the first is in the European tradition. Rooms are spacious, with very large bathrooms, but also afford the very best of New World comforts. The restaurants, convention and ballrooms closely follow American precedent and are of especially large size. Airline offices are ranged in a row and an enclosed shopping gallery offers the wares of Rome's leading boutiques without the trouble of leaving the hotel. The public rooms are planned as parts of a

functionally independent unit and can at any moment be placed under separate administration.

The service block providing for the other two sections obviously had to be on an equally large scale. It has an industrial character, functioning with the precision of a production line. The system makes impossible any conflict between the operation of the guest-room and public sections: the project was for some time based entirely on functional diagrams, which were only gradually developed into plans. It was no small task to fit a building with a volume of 228000 m³ into a sloping site, and the task was complicated by the requirements of the city authorities and the ministry of public works, which forced large areas of the building underground, but succeeded in safeguarding the charm of the naturally sloping site. More than half the enclosed space (52% or 118000 m³) was actually built below ground level. The huge block of the basement reaches down to an excavated depth of as much as 20 m. The podium is three full floors deep below the floor level of the lobby, and contains restaurants for 1200 persons, a ballroom and convention facilities for 2200, the kitchens and storage rooms, the steam baths and locker section, garages for 300 cars, staff rooms, mechanical installations, and a water tank holding 1200000 liters.

The upper lounge is of gigantic size and extends, following the slope, into a second equally large lounge; the two are joined by a broad curving double stairway. The lower lounge is virtually isolated from such hotel functions as reception, shopping and management. It is the hub of conventions and social affairs on its own floor. The ballroom and the elliptical dining club are interior rooms, while the lounge, main restaurant, cocktail lounge, and gallery for art exhibitions open onto the garden areas

1. The east façade overlooking the park and an unrivaled panorama—modern, ancient, and papal Rome.
2. The north wing toward the Monte Mario observatory—precast balcony fronts with facing of terracotta tiles.

1. Die Ostseite mit dem Blick auf den Park und ein Panorama ohne Beispiel: das moderne, das alte und das päpstliche Rom.
2. Der Nordflügel gegen das Observatorium auf dem Monte Mario. Vorgefertigte Brüstungen mit Verblendung aus Terracottaplatten.

Hotel Cavalieri Hilton, Rom

Architekten: Ugo Luccichenti, Emilio Pifferi, Alberto Ressa

Rom ist für Besucher aus aller Welt die Stadt der sieben Hügel und unzähliger Monumente. Es ist nur sinnvoll, daß das neueste Luxushotel der Ewigen Stadt auf einem Hügel, dem Monte Mario, liegt und alle Monumente Roms zu Füßen hat.

Das Hilton ist vom Flughafen Fiumicino leicht zu erreichen und liegt günstig zu den Fernstraßen, der Via Aurelia und der Autostrada del Sole. Daß man mit dem Wagen gut 15 Minuten von der City zum Hotel braucht, spielt kaum eine Rolle. Es gibt stündlich Verbindungen mit Roma Termini und Via Veneto, und das Hotel ist eine Stadt für sich, die mit Recht den Namen »Hilton-City« tragen könnte. Seine Geschoßfläche von über 56000 qm entspricht einem Siebentel der Vatikanstadt. Diese neue Formel für ein römisches Hotel fand bei den ausländischen Gästen sofort großen Widerhall; italienische Reisende, an kleinere Stadthotels gewöhnt, fanden langsamer den Weg nach dem Monte Mario.

Das Cavalieri Hilton umfaßt, im echten Sinne des Wortes, ein Gelände von 6 Hektar in einer vornehmen Wohngegend beim Observatorium des Monte Mario. Das Panorama ist eines der schönsten, die man finden kann. Der Vatikan mit der Kuppel von Sankt Peter flankiert die Aussicht, das Bild der Stadt entrollt sich wie auf einer Breitwand. Im Südosten tauchen die Albaner Berge aus dem Dunst und nach Osten zu die Abruzzen.

Von den drei Bereichen, die ein modernes Hotel ausmachen – Bettenblock, öffentliche Räume und Service –, ist der erste in der europäischen Tradition gehalten. Die Zimmer sind geräumig, haben große Bäder, sind aber ausgestattet mit dem höchsten Komfort der Neuen Welt. Die Restaurants, Konferenz- und Feständer dagegen halten sich ganz an amerikanische Vorbilder und sind

(Fortsetzung Seite 64)

3. The restaurant and pool area seen from the park—the ribbon pattern of the guest-room floors, slim partitions of travertine.
4. The glass-walled light-well of the lower lounge area— cacti, Japanese maples, ancient grindstones.
5. View from above of the restaurant and lower lounge roof with its elaborate mosaics, pierced by the atrium and four small patios.

3. Restaurants und Schwimmbad vom Park aus gesehen. Darüber die Bandstruktur der Gästegeschosse, schmale Balkonwände aus Travertin.
4. Atrium mit Glaswänden in der unteren Halle: Kakteen, japanische Ahornbüsche, antike Schleifsteine.
5. Das Restaurantgeschoß mit der unteren Halle unter einem Dach aus reich ornamentierten Mosaiken, darin ausgestanzt das Atrium und vier kleine Patios.

(Continued from page 62)
walls and balcony fronts clad with precast concrete panels, faced with terracotta tiles. The three floors of the basement have exterior walls sheathed with large areas of pinkish peperine stone.

The apartments in the long zigzag slab have a spacious vestibule, almost a dressing room, next to the corridor. Luggage, which porters bring up from the outer entrance, can be easily accommodated, so that not a single bulky suitcase has to be put in the bedroom. The vestibule is closed at night by a large door with a mirror surface, that fills the passage exactly and fits flush with the living room wall. Each apartment has a usable area of at least 30 m², enlarged outside the window wall by a loggia of 8 m².

The great importance attached to service is clearly expressed in the plan. For every three guest elevators there are three service elevators, plus another for luggage. Room service has been planned to obviate the need for kitchens on every floor, which are hard to control. The breakfast trolleys arrive direct by service elevator from a special part of the main kitchen. The kitchen complex of 1460 m² (for a restaurant floor area of 3000 m²) can serve 2200 meals at a time. The kitchen is between the ballroom and the main restaurants, and can also serve ready-made dishes to the café above. All preparation and storage rooms for meat, vegetables, fish and pastries are below, on the second basement level. They deliver a partly prepared product to the main kitchen. Large though the main cooking plant may be, the chef is still able to supervise all sections from his central control point.

The gardens of the Cavalieri Hilton cover two small hills —some 27000 m²—with greenery, creating with their pines a landscape as natural as that of any of the hills round Rome. The hills are artificial, however; 30000 of the 300000 m³ of earth excavated for the basements was deposited here. Several hundred trees were planted to turn the bare hillside into a landscaped park. A hundred pines (pinus pinea) up to 15 m high were planted, as were large numbers of oaks, magnolias, cedars, palms, cypresses and laurels. The trees and shrubs were grouped to open unexpected views of the city, or, from other points, to unfold gradual ones. Views may be simply framed, or emphasized by sharp perspective. The gardens took three years to complete, and so many trees were planted that they had to be given names of their own: for the gardeners, every tree still bears the name of the saint on whose day it was planted.

(Fortsetzung von Seite 63)
besonders großzügig gestaltet. Die Büros der Luftlinien bilden eine eigene Ladenzeile, und die Einkaufspromenade zur anderen Seite der Halle bietet die besten Boutiquen Roms, ohne daß man einen Schritt vor die Tür setzen müßte. Der Bereich der öffentlichen Räume ist funktionell so unabhängig konzipiert, daß er jederzeit einer autonomen Verwaltung unterstellt werden könnte. Der Serviceblock, der hinter den beiden ersten Bereichen steht, ist zwangsläufig ebenfalls groß entwickelt. Er hat industriellen Charakter und produziert mit der Präzision eines laufenden Bandes. Das System schließt jede Überschneidung mit den Funktionen der Gästebereiche aus. Die Planungsarbeit stützte sich lange Zeit nur auf Funktionsdiagramme, die nach und nach in Bauskizzen umgesetzt wurden. Eine Baumasse von 228000 cbm dem Hang anzufügen, war keine geringe Aufgabe, sie wurde erschwert durch Forderungen der Stadt und des Ministeriums für öffentliche Arbeiten; Forderungen, die ganze Trakte unter die Erde zwangen und dafür den Reiz der Hügelhänge schützten. Tatsächlich liegt mehr als die Hälfte des umbauten Raumes (52% oder 118000 cbm) unter Terrain. Der gewaltige Block der Breitfußbasis steckt tief im Boden, bis zu 20 m Tiefe ausgehoben. Er hat drei volle Geschosse, sein Dach liegt auf dem Bodenniveau der Eingangshalle. In dieser Basis finden sich Restaurants für 1200 Personen, Festsaal und Tagungsstätten für 2000 Menschen, die Küchen und die Lager, weiter die Bäderabteilung, Garagen für 300 Wagen, Personalräume und technische Zentralen, schließlich einem Wasserreservoir für 1200000 Liter.

Die obere Halle, riesig in ihren Ausmaßen, setzt sich dem Hang folgend über eine groß geschwungene Doppeltreppe in einer zweiten Lounge von gleichen Dimensionen fort. Diese untere Halle ist faktisch aus dem Hotelbetrieb mit Empfang und Concierge, Läden und Büros herausgenommen. Sie dient als Drehscheibe des gesellschaftlichen Lebens und der Tagungen in diesem Geschoß. Der Festsaal und der elliptische Supper-Club liegen im Innern, doch Halle, Hauptrestaurant, Bar und Ausstellungsgalerie öffnen sich auf der Talseite zu den Gartenanlagen um das Schwimmbad. Ein offenes Atrium – japanischer Ahorn und Euphorbia um vier alte Schleifsteine aus den Korallen-Werkstätten von Livorno – bringt Licht in den Kern der Halle. Vier kleinere Patios sind den Salons für private Veranstaltungen vorgelagert. Der erste in der Art eines italienischen Gartens aus dem 16. Jahrhundert mit Buchsbaumhecken und Begonien, der zweite ein Wüstengarten, die anderen mit Wiesengräsern und Pflanzen aus der Nähe des Wassers besetzt. Diese vier Gartenvarianten auf wenigen Quadratmetern wirken von oben als übergrünter Rahmen in der weitgestreckten Mosaikterrasse – beige, graue und bräunliche Pastelltöne – des Eingangsgeschosses.

Die breite Basis der Grundgeschosse, breit im Schnitt, selbst im Verhältnis zu der großen Tiefe des Bettenhau

ses, wird nur aus bestimmten Perspektiven um das Schwimmbad sichtbar, sonst bleibt sie auf ferne oder nahe Sicht im Boden. Darüber gehen die sechs Zimmergeschosse hoch, von dem Grundblock nur durch ein dünnes Polster getrennt. Das halbe Zwischengeschoß hat nicht genug statische Höhe, um die Stützenlasten von oben aufzunehmen. Die Auffangkonstruktion geht noch durch das unterste Wohngeschoß und liegt dort in den Wänden. Sie reduziert die Zahl der Stützenlasten von sechs in den Obergeschossen auf zwei in der Basis. Die Ingenieure, unter ihnen P. L. Nervi, entwarfen sechs verschiedene statische Systeme, zwei in Stahlbau, die anderen vier in Stahlbeton. Eine Metallkonstruktion schied als zu teuer aus, doch wurde unter den Vorschlägen in Stahlbeton nicht die preislich günstigste genommen, sondern eine Lösung, die den Installationssträngen die wenigsten Hindernisse bot. Der hohe Baukörper der sechs Wohngeschosse ist an den Außenwänden und Brüstungen durch vorgefertigte Zementtafeln mit eingelassenen Terracottaplatten verkleidet. Der Block der Untergeschosse zeigt als Außenhaut große Flächen von rötlichem Travertin.

Die Apartments in dem langen S-förmig abgekanteten Block haben zum Flur ein geräumiges Vestibül, fast ein Schrankzimmer. Das Gepäck, das vor dem Eingang des Hotels – und nicht in der Halle – entgegengenommen wurde, findet hier reichlich Platz, kein Koffer steht sperrig im Zimmer. Der Vorraum wird nachts durch eine verspiegelte Drehtür geschlossen, die genau den Durchgang füllt und in der Wand des Wohnschlafraumes aufgeht. Jede Einheit hat wenigstens 30 qm Fläche, erweitert durch eine Loggia von 8 qm.

Die große Bedeutung, die dem Service beigemessen wird, drückt sich schon im Plan aus. Auf drei Fahrstühle

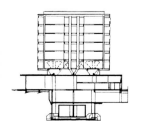

Section A-A / Schnitt A-A.

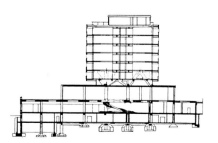

Section B-B / Schnitt B-B.

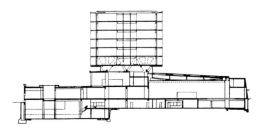

Section C-C / Schnitt C-C.

6. View to the south with the dome of Saint Peter's in the distance.

6. Blick nach Süden mit der Kuppel von Sankt Peter im Hintergrund.

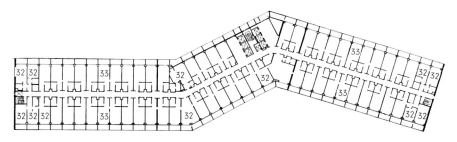

Plan, typical floor / Grundriß Normalgeschoß.

für Gäste kommen drei weitere für das Personal und dazu noch ein Gepäcklift. Für den Zimmerservice wurden die kaum kontrollierbaren Etagenküchen vermieden. Die Frühstückswagen kommen über die Aufzüge direkt aus einem Teil der Hauptküche. Der Küchenkomplex von 1460 qm (bei Restaurantflächen von 3000 qm) kann gleichzeitig 2200 Gedecke anrichten. Er liegt zwischen dem Festsaal und den Abendrestaurants, kann aber auch die Cafeteria darüber mit fertigen Gerichten beliefern. Alle Vorbereitungs- und Lagerräume für Fleisch, Gemüse, Fisch und Gebäck liegen ein Geschoß tiefer im zweiten Untergeschoß. Sie liefern an die Küche eine Art Halbfabrikat. Spezialgerichte werden aber ausschließlich in der Hauptküche zubereitet. So groß sie ist, der Küchenchef kann von einem zentralen Platz alle Abteilungen übersehen.

Die Gärten des Cavalieri Hilton übergrünen zwei kleine Hügel von 27000 qm und wirken mit ihren Schirmpinien so natürlich wie irgendeiner der Hänge um Rom. Die Hügel sind jedoch künstlich aufgeschüttet (30000 von den 300000 cbm Aushub des Hotels fanden hier ihren Platz). Mehrere hundert Bäume wurden gepflanzt, um das kahle Gelände zu einem Aussichtspark zu machen. Allein hundert Stämme Pinus Pinea, bis zu 15 m hoch, wurden verpflanzt, dazu Steineichen, Magnolien, Palmen, Zedern, Zypressen und Lorbeer. Die Baumgruppen und Gebüsche wurden räumlich so placiert, daß Ausblicke auf Rom sich plötzlich auftun, oder, von anderen Plätzen, sich langsam entfalten, daß diese Ausblicke ruhig gerahmt erscheinen oder perspektivisch forciert. Die Gärten wurden im Laufe von drei Jahren angelegt, und es wurden so viele Bäume gepflanzt, daß sie Namen bekommen mußten. Für die Gärtner trägt jeder Stamm bis heute den Namen des Heiligen, an dessen Festtag er gepflanzt wurde.

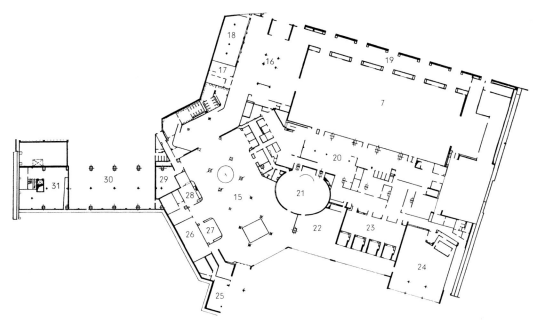

Plan, entrance floor / Grundriß Eingangsgeschoß.

Key to plans: 1 Access, main entrance, 2 Front desk, 3 Cash office, 4 Lobby, 5 Luggage, 6 Airline offices, 7 Ballroom, 8 Service gallery, 9 Cafeteria, 10 Terrace, 11 Shopping gallery, 12 Bank, 13 Ladies' hairdresser, 14 Administration, 15 Lounge, 16 Ball room foyer, 17 Office for conventions, 18 Coats, 19 Gallery, 20 Main kitchen, 21 Supper club, 22 Bar, cocktail lounge, 23 Private dining room, 24 Main restaurant, 25 Snack bar, 26 Green saloon, 27 Red saloon, 28 Restaurant management, 29 Telephone exchange, 30 Garage, 31 Basements of shops, 32 Suites, 33 Guest-rooms.

Legende zu den Plänen: 1 Vorfahrt, Haupteingang, 2 Empfang, 3 Kasse, 4 Lobby, 5 Gepäck, 6 Büros der Luftfahrtgesellschaften, 7 Ballsaal, 8 Servicegalerie, 9 Cafeteria, 10 Terrasse, 11 Ladenstraße, 12 Bank, 13 Damenfriseur, 14 Verwaltung, 15 Lounge, 16 Foyer des Ballsaals, 17 Kongreßbüro, 18 Garderobe, 19 Galerie, 20 Hauptküche, 21 Supper-Club, 22 Bar, Cocktail Lounge, 23 Räume für Privatparties, 24 Hauptrestaurant, 25 Snackbar, 26 Grüner Salon, 27 Roter Salon, 28 Direktion der Restaurants, 29 Telefonzentrale, 30 Garage, 31 Lagerräume der Läden, 32 Suiten, 33 Gästezimmer.

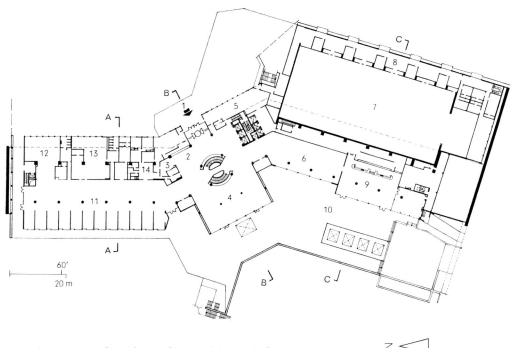

60'
20 m

Plan, first basement floor / Grundriß erstes Untergeschoß.

7. The upper and lower lounges connected by a springy steel stairway. Vaulted ceilings of aluminium strips.

8. Central feature of the grand stairway—a sculpted marble fountain with spiral channels.

9. Art gallery in the lower lounge area, close to the atrium and the garden view. Serial lighting fixtures of Murano glass.

10. The great ballroom, seating arranged in rows for a major convention.

11. The supper club with its large round tables set for a dinner.

7. Die obere und untere Hotelhalle verbunden durch eine Stahltreppe. Gewölbte Sichtdecken aus Aluminiumstreifen.

8. Kernstück der großen Treppenanlage: eine in Marmor gehauene Fontäne mit spiralig zulaufenden Rillen.

9. Kunstgalerie in der unteren Hotelhalle, nahe dem Atrium, mit Blick auf den Garten. Bandartig gereihte Beleuchtungskörper aus Muranoglas.

10. Der große Ballsaal, in Reihen bestuhlt für einen Kongreß.

11. Der Supper-Club mit großen runden Tischen hergerichtet für eine Dinnerparty.

12. A standard twin-bed apartment overlooking the city. All rooms have large balconies, richly textured fabrics, single-coloured carpeting. Heated or cooled air is distributed from unit next to window.

12. Ein Standard-Apartment mit getrennten Doppelbetten. Alle Räume haben Balkone, kontrastreich gewirkte Stoffe, einfarbige Teppichböden. Warme oder gekühlte Luft wird von einem Klimagerät unten am Fenster verteilt.

Hotel Royal, Munich

Architects: Richard Heller and Ernst M. Lang

Hotel Royal, München

Architekten: Richard Heller und Ernst M. Lang

This building, erected on a crowded city site, was originally intended to be an office block. The architects had to fit hotel accommodation into a tight existing plan after the structural framework was in place. Lined up along the street front are the hotel entrance, a jeweler's shop, a branch bank, a snack bar and the entrance to a basement night club. The lobby, breakfast room and bar corner occupy the second floor; six further floors contain a total of 48 guest-rooms, each with a shower bath. The interiors, designed by R. Heller, were of particular importance in such a tight plan. The designer has succeeded in creating continuity of line and articulation of space in the lobby and dining-breakfast room; privacy is achieved by partial screening. Ceilings and walls are deeply textured, wood predominates in the comparatively narrow range of materials used (wicker, unpolished glass, wall-to-wall carpets). The front elevation is composed of simple ribbons—precast concrete panels, aluminium windows with exterior sunblinds, and illuminated lettering of regular shape and uniform design. The architects meant this regularity and sobriety to distinguish the hotel from its gaudily-lettered neighbours.

Das Gebäude entstand in einer Baulücke der Innenstadt und sollte ursprünglich ein Bürohaus werden. Die Architekten mußten Hotelfunktionen in den knappen Grundriß einplanen, als das tragende Skelett bereits stand.
An der Straße liegen dicht nebeneinander Hoteleingang, Juwelierladen und Bankfiliale, ein Imbißlokal und der Zugang zu einem Night-Club im Keller. Empfang, Frühstücksraum und Barecke nehmen das erste Obergeschoß ein, darüber kommen die sechs Normalgeschosse mit zusammen 48 Zimmern, alle mit Duschbad. Der Raumgestaltung von R. Heller kam bei einem so beengten Projekt besondere Bedeutung zu. Es gelang, im Empfang und im Speiseraum durchgehende Linien und Raumzonen zu schaffen und durch teilweise Abschirmung Räume intim abzusondern. Decken und Wände sind stark strukturiert, Holz überwiegt unter den wenigen Materialien (Korbgeflecht, Dickglas, Teppichboden).
Die Fassade ist bandmäßig schlicht – Brüstungen aus Sichtbetonplatten, Aluminiumfenster mit äußerem Lamellenschutz –, ihre Leuchtschrift streng und einheitlich. Durch dieses Mittel hob sie der Architekt heraus aus den Fronten der Nachbarhäuser mit ihren grellen Reklamen.

Plan, first floor. Key: 1 Breakfast room, 2 Kitchen, 3 Bar, 4 Reception.
Plan typical floor. Key: 1 Corridor, 2 Guestroom with shower bath, 3 Service room.

Grundriß erstes Obergeschoß. Legende: 1 Frühstücksraum, 2 Küche, 3 Bar, 4 Empfang.
Grundriß Normalgeschoß. Legende: 1 Erschließungsgang, 2 Zimmer mit Duschbad, 3 Putzraum.

1. A façade of shallow bands; plain, strictly co-ordinated illuminated lettering.
2. The front desk seen from the waiting corner.

1. Fassade in flachen Bändern; schlichte, streng koordinierte Leuchtschrift.
2. Der Empfang von der Warteecke gesehen.

3. Breakfast room. In the background, the bar with continuous seating.
4. Harry's Inn, a snack bar on the ground floor.
5. Heavy slabs of glass, wicker ceiling, controlled lighting.

3. Frühstücksraum. Im Hintergrund die Bar mit bandartig zusammengezogenen Sitzen.
4. Imbiß »Harry's Inn« im Erdgeschoß.
5. Dickglas, Korbdecke, Lichteffekte.

Europahotel, Recklinghausen, Germany

Architect: Hans Joachim Lenz

The project is one of a chain of Europahotels built in Germany and elsewhere. It is reputed to be the most modern hotel in the Ruhr district, a prestige hotel for businessmen and visitors to the Ruhr Festival. Though it is not a big hotel its operation is thouroughly rationalised and even automated, with the double purpose of achieving a lower running cost and of providing an unusual degree of comfort.

The exterior is restrained and free from contemporary clichés. The interiors, designed down to the last detail, show a sensitive combination of rich materials. The ribbon pattern of the balcony slabs and railings, of differing widths, gives the street front a lively striated texture; the massive roof slab is pierced above the restaurant terrace to form a lighter-looking concrete grid. The colors and materials: ceilings and parapets of white exposed concrete, columns and balcony screen walls of exposed concrete painted dark gray, a single touch of rough-textured slate beside the entrance. The cantilevered roof canopy projects far across the sidewalk and entrance drive. Its neat shape, which also extends deep into the hall, is defined after dark by strip-lights along the edges.

The lobby joins the sidewalk without any change of level; it has formally-grouped chairs with white upholstery, on an island carpet of blue velours. The partition between the lobby and the restaurant is of fire-blackened forged iron plates: a symbol of this region of coal and iron. Between the elevator and the front desk, the wall bears a pattern of small blue metal plates: the key safe. It guards keys and mail in its pigeon holes and is part of the technical schema of the hotel, which is entirely controlled from the front desk. The man at the controls behind the desk pushes a button and a particular pigeonhole flips open. This hall porter-receptionist controls much more than the key safe from his desk; he also runs the entire backstairs operation of the hotel. He controls all lighting installations, ventilation and heating equipment, all pumps and laundry machines. He is connected by an intercom system with all exits, kitchens, preparation rooms and restaurants. Bills arrive within seconds by tube from the restaurant, and are added by electronic equipment to the total account. He also controls the chambermaids from his desk. The maid inserts a plug into a socket provided in each room, and an indicator at the desk lights up to show where she is working. Bell-boys can be called and guided by a monitoring system with ten portable receivers. Even the loudspeaker system of the conference and lecture rooms and the choice of radio programs for the guest-rooms are controlled from the front desk.

Each of the five typical floors has six double rooms facing the street, glazed from ceiling to floor and screened by a large balcony. Six single rooms, also having a bathroom with tub, share the rear face with the elevators, stairs and service rooms. Several double rooms have been furnished and decorated with special care. The architect has named them the Continent Rooms. However he did not wish merely to decorate the walls with pictures and souvenirs, but chose instead to "refer to the continents, not pictorially but emotionally, using the associations attached to a color or material." The Africa Room has finishes of macassar ebony, easy chairs covered with calf skin, rich shades of blue, red and yellow; the American Room chrome, steel and plastics. An oriental atmosphere is conveyed by Sen ash, Japanese mats, Honan silk, grass wall covering. Australia is represented by smoked oak, chairs in black leather, rough natural fabrics and lambskin.

1. Exposed gray and white concrete; broad bands of glass. The illuminated lettering is kept strictly within the depth of the roof fascia.
2. The canopy with its lighted edges. The neon lettering forms a neat ribbon.

1. Sichtbeton in Weiß und Grau, Glas in breiten Bändern. Die Leuchtschrift ordnet sich ganz dem Dachsims ein.
2. Das Vordach mit seinen Lichtkanten, die Leuchtschrift als ein knappes Band.

Europahotel, Recklinghausen, Deutschland

Architekt: Hans Joachim Lenz

Das Projekt gehört zu einer Reihe von Europahotels in Deutschland und im Ausland. Es gilt als das modernste Hotel im Industriegebiet, als ein repräsentatives Haus für Geschäftsreisende und für Gäste der Ruhrfestspiele. Obwohl kein Großhotel, ist es im Betriebsablauf außerordentlich rationalisiert, ja automatisiert, nicht nur um wirtschaftlich zu arbeiten, sondern auch um ungewöhnliche Bequemlichkeit zu bieten.

Die Architektur wirkt nach außen kühl, frei von herrschenden Klischees; der Ausbau, bis in die Einzelheiten durchgestaltet, zeigt ein sensibles Beieinander ausgesuchter Materialien. Die wechselnd breiten Bänder der Balkonplatten und Brüstungen geben der Straßenfassade eine lebendig gestreifte Struktur; die massige Dachplatte über dem Terrassen-Restaurant ist als Betonraster aufgelöst und verliert an Schwere. Die Farben und Materialien: Decken und Brüstungen in Sichtbeton, weiß, Stützen und Balkon-Trennwände Sichtbeton dunkelgrau gestrichen, ein Akzent von bruchrauhem Schiefer neben dem Eingang. Das freitragende Vordach stößt weit über Gehsteig und Anfahrt vor; seine einfache Form, durchgehend in die Tiefe der Halle, wird nachts von Leuchtstreifen an den Kanten nachgezeichnet.

In der Halle, die ohne eine Stufe an den Gehsteig anschließt, findet der Gast architektonisch gereihte Sitzmöbel, weiß, auf einer Insel von blauem Velours. Die Wand zwischen Halle und Restaurant ist aus eisernen Platten geschmiedet und feuergeschwärzt: grauschwarzes Symbol des Landes von Kohle und Eisen. Zwischen Fahrstuhl und Empfang ist die Wand aufgeteilt in kleine, blaue Metallplatten: der Schlüsseltresor verbirgt in seinen Fächern diskret Post und Schlüssel und ist Teil der Tech-

nik des Hauses, die vom Empfang gesteuert wird. Der Mann am Schaltpult hinter dem Tresen drückt auf einen Knopf, und das Fach des Gastes öffnet sich. Aber der Empfangschef lenkt von seinem Platz aus viel mehr – das Leben hinter den Kulissen des Hotels. Er reguliert sämtliche Beleuchtungen, Lüftungs- und Heizungs-Anlagen, Pumpen und Wäschereimaschinen. Er ist mit allen Ausgangstüren, Küchen, Vorbereitungsräumen und Restaurants über Wechselsprechanlagen verbunden. Eine Rohrpost bringt die Restaurantrechnung in Sekunden zum Empfang, wo modernste Buchungsmaschinen die Endrechnung addieren. Der Empfangschef, eine besonders geschulte Kraft, kontrolliert von seinem Regiepult die Zimmermädchen. Sie stecken in den Zimmern ihren Schlüssel in eine Kontaktdose, ein Licht leuchtet beim Empfang auf und zeigt, in welchem Raum das Mädchen arbeitet. Über eine Rufanlage mit zehn Empfängern können Hotelboys und Hausdiener prompt dirigiert werden. Auch die Lautsprecheranlage der Sitzungs- und Vortragsräume und die Programmwahl für das Radio in den Gastzimmern werden vom Empfang bedient.

Die fünf Normalgeschosse haben zur Straße hin je sechs Doppelzimmer, bis zum Fußboden verglast, mit breitem Balkon. Auf der Rückseite liegen sechs Einzelzimmer, auch sie mit Wannenbad, dazu Fahrstühle, Treppen und Servicezimmer. Eine Reihe der Doppelzimmer sind mit besonderer Sorgfalt gestaltet. Der Architekt nannte sie die Erdteilzimmer. Er wollte nicht irgendwelche Bilder und Requisiten bringen, wollte »nicht vom Äußerlichen, sondern vom Gefühlsmäßigen, von den Stimmungswerten her, die von jeder Farbe oder von jedem Material ausgehen, auf die Kontinente Bezug nehmen«. So findet man

im Afrikazimmer Makassarholz, Sessel in Kalbfell und die Farben Blau, Rot und Gelb, im Amerikazimmer Chrom, Stahl und Kunststoffe. Orientalisches Flair wird in Sen-Esche, Japanmatte, Honanseide, Grastapeten nahegebracht, für Australien treten geräucherte Eiche, Stühle in schwarzem Leder, Rupfen und Lammfell ein.

A Plan, ground floor / Grundriß Erdgeschoß.
B Plan, typical floor / Grundriß Normalgeschoß.
C Plan, roof floor / Grundriß Dachgeschoß.
Key to plans: 1 Entrance lobby, 2 Large conference room, 3 Small conference room, 4 Winter garden, 5 Coats, 6 Toilets, 7 Service kitchen, 8 Switch room, 9 Passenger elevators, 10 Staff elevator, 11 Shop, 12 Delivery entrance, 13 Storage, 14 Transformer room, 15 Continent Room, 16 Double bedroom, 17 Single bedroom, 18 Room service, 19 Chute for dirty linen, 20 Bar, 21 Grill room, 22 Terrace, 23 Kitchen, 24 Dishwashing, 25 Grill, 26 Wine refrigeration room.

Legende zu den Plänen: 1 Empfangshalle, 2 Großer Konferenzraum, 3 Sitzungssaal, 4 Wintergarten, 5 Garderobe, 6 Toiletten, 7 Kaffeeküche, 8 Schaltraum, 9 Personenaufzüge, 10 Personalaufzug, 11 Laden, 12 Lieferanteneingang, 13 Nebenraum, 14 Trafostation, 15 Erdteilzimmer, 16 Doppelzimmer, 17 Einzelzimmer, 18 Kelleroffice, 19 Wäscheschacht, 20 Bar, 21 Grillrestaurant, 22 Terrasse, 23 Küche, 24 Spülküche, 25 Grill, 26 Weinkühlraum.

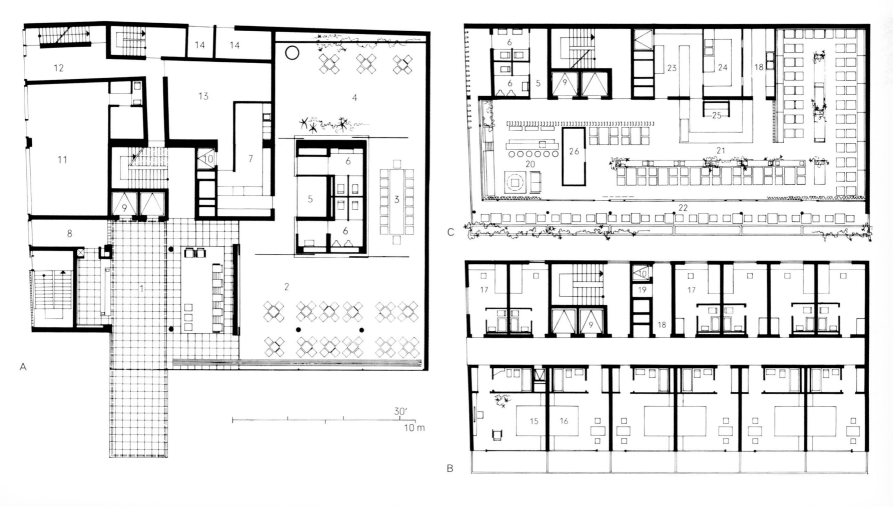

3. A wall of blackened iron plates; white fabrics, light-grey marble floor; front desk and wall paneling in walnut and rosewood, ceiling light-blue.
4. The grill unit.
5. The grill restaurant on the roof. Grill block of charcoal-gray hand-made clinker bricks, teak counter top.
6. Little built-in furniture, a general freedom from clutter.
7. The Europe Room. Dark walnut finish, green carpeting, light fabrics.

3. Wand in schwärzlichen Eisenplatten, weiße Stoffe, lichtgrauer Marmorfußboden, Empfangstheke und Wandverkleidung Nußbaum und Palisander, Decke hellblau.
4. Die Grillanrichte.
5. Grillrestaurant auf dem Dach. Grillblock aus anthrazitfarbenen handgeformten Klinkern, Teakplatte.
6. Wenige feste Einbauten, kein Zuviel in den Räumen.
7. Europazimmer. Dunkles Nußbaumholz, grüner Teppich, leichte Gewebe.

Europahotel, Ludwigshafen/Rhine, Germany

Architect: Hans Joachim Lenz

Planned in a high-density area of the city, the hotel presents a smooth unperforated front to the square it faces. At the rear the podium building occupies the last square meter of the site. The T-shaped guest-room block is above the podium but clear of it, as guest-rooms begin only at the second floor level. The central atrium is not touched: it gets its daylight from the void under the guest-room block, which straddles it. Two floors of staff quarters (25 rooms) stretch across the kitchen and service alley. The plane of the entrance front is broken only by the main dining room, which projects to cover the entire length of the sidewalk and the shop fronts. The lobby and lounge area is divided in two by the front desk; to the left are quiet groups of easy chairs, while the other part of the lounge is dominated by the free-standing staircase, descending from the upper floors. The elevators and main stairway are, for once, visibly together. The atrium in the center contains a winter garden, a place for dancing and a swimming pool; its glass roof opens in summer. To left and right of it are two narrow rooms, the cocktail lounge and a luxury restaurant with seven tables. At the rear of the building there are a conference room as well as breakfast rooms for 100 to 180 persons.

The grill restaurant on the first floor, seating more than 100 guests, is, like the conference room, divided from the kitchen and lobby areas by a determinedly straight wall. The tables are arranged in the French manner—tables for six occupy the glazed front section which projects over the square, and are separated by plant boxes with built-in service counters; larger bays at the ends have 4 small tables for two, which can be put together to seat 8, in the more secluded corners; there are very few tables for four. The whole is symmetrically arranged, the grill unit having a counterpart in the wine block ,where selected wines are stocked for guests to see behind sheets of green glass. The architects managed to limit the number of columns in the grill restaurant to six. Double longitudinal beams carry the wall loads from the guest-room floors without increasing the depth of the exposed ceiling structure. The dimensions of the structural ceiling elements are very carefully scaled to the size of the room: the longitudinal beams are divided along the middle, thus losing their heavy look. With their natural gray tone they also provide a background for

the color scheme. The ceiling panels are plastered and painted dark green. The floor is covered with velours carpeting, walls are finished in East Indian rosewood and raw clinker bricks. Gray-red brick walls reappear in the ground floor rooms, with flooring of Belgian granite. The structure of concrete beams and columns is exposed throughout the building and gives the interiors, from the lounge and bar to the conference room, a certain simplicity. In the winter garden the concrete structure again becomes a dominating element. The basic theme of concrete-and-clinker is carried through all the 95 apartments. Colors and textures in the guest-rooms are: charcoal gray velours carpets, curtains a light yellow, concrete ceilings rough with form marks, unpainted; walls of gray-red clinker bricks. The rough textures are complemented by the smooth surfaces of the wood paneling under the windows and on the beds.

There are Continent Rooms like those of the Europahotel in Recklinghausen, and two luxury suites on the top floor, set back from the building line. Their living rooms occupy the width of one standard apartment, but are double-height near the window. A spiral staircase leads up to a dressing area and bedroom occupying the width of two standard apartments.

Advanced mechanical services are a major feature of this project—built in 1963—as of all other Europahotels. Visitors are announced by a gong in the guest-rooms; at the touch of a button a "please enter" sign lights up at the door. A tiny service elevator in the corridor replaces the room waiters, and serves drinks and cold dishes noiselessly at any hour of the night. Guests need only insert tokens bearing their room number into the tube next to the elevator to be almost automatically served. This service, too, is registered by the control center at the

front desk. In addition to its many other functions, this center, described in the account of the Recklinghausen hotel, is also designed to handle all local and trunk calls and teleprinting services. There is even a closed-circuit television system between the basement garage and the front desk. Guests arriving in their own cars may speak to the receptionist who guides them from his desk.

1. View from Ludwig Square: entrance and shops under the shadow of the projecting grill restaurant. Colors: gray and white concrete.
2. The main stair from the bedroom floors ends in full view in the lobby. To the left: the key safe, and at the back of the picture, the winter garden.
3. The lobby-lounge area. A coffered ceiling of concrete beams; brick walls, granite floor and island carpets. Beyond are the bar and atrium.
4. The winter garden seen from the bar. It has a sliding glass roof; lofty concrete beams and top lighting are important to its character.

1. Ansicht vom Ludwigsplatz. Im Schatten des vorgebauten Grillrestaurants Eingang und Läden. Farben betongrau und weiß.
2. Die Haupttreppe aus den Wohngeschossen endet sichtbar in der Halle. Links der Schlüsseltresor, in der Tiefe des Bildes der Wintergarten.
3. Die Halle. Rasterdecke aus Betonstegen, Klinkerwände, Boden aus Granit und Teppichinseln. Im Hintergrund Bar und Atrium.
4. Der Wintergarten aus der Bar gesehen. Schiebedach in Glas. Hohe Betonbalken, in Licht aufgesogen, als beherrschender Raumfaktor.

Europahotel, Ludwigshafen am Rhein, Deutschland

Architekt: Hans Joachim Lenz

In einer Baulücke der Innenstadt errichtet, zeigt das Haus zum Ludwigsplatz eine geschlossene Fassade. Die Breitfußanlage nimmt auf der Rückseite den letzten Quadratmeter des Grundstücks ein. Das Bettenhaus setzt sich in T-Form darüber, doch erst vom 2. Obergeschoß an. Das zentrale Atrium des Erdgeschosses wird nicht berührt, sein Glasdach bleibt durch den offenen Raum unter dem Bettenflügel durchgehend belichtet. Die 25 Personalzimmer überspannen in zwei Geschossen die Küche und den Wirtschaftsweg. Die Eingangs-Fassade ist flächig, nur das Hauptrestaurant tritt hervor und überdeckt den ganzen Gehsteig mit den Ladenfronten. Die Halle wird durch den Empfangsblock zweigeteilt, links sind ruhige Sitzgruppen angeordnet, der rechte Teil wird von der freigestellten Treppe aus den Wohngeschossen beherrscht. Fahrstühle und Haupttreppe sind hier – ein seltener Fall – sichtbar eng zusammengebracht. Das Atrium in der Mitte ist Wintergarten, Tanzfläche und Schwimmbad, sein Glasdach läßt sich im Sommer öffnen. Zu beiden Seiten liegen ganz schmal die Bar und das Luxusrestaurant mit sieben Tischen; in der Tiefe des Baues ein Konferenzsaal und Frühstücksräume für 100 bis 180 Personen.

Das Grillrestaurant im ersten Obergeschoß (über 100 Plätze) ist wie der Konferenzsaal von den Küchen und Vorräumen durch eine glatte Wand getrennt. Die Tischordnung ist französisch inspiriert, in der gläsernen Kanzel zum Ludwigsplatz hin Sechsergruppen, abgeteilt durch Pflanzenbecken mit angebauter Servierfläche, in den ruhigeren Raumecken größere Buchten mit je acht Stühlen an kleinen Tischen für zwei, die man zusammenrücken kann, und ganz wenige Tische für vier Personen. Alles ist symmetrisch angeordnet, der Grillinsel entspricht auf der anderen Seite ein Weinblock in grünem Glas; kostbare Weine sind sichtbar für den Gast gelagert. Die Architekten kamen im Grill mit sechs Stützen aus. Doppelte Längsträger fangen die Wandlasten aus den Wohngeschossen in der freiliegenden Deckenkonstruktion auf. Sie ist in Höhe und Breite ganz auf die Dimension des Raumes abgestimmt – die Längsträger verlieren durch die gespaltene Ausführung an Schwere – und geben mit ihrem natürlichen Grau den Grundton für die Raumgestaltung. Die Deckenfelder sind verputzt und dunkelgrün gestrichen. Zum Veloursboden kommen Wände in ostindischem Palisanderholz und in rohen Klinkern. Die graurote Backsteinwand kehrt auch in den Erdgeschoßräumen wieder, hier kombiniert mit Bodenplatten aus belgischem Granit. Das tragende System von Betonstützen und Balken, nirgends kaschiert, gibt allen Räumen von der Lounge und Bar bis zum hinteren Saal einen Zug ungezwungener Frische; es wird im Wintergarten zum dominierenden Raumelement.

Das Thema Sichtbeton und -klinker ist durch alle 95 Apartments getragen. Farbe und Strukturen in den Räumen: Teppiche in anthrazitfarbenem Velours, lichtgelbe Vorhänge, Betondecke schalungsrauh, natur; Wände grauroter Backstein. Den rauhen Oberflächen werden in den glatt verarbeiteten Hölzern der Brüstung und des Bettenrahmens präzise Obertöne aufgesetzt. Lose flauschige Bettspreiten wirken anheimelnd improvisiert.

Es gibt – wie in Recklinghausen – Erdteilzimmer, und es gibt wie dort zwei Luxusapartments, zurückgesetzt im Dachgeschoß. Der Wohnraum nimmt eine normale Raumbreite ein, ist zum Fenster zweigeschossig. Über eine Wendeltreppe erreicht man Ankleide- und Schlafzimmer, verteilt über zwei Raumbreiten. Im Dachgeschoß liegen noch drei Fahrerzimmer.

Die Technik ist auch in diesem Europahotel – Baujahr 1963 – voll ausgespielt. In den Zimmern meldet ein Gong Besucher an der Tür; ein Knopfdruck und draußen

leuchtet das Zeichen »Bitte eintreten« auf. Ein Kleinstlift im Flur ersetzt den Etagenkellner, serviert zu jeder Nachtstunde lautlos Getränke und kalte Speisen. Der Gast wirft nur Metallmarken mit seiner Zimmernummer in die Rohrpost neben dem Aufzug und wird fast automatisch bedient. Auch dieser Service wird vom Regiepult in der Halle gesteuert. Neben den vielen Funktionen, die

für das Recklinghausener Hotel beschrieben sind, werden am Pult noch alle Telefongespräche und Fernschreiben vermittelt. Es gibt sogar eine Fernsehanlage zwischen der Tiefgarage und dem Portier. Wer im Wagen anreist, spricht über einen Fernsehschalter mit der Halle; der Portier weist ihn von seinem Platz aus über den Bildschirm ein.

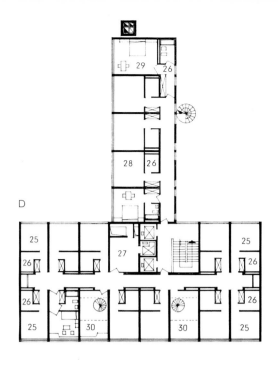

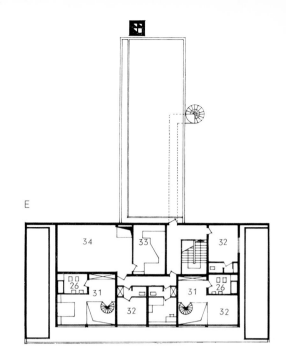

C

D

E

A Plan, ground floor / Grundriß Erdgeschoß.
B Plan, first floor / Grundriß 1. Obergeschoß.
C Plan, 3rd–5th floor / Grundriß 3.–5. Obergeschoß.
D Plan, 6th floor / Grundriß 6. Obergeschoß.
E Plan, roof floor / Grundriß Dachgeschoß.

Key to plans: 1 Main entrance hotel, 2 Entrance to wine restaurant in the basement, 3 Lobby, 4 Front desk, 5 Lounge, 6 Bar, 7 Atrium, 8 Conference room, 9 Breakfast room, 10 Luxury restaurant, 11 Coats, 12 Shops, 13 Office, 14 Electrical equipment, 15 Kitchen, 16 Service alley,

17 Grill restaurant, 18 Grill unit, 19 Wine storage block, 20 Kitchen, grill restaurant, 21 Service corridor, 22 Glass roof atrium, 23 Staffs' living room, 24 Staff bedrooms, 25 Single bedroom, 26 Bathroom—W.C.—Wardrobe, 27 Service, 28 Double bedroom, 29 Continent room, 30 Luxury suite, living room, 31 Luxury suite, bedroom, 32 Room for chauffeur, 33 Elevator machinery, 34 Fan room.

Legende zu den Plänen: 1 Haupteingang Hotel, 2 Eingang zur Weinstube im Untergeschoß, 3 Lobby, 4 Emp-

fang, 5 Lounge, 6 Bar, 7 Atrium, 8 Konferenzraum, 9 Frühstücksraum, 10 Luxusrestaurant, 11 Garderobe, 12 Läden, 13 Büro, 14 Elektro-Schaltraum, 15 Küche, 16 Wirtschaftsweg, 17 Grillrestaurant, 18 Grill, 19 Weinlagerraum, 20 Küche Grillrestaurant, 21 Kellnergang, 22 Glasdach Atrium, 23 Aufenthaltsraum für Angestellte, 24 Schlafraum für Angestellte, 25 Einzelzimmer, 26 Bad – WC – Garderobe, 27 Etagenservice, 28 Zweibettzimmer, 29 Erdteilzimmer, 30 Luxusapartment, Wohnraum, 31 Luxusapartment, Schlafraum, 32 Fahrerzimmer, 33 Aufzugmaschinen, 34 Lüftungszentrale.

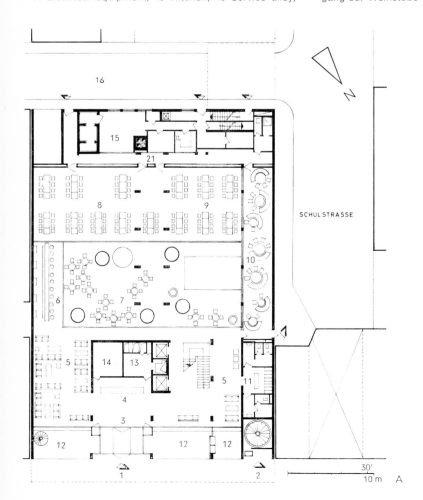

SCHULSTRASSE

A

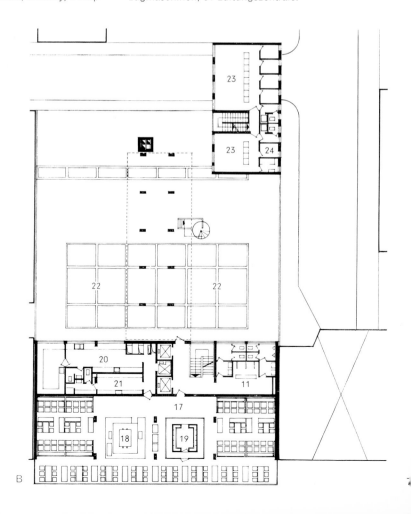

B

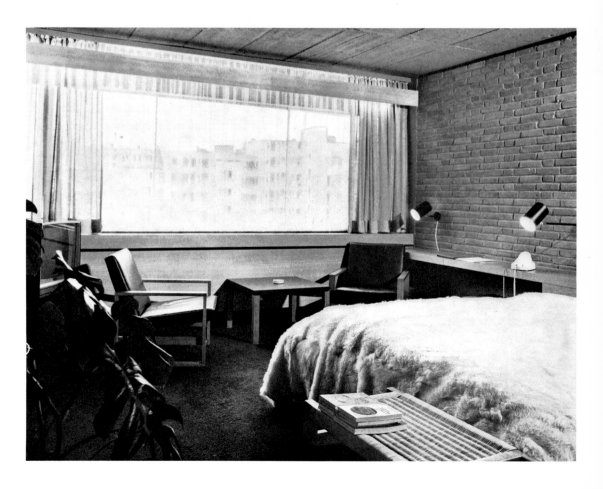

5. The bar is narrow, with brick walls and a concrete ceiling with very shallow coffering. Light floods in through glass bricks.

6. The grill restaurant. The concrete structure, poured in smooth formwork, is exposed. Ceiling panels are deep green.

7. A lively-looking room and no mere mass-produced cell: some textures are rough, there is smooth Sen-ash, light yellow curtains and a furry bedspread.

5. Ein schmaler Raum, die Bar. Ziegelwände, Betonkassetten fast bündig ausgefüllt. Flutendes Licht durch Glasbausteine.

6. Das Grillrestaurant. Die statische Struktur der Decken ist freigelegt in glattgeschaltem Beton. Tiefgrüne Dekkenfelder; hinter dem Grill eine zweite Insel: das Weinlager mit grünen Glaswänden.

7. Statt einer organisierten Wohnzelle ein lebendiger Raumeindruck: rauhe Strukturen, glatte Sen-Esche, lichtgelbe Vorhänge, flauschig-lose Tagesdecke.

Grand Hotel, Cannes

Architect: L. Lafond

The new Grand Hotel de la Croisette has inherited from its famous 19th-century predecessor its name, its bronze door numbers and key tags and its splendid avenue of palm trees opening towards the sea. Also in the spirit of the past is the generous size of the guest-rooms, the distinction of the exteriors, which have a modern form of travertine façade—and the largeness of the building. The hotel proper is reduced in size, however, occupying only the center part of the long L-shaped building; continuing on the left and right are the Résidences du Grand Hotel, small, very comfortable apartments without hotel service.

The ten typical floors of the hotel section accommodate 70 guest apartments. The main living-bedroom area alone covers 25 or 30 m²; in addition there are a closed entrance hall, a large bathroom with bath and bidet, and a separate toilet. The living area has a floor-to-ceiling glass wall and a deep balcony terrace. Railings are as light as possible: they are supported by plexiglas uprights about as wide as one's hand, which do not interrupt the view of palms and sea. Rooms at the rear of the building also have balconies with a view of the city and the hills to the north.

The Parc du Grand Hotel is a quiet expanse of lawn with a few colored borders flowering at different seasons. The marble-paved promenade in front of the hotel and the adjoining group of shops and the few curving paths under the palm trees are for pedestrians only. The great depth of the park considerably reduces traffic noise in the rooms. The access route leads through several side streets to the parking lot on the north side of the hotel. The lobby and restaurant, both intimate in scale, are screened from the parking lot by a band of windows covered with vines. In the lobby-lounge—its area of some 350 m² is seven times that of the restaurant—the reception section is marked by a few heavy columns; they do not impair the continuity of this large space. Its various zones are defined by changes in furniture—colorful upholstered seats alternate with white molded chairs by Eero Saarinen—and subdivided only by narrow plant boxes. A single work of ancient art, a painted wooden screen from China, fills most of the east wall, and is a surprising object to find in an entirely modern décor; but its rust-brown tones go well with the light brown and beige of the lounge. There is no piped music in the guest-rooms, and television can only be watched in the conference room. The house offers every other luxury, however, in the form of choice fabrics and carpets, well-finished wood paneling and mosaic bathrooms, but above all in the heating system (electric radiant heating) and in the sound insulation of the rooms. It is remarkable that this new luxury hotel, one of the few recent hotels in France to have entirely modern interiors and exteriors, should be frequented by so many guests who belong to an older generation.

1. The hotel seen from the Croisette: quiet lawns under palm trees. The hotel proper is flanked by residential wings.

1. Das Hotel von der Croisette gesehen, ruhige Rasenflächen unter Palmen. Der Hotelbau flankiert von Wohnflügeln.

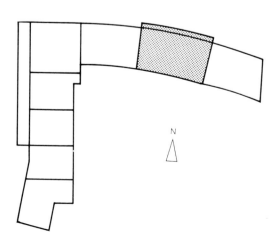

Site plan with hotel ground floor / Lageplan mit Hotel-Erdgeschoß.

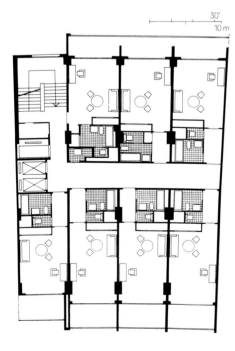

Plan, typical floor / Grundriß Normalgeschoß.

Grand Hotel, Cannes

Architekt: L. Lafond

Das neue Grand Hotel an der Croisette hat von seinem berühmten Vorgänger aus dem 19. Jahrhundert den Namen übernommen, die Schlüssel- und Türschilder und den großartigen Palmengarten zum Meer hin. Geblieben ist auch der Komfort der großen Räume, die Distinktion des Äußeren – eine Travertinfassade in zeitgemäßer Fassung – und die Ausmaße der Gesamtanlage. Doch das Hotel selbst ist klein geworden, es nimmt nur den Mittelteil des großen Winkelbaues ein; links und rechts schließen sich die »Résidences du Grand Hotel« an, kleine, sehr komfortable Wohnungen ohne Hotelservice.

In den 10 Normalgeschossen verfügt das Haus über 70 Gästezimmer. Allein die Salons – Wohn-Schlafräume – haben 25 oder 30 qm, dazu kommt ein abgeschlossener Eingangsflur, ein geräumiges Badezimmer mit Wanne und Bidet und eine getrennte Toilette. Der Salon hat nach außen eine reine Glaswand und einen tiefen Balkon. Die Brüstungen sind so leicht wie möglich in handbreiten Streifen von Plexiglas ausgeführt; sie stören nicht die Sicht auf die Palmenkronen und das Meer. Auch die Zimmer der Rückseite haben Balkone mit einem Blick auf die Stadt und die Hügel nach Norden.

Der Parc du Grand Hotel ist behutsam in großen Rasenflächen und wenigen, im Wechsel der Jahreszeiten blühenden Beeten gestaltet. Die marmorbelegte Promenade vor dem Hotel und der Ladenzeile im Winkel dazu, die wenigen geschwungenen Pfade unter den Palmen stehen nur Fußgängern offen. Der Park mit seiner großen Tiefe nimmt dem Hotel den Verkehrslärm. Die Anfahrt führt über Nebenstraßen zum großen Parkplatz des Hotels auf der Nordseite. Die Halle und das Restaurant, in sehr intimem Maßstab, sind durch ein grünberanktes Fensterband gegen den Parkplatz abgeschirmt. In der Halle von über 350 qm – das ist die siebenfache Fläche des Restaurants – markieren ein paar schwere Stützen die Eingangslobby, ohne daß der große Raum an Kontinuität verlöre. Seine Zonen sind durch wechselnde Möblierung stark farbiger Polstermöbel oder weißer Sitzschalen von Eero Saarinen definiert und höchstens durch schmale Pflanzenkästen leicht abgegrenzt. In dem völlig modernen Dekor à la Knoll fällt ein einziges altes Stück auf, eine wandfüllende chinesische Tafelmalerei an der Ostseite, die mit ihren rostbraunen Tönen sich farblich gut in die lichtbraunen und beigen Töne der Halle einfügt. In den Gästezimmern gibt es kein Radio, und fernsehen kann man nur im Konferenzraum. Dafür bietet das Haus ausgesuchten Komfort in der Verarbeitung der Hölzer, in den Mosaikverkleidungen der Bäder, in den wertvollen Bezügen und Teppichen, vor allem aber in der Heizung (elektrische Strahlungsheizung) und der akkustischen Abschirmung von Raum zu Raum. Es fällt auf, daß dieses Hotelgebäude, einer der wenigen Hotelneubauten in Frankreich, die im Äußeren und in der inneren Gestaltung ganz unserer Zeit entsprechen, auch von vielen Gästen der älteren Generation besucht wird.

2. The lounge and lobby, a continuous space articulated by contrasting groups of low easy chairs and white molded chairs by Saarinen.

2. Lounge und Eingangshalle; ein durchgehender Raum, differenziert durch kontrastierende Gruppen von niedrigen Sesseln und weißen Schalenstühlen von Saarinen.

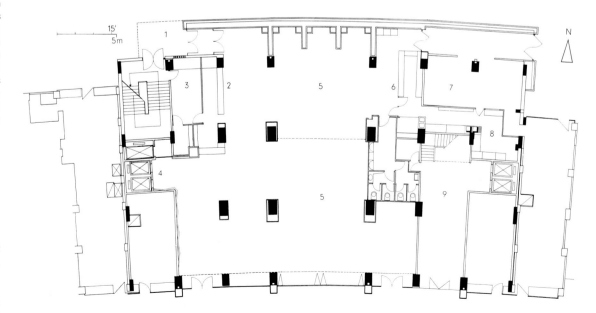

Plan, ground floor / Grundriß Erdgeschoß.

Key to ground floor plan: 1 Hotel entrance, 2 Front desk, 3 Office, 4 Elevators, 5 Lounge, 6 Bar, 7 Restaurant, 8 Kitchen, 9 Entrance to private apartments.

Legende zum Grundriß Erdgeschoß: 1 Hoteleingang, 2 Empfang, 3 Büro, 4 Aufzüge, 5 Lounge, 6 Bar, 7 Restaurant, 8 Küche, 9 Eingang zu den Privatwohnungen.

3. The lobby and the dark-paneled bar; low plant-boxes,
a Chinese painted screen in the lounge.

3. Die Eingangshalle und dunkel getäfelte Bar; niedrige
Pflanzenkästen, in der Lounge ein gemalter chinesischer
Wandschirm.

4. A guest-room balcony. Light plexiglas railings and an unobstructed view of the Croisette and the bay.

4. Balkon vor einem Gastzimmer. Leichte Brüstungen aus Plexiglas und ungehinderter Ausblick auf die Croisette und die Bucht.

Plan, typical guest room / Grundriß eines Gästezimmers.

5, 6. A guest apartment and bathroom. All-glass window-wall, radiant heating, integrated lighting fixtures.

5, 6. Gästeapartment und Baderaum. Fensterwand in Ganzglas, Strahlungsheizung, integrierte Beleuchtung.

Hotel Airport, Glattbrugg-Zurich

Architects: Manfred and Helen Heuss

This small hotel is not an airport hotel, as the name might suggest, but a hotel for businessmen, sited far from the landing approach to the airport, but less than 200 m from the two main road connections between the city center and the airport. The building has 47 rooms (82 beds) and achieves a high standard of comfort and service. An underground garage holds 20 cars and 30 more can be parked on an open parking lot.

In addition to the 54-seat restaurant there is a grill room for 41 guests; the two rooms are separated by a bar and buffet. The kitchen is in the basement. It serves Japanese and European specialities, sending them up by two kitchen elevators. The guest-rooms are carefully tailored to the needs of the clientèle. On the four typical floors, twin-bed rooms, single rooms and double-bedded rooms alternate. The top floor, of smaller area, houses three larger apartments and a conference room. Each floor has a servery with kitchen elevator. The architects tried to use the same furniture in all rooms, in order to furnish this small hotel as economically as a larger project.

The modest size of the rooms and their widely differing dimensions raised problems. The furniture in the guest-rooms is light and small in scale so as to make the rooms seem larger. All sectional elements are rectangular in shape and made of walnut, like the wall paneling, which is continuous up to sill height. In the recessed lobby the architects have managed to create a quiet lounge corner in spite of the lack of space. A deep-pile Berber carpet in a natural beige sets off the black leather easy chairs and the polished concrete floor. Large chromed lighting fixtures concentrate their light on the glass tables. The walnut paneling of the guest-rooms is repeated in the two restaurant rooms and combined with dark red linen curtains, a dark, textured wall-to-wall carpet and red and olive-green upholstery. The hotel is in all parts distinguished by the "dry elegance" which the architects aimed to achieve.

A Plan, ground floor / Grundriß Erdgeschoß.
B Plan, typical floor / Grundriß Normalgeschoß.
Key to plans: 1 Restaurant, 2 Grill room, 3 Lobby, 4 Reception, 5 Lounge corner, 6 Manager, 7 W.C., 8 Single bedroom, 9 Twin bedroom, 10 Double-bedroom, 11 Room service, 12 Bathroom.

Legende zu den Plänen: 1 Restaurant, 2 Grill, 3 Halle, 4 Empfang, 5 Sitzecke, 6 Direktion, 7 WC, 8 Einzelzimmer, 9 Doppelzimmer, 10 Grandlitzimmer, 11 Etagenservice, 12 Bad.

A

B

Hotel Airport, Glattbrugg-Zürich

Architekten: Manfred und Helen Heuss

Kein Flughafenhotel, wie der Name vermuten ließe, sondern ein »Haus für Geschäftsleute«, weit außerhalb der Einflugschneise, aber kaum 200 m von den beiden Haupt-Straßenverbindungen zwischen der Innenstadt und dem Flugplatz gelegen. Mit seinen 47 Zimmern (82 Betten) bietet es baulich und im Service einen ausgewogenen Komfort. Eine Unterflur-Garage nimmt 20 Wagen auf, auf dem Parkplatz können weitere 30 Fahrzeuge stehen. Neben dem Restaurant mit 54 Plätzen gibt es einen Grill für 41 Gäste, beide in ihren Funktionen gegliedert durch den Bar- und Buffetblock. Die Küche ist im Kellergeschoß untergebracht, sie serviert über zwei Speiselifts japanische und europäische Spezialitäten. Auch die Zimmer des Hauses sind sehr genau auf die Wünsche der Gäste abgestimmt. In den vier Normalgeschossen wechseln Doppelzimmer mit Einzel- und Grandlitzimmern (französische Betten) ab. In dem zurückgesetzten Dachgeschoß sind drei etwas größere Apartments und ein Konferenzzimmer untergebracht. Jedes Geschoß hat eine Anrichte mit Speiseaufzug. Die Architekten strebten an, in allen Zimmern einheitliche Möbelelemente zu verwenden, um in diesem Haus mäßiger Größe so rationell zu arbeiten wie in einem Großhotel.

Die geringe Größe der Zimmer und die stark wechselnden Maße boten Probleme. Die Möbel in den Räumen sind leicht und maßstäblich so gewählt, daß sie den Raum größer erscheinen lassen. Alle Anbauteile sind kubisch und im selben Nußbaumholz wie die umlaufenden Brüstungen gehalten. In der zurückgesetzten, ganz verglasten Hotelhalle gelang es bei knappem Raum eine ruhige Sitzecke zu schaffen. Auf dem geschliffenen Betonboden hebt ein hochfloriger, naturfarbener Berberteppich die Sitzgruppe aus schwarzen Ledersesseln hervor. Große verchromte Pendelleuchten konzentrieren ihr Licht auf die Glastische. In den beiden Restauranträumen ist das Nußbaumholz der Zimmer wiederholt und mit dunkelroten Leinenvorhängen, einem dunkel strukturierten Spannteppich und roten und olivgrünen Möbelstoffen kombiniert. Das Haus zeigt in allen Teilen die »trockene Eleganz«, die das Ziel der Architekten war.

1. The undercut cube of the bedroom floors: the horizontal bands of the façades are interrupted by verticals marking the external bathrooms. Long slots pierce the white panels under the windows; columns and mullions are a metalic gray to blend with the glass. The low restaurant wing is to the right.
2. The restaurant and buffet: the entrance is in the background. American walnut paneling and 'drily elegant' dark colors.
3. The lounge. Black leather chairs, some chromium, glass tables lit by low hanging fittings, a Berber rug.
4. A corner room. Continuous paneling is walnut: the only species of wood used in the building.

1. Der unterschnittene Würfel der Bettengeschosse; Bandstruktur der Fassaden, unterbrochen bei außenliegenden Bädern. Weiße Brüstungen, durch Schlitze perforiert. Pfeiler und Fensterprofile gehen metallisch-grau in den Glasbändern auf. Rechts der flache Restaurantbau.
2. Das Restaurant und Buffet gegen den Eingang gesehen. Trockene Eleganz in dunklen Tönen und amerikanischem Nußbaumholz.
3. Die Halle. Schwarze Ledersessel, Glastische aus niedrigen Leuchten angestrahlt, Chromgestelle und ein Berberteppich.
4. Ein Eckzimmer, umlaufende dunkle Brüstung: eine einheitliche Holzart (Nußbaum) für den ganzen Bau.

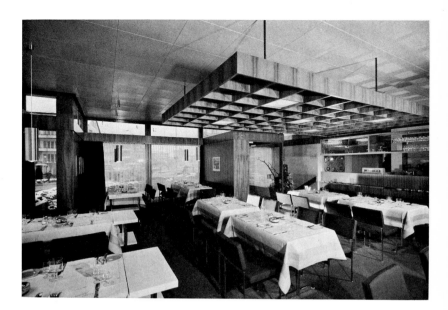

Humber Royal Hotel, Grimsby, England

Architects: Howard V. Lobb and Partners

The Humber Royal has 49 guest-rooms and 96 beds, and is a good example of hotel development in England's provincial centers. It was built in the large fishing port of Grimsby, to replace the recently demolished Royal Hotel, and to serve the whole Humber river industrial region (which has sea connections to North Europe) and in particular the rapidly growing new port of Immingham. It is a hotel for businessmen, with a large well-planned entertainment section. Its location outside the town made it easier for the architects to satisfy their wish to provide quiet accommodation. Views are out to the west, across unspoiled open country, and traveling businessmen find a golf course at their doorstep. The architects managed to cut off any views to the east, of the car park and an unsightly scatter of housing beyond it. The bedroom areas are also kept undisturbed by the noise of dance bands and late leaving guests from the banqueting section. Semi-mature trees were planted to obscure the parking area: the public rooms and bedrooms have views of lawns and fully-grown trees.

The ground floor layout shows tendencies typical of many recent hotel projects in the United Kingdom. The various sections have clearly separated entrances and foyers, intimacy is the keynote of the lobby, lounge and bar areas. At the Humber Royal, the restaurant and the banquet room are separated by a variety of spaces – among them a lounge bar, dance bar, cocktail bar, several foyers and a small patio. The restaurant has balanced natural lighting from both sides, and the banquet room a quietly pleasant outlook. A residents' lounge above the reception area improves the hotel's rating in tourist guides like the Automobile Association handbook. Typical rooms on the three bedroom floors have one bed and one daybed; there are several larger rooms with two beds and a daybed for a child. Staff bedrooms are on the third floor; the manager's flat above has a sitting room at roof level. There are 15 guest-rooms to each floor, all with their own bathrooms. In addition to the residents' lounge, guests can use a special television room and a washing and ironing room on the first of the upper floors. With bedrooms on only one side of the corridor, facing west, quiet accommodation is assured. The narrow vertical window slits along one side of the corridor avoid views of the kitchen roofs below. Bedrooms, have window walls from floor to ceiling, opening onto balconies.

The building's exteriors are unified by the use on all wall surfaces of the same gold-colored brickwork, with long bands of white mosaic. Elements are neatly articulated, with the main staircase and lifts set apart as a separate tower, showing hints of traditional and bay windows, in contrast with the almost monolithic bedroom block. The long lines of the elevations are reflected inside the bedrooms, where there are long wooden fascias, box-type light fittings and wood railings.

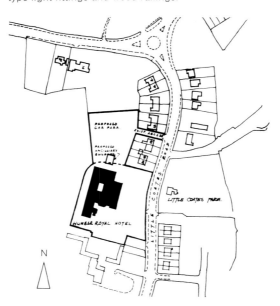

1. The building is composed of three main elements: the bedroom block, a separate staircase tower and a lower section housing the public rooms, kitchen and staff facilities. The hotel, bar and ballroom areas have separate entrances and are reached directly from the car parks.
2. The building seen from the east. The three entrance canopies are well differentiated, exterior brick walls unified in color, the golden brick tone heightened by white mosaic fascias. The ample fenestration of the staircase tower introduces a residential scale.
3, 4. The west elevation, entirely glass-walled. The first floor accommodates a residents' lounge, a gallery grill-room and several larger guest apartments. Bedrooms on upper floors have balconies.

1. Das Gebäude ist aus drei Hauptelementen zusammengefügt: dem Schlafraumblock, einem abgesetzten Treppenturm und einem niederen Teil mit den öffentlichen Räumen, der Küche und den Personalräumen. Hotel, Bars und Ballsaal haben getrennte Zugänge und sind unmittelbar von den Parkplätzen aus zu erreichen.
2. Das Gebäude von Osten gesehen. Die drei Vordächer sind deutlich verschieden gestaltet, die äußeren Ziegelflächen in der Farbe einheitlich, der goldene Ton der Ziegel verstärkt durch Bänder aus weißem Mosaik. Der Treppenturm mit seinen großen Fensterflächen gibt einen wohnlichen Maßstab.
3, 4. Die Westansicht, ganz in Glas aufgelöst. Das erste Obergeschoß enthält die Lounge für Hotelgäste, einen Grillraum über dem Restaurant und einige größere Gästeapartments. Die Schlafräume der oberen Geschosse haben Balkone.

Site plan / Lageplan.

Hotel Humber Royal, Grimsby, England

Architekten: Howard V. Lobb and Partners

Dieses Hotel mit 49 Schlafräumen und 96 Betten ist ein gutes Beispiel für den Hotelbau in englischen Provinzstädten. Es wurde in dem großen Fischereihafen Grimsby gebaut, um das alte abgerissene Royal-Hotel zu ersetzen und für den ganzen Industriebezirk am Humber-Fluß – mit seinen Seeverbindungen nach Nordeuropa – ein zentrales Hotel zu schaffen, besonders auch für den schnell wachsenden neuen Hafen von Immingham. Es handelt sich um ein Hotel für Geschäftsreisende mit einem großen, gut geplanten Trakt für gesellschaftliche Veranstaltungen. Die Lage außerhalb der Stadt erleichterte den Architekten ihre Aufgabe, ruhige Schlafräume anzulegen. Die Aussicht nach Westen geht über offene unverbaute Landschaft, und die Geschäftsreisenden haben einen Golfplatz vor der Tür. Den Architekten gelang es, Ausblicke auf die Parkplätze nach Osten und auf eine unschöne Gruppe verstreuter Häuser dahinter auszuschließen. Der Schlaftrakt ist ebenfalls so gelegt, daß Störungen durch Lärm von Tanzkapellen und späten Restaurantgästen ausgeschlossen sind. Auf dem Parkplatz wurden Schattenbäume von einiger Größe gepflanzt; die Schlafräume und öffentlichen Räume haben weite Rasenflächen und voll ausgewachsene Bäume im Blick.

Die Anlage des Erdgeschosses zeigt Tendenzen auf, die für eine Reihe neuerer Hotelprojekte in England typisch sind. Die verschiedenen Sektionen haben klar getrennte Zugänge und Eingangshallen, der intime Rahmen steht in den Hallen, Foyers und Bars im Vordergrund. Beim Humber Royal sind die verschiedenen Bereiche und Funktionen – darunter eine Loungebar, eine Tanzbar, eine Cocktailbar und mehrere Foyers – gut artikuliert und sorgfältig zusammengefügt, so daß Folgen ruhiger Buchten an langräumigen Flurzügen entstehen. Ein zentraler Patio wurde sehr geschickt östlich des Bettenblocks eingeplant; er trennt das Restaurant vom Festsaal. Das Restaurant bekommt dadurch ausgewogenes natürliches Licht von zwei Seiten und gibt dem Festsaal eine ruhige, angenehme Aussicht. Eine besondere Lounge für Hotelgäste wurde eingerichtet, um dem Hotel eine höhere Einstufung in Touristen-Handbüchern, wie den Listen des englischen Automobilclubs, zu sichern.

Die typischen Räume der drei Schlafgeschosse haben ein Bett und eine Tagescouch, daneben gibt es größere Räume mit zwei Betten und einer Couch für ein Kind. Das Personal wohnt in Räumen im dritten Obergeschoß, darüber liegt die Wohnung des Hoteldirektors, mit einem Wohnraum auf dem Dach. Jedes Geschoß hat 15 Schlafräume, alle mit eigenen Bädern. Neben der Residents' Lounge können die Gäste einen Fernsehraum benutzen und ein Wasch- und Bügelzimmer, alle im ersten Obergeschoß. Da die Gästezimmer nur einhüftig angelegt und nach Westen orientiert sind, ist völlige Ruhe gewährleistet. Die schmalen senkrechten Fensterschlitze in den Korridoren, durchscheinend verglast, vermeiden Ausblicke auf das tieferliegende Küchendach. Die Schlafräume auf der anderen Seite haben Glaswände vom Boden bis zur Decke, die sich auf Balkone öffnen.

Das Äußere des Gebäudes, im Gesamteindruck einheitlich gestaltet durch die Verwendung einer einzigen goldgetönten Ziegelsorte für alle Wandflächen und lange Bänder in weißem Mosaik, ist klar gegliedert; das Haupttreppenhaus mit den Fahrstühlen ist als Turm herausgesetzt und zeigt Anklänge an traditionelle Glaserker und Eckfenster im Gegensatz zu dem fast monolithischen Bettenhaus. Die gestreckten Linien des Äußeren sind in den Schlafräumen wieder aufgenommen in langen Holzborden, Lichtleisten und Geländern.

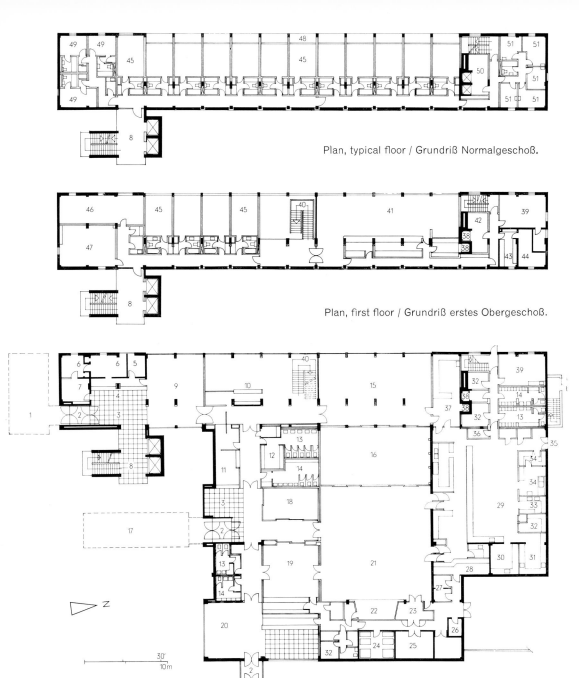

Plan, typical floor / Grundriß Normalgeschoß.

Plan, first floor / Grundriß erstes Obergeschoß.

30'
10m

Plan, ground floor / Grundriß Erdgeschoß.

Key to plans: 1 Hotel entrance canopy, 2 Porch, 3 Lobby, 4 Front desk, 5 Porter, 6 Office, 7 Manager, 8 Stair hall and guest lifts, 9 Foyer lounge, 10 Cocktail bar, 11 Cloakroom, 12 Powder room, 13 Ladies' W.C.s, 14 Gentlemen's W.C.s, 15 Restaurant, 16 Patio, 17 Ballroom entrance canopy, 18 Reception, 19 Dancing bar, 20 Lounge bar, 21 Ballroom, 22 Stage, 23 Furniture storage, 24 Beer tanks, 25 Beer crates, 26 Spirits, 27 Wine, 28 Wines and glasses counter, 29 Main kitchen, 30 Pastry, 31 Meat and fish, 32 Refrigeration room, 33 Pot washing, 34 Vegetable storage and preparation, 35 Service entrance, 36 Kitchen chef, 37 Service lobby, restaurant, 38 Service lift, 39 Staff room, 40 Stairs to grillroom, 41 Grillroom, 42 Linen sorting room, 43 Linen storage, 44 Ventilation plant, 45 Guest room, 46 Residents' lounge, 47 TV room, 48 Balcony, 49 Single bedroom, 50 Room service, 51 Staff bedroom.

Legende zu den Plänen: 1 Schutzdach über Hotelvorfahrt, 2 Windfang Hoteleingang, 3 Lobby, 4 Empfang, 5 Portier, 6 Büro, 7 Manager, 8 Treppenhalle und Gästeaufzüge, 9 Foyerlounge, 10 Cocktailbar, 11 Garderobe, 12 Schminkraum, 13 Damentoiletten, 14 Herrentoiletten, 15 Restaurant, 16 Patio, 17 Schutzdach über Ballsaal-Eingang, 18 Rezeption, 19 Tanzbar, 20 Loungebar, 21 Ballsaal, 22 Bühne, 23 Möbellager, 24 Biertanks, 25 Bierkästen, 26 Spirituosen, 27 Wein, 28 Wein- und Gläserausgabe, 29 Hauptküche, 30 Konditorei 31 Fleisch und Fisch, 32 Kühlraum, 33 Topfspülküche, 34 Gemüselagerung und -vorbereitung, 35 Lieferanteneingang, 36 Küchenchef, 37 Kellnervorraum des Restaurants, 38 Personalaufzug, 39 Personalraum, 40 Treppe zum Grillraum, 41 Grillraum, 42 Wäschesortierraum, 43 Wäscheraum, 44 Lüftungsanlage, 45 Gästezimmer, 46 Lounge für Hotelgäste, 47 Fernsehraum, 48 Balkon, 49 Einzelzimmer, 50 Etagenservice, 51 Personalschlafräume.

5. Night view. Well-lit ground floor areas; rhythmically spaced slit windows with obscured glass on upper floor corridors.
6. Patio between restaurant and ballroom (right).

5. Nachtansicht. Gut beleuchtete Räume im Erdgeschoß, Rhythmus der doppelten Fensterschlitze in den oberen Fluren, mit durchscheinenden Scheiben verglast.
6. Patio zwischen dem Restaurant und dem Ballsaal zur Rechten.

7. Stairs from terrace and cocktail bar to gallery grill have teak steps, and cantilever from a central beam.
8. The foyer lounge at ground floor level overlooking the golf course and tall trees. Paneling of rosewood and travertine.
9. A bedroom. Quiet tones of tan-colored fabrics and natural wood. Extended lines of head boards and lighting troughs in cherry wood, and of balcony handrails in teak. All-glass window wall, balcony railing of glass.
10. The grillroom on the first floor. Warm tones of wood, strong colors in carpet, furniture fabrics and curtains.
11. The lounge bar with separate access from the southern parking area.

7. Treppe von der Terrasse und der Cocktailbar zum Grill im ersten Obergeschoß. Teakholzstufen kragen von einem Mittelbalken aus.
8. Die Foyerlounge im Erdgeschoß mit Blick über den Golfplatz und hohe Baumgruppen. Vertäfelung in Palisander und Travertin.
9. Ein Gastzimmer. Ruhige Brauntöne in Geweben und Naturholz. Lange Linien der Wandborde und Lichtleisten in dunkel gebeiztem Kirschholz, der Balkonbrüstungen in Teak. Ganzglaswand und Balkonbrüstung aus Glas.
10. Der Grillraum im ersten Obergeschoß. Warme Holztöne; Teppich, Bezüge und Vorhänge in starken Farben
11. Die Loungebar mit eigenem Eingang vom südlichen Parkplatz her.

Atrium Hotel, Brunswick, Germany

Architects: Friedrich Wilhelm Kraemer, Günter Pfennig,
Ernst Sieverts

The Atrium Hotel is one of the few recent examples to be built near a railway station. The hotel faces Brunswick's main station across a plain and empty square with little planting. Traffic noise was a major problem. F. W. Kraemer, an architect who has several times made use of courts in his designs, chose an atrium plan not so much to fill a gap between existing buildings, as to introduce something solid into a place where the texture of the city thins and weakens.

On three outer sides of the building, corridors block out traffic noise and shield the rooms from uninviting views. These three outside elevations are solids, finished in red granite and punctured only where the corridors end in ample windows.

On every guest-room floor of the fourth side there is a central corridor with 12 rooms on each side of it. The windows of the outward-facing rooms on this side form three horizontal bands and have a view of a small park. Similar low continuous strips of guest-room windows are repeated on all four sides of the inner court, which is tightly planned, almost square and endowed with a fountain and raised plant-boxes.

The proportion of single to double rooms is 5 to 1, with a total of 126 beds—6 double units (one with a sauna), 12 double and 90 single rooms, of which latter 42 can be used by two persons—bringing the total to a maximum of 168 beds. A few of the rooms can be combined to form suites. Apart from the standard rooms (all with bath or shower), there are 12 long-stay apartments in the west wing, which has a separate entrance. They possess kitchenettes and are rentable for a minimum period of four weeks. Rooms are small, the main partitions being spaced at 3,00 m centers, with the smallest single apartment measuring 5,92 m in depth, or a total usable floor area of about 15 m², an indication that the hotel will cater mainly

for travelling salesmen and passing tourists staying overnight. Storage units, luggage racks and writing desks are wall-hung in all rooms to avoid cluttering the small spaces.

The kitchens are as diverse as the room types. The main kitchen has a conveyor belt system connecting the various sections, from the gardemanger (for cold dishes) to the patissier (for sweets and desserts). As well as the breakfast kitchen, which is an entirely separate unit, there are the ballroom kitchen, which also serves food after the main kitchen is closed, and the bar kitchen, likewise able to handle hot dishes till late at night.

The overall form of the Atrium Hotel complements the almost unbroken solid of the three guest-room floors with a base of two floors walled largely with glass, whose height is halved on all four sides by a terrace faced with slabs, which projects for a varying distance and creates a shaded arcade beneath. Shops extend along two sides of the building and there are even some on the first floor level, where a large raised terrace is used as an outdoor café, linked with the public square by an open stairway.

The upper part of the atrium is surrounded by walls pierced by the strip-windows not of corridors but of guest-rooms. Horizontal slabs project from all four sides, but are not used as guest-room balconies; they merely shield and shade part of the court area at the restaurant and bar level (first floor). Since the atrium floor is also the ballroom roof, the space is less deep than the exterior proportions of the building suggest. In the center is a fountain crowned by a carved capital from the former Brunswick Castle, and surrounded by a pleasantly meandering pattern of raised plant-boxes.

The Atrium Hotel, built at the cost of about 1,6 million dollars for construction and 300 000 dollars for furnishings

and equipment, is the first phase of a major urban development, comprising three tall apartment buildings and a pedestrian shopping mall, to be built during the next few years. The new mall will be connected with the railway station by a footbridge and escalator ramps, leading shoppers and visitors past the hotel terrace, along the mall and further into the city, unmolested by vehicular traffic.

1. The hotel from the railway station. A granite-clad solid three storeys high, above a glass-walled base. A pedestrian bridge will tie in with the opening at the right-hand end of the terrace railing.

1. Das Hotel vom Bahnhof aus gesehen: ein geschlossener, granitverkleideter Block von drei Geschossen auf verglastem Unterbau. In die Brüstungslücke der Terrasse (hinter dem Lichtmast) wird später ein Fußgängersteg einmünden.

Atrium-Hotel, Braunschweig, Deutschland

Architekten: Friedrich Wilhelm Kraemer, Günter Pfennig, Ernst Sieverts

Das Atrium-Hotel ist eines der wenigen Projekte der letzten Jahre, die in der Nähe von Hauptbahnhöfen gebaut wurden. Es liegt dem Bahnhofsgebäude gegenüber, auf der anderen Seite eines etwas leeren Platzes mit wenigen Ansätzen von Grün. Verkehrslärm war eines der Hauptprobleme. F. W. Kraemer, ein Architekt, der schon öfter Gebäude um Innenhöfe entworfen hatte, entschied sich für einen Atriumplan, nicht, weil er eine Lücke zwischen bestehenden Gebäuden zu füllen gehabt hätte, sondern in der Absicht, einen massiven Akzent zu setzen, wo das Gefüge der Stadt dünn und brüchig wird. Drei Flure liegen auf den Außenseiten des Gebäudes, um die Räume gegen Verkehrsgeräusche und wenig schöne Ausblicke abzuschirmen.

Die Räume gehen mit ihren Fenstern auf einen straff entworfenen Innenhof mit einem Brunnen und aufgesetzten Pflanzenbecken. Nur auf der vierten Seite des fast quadratischen Planvierecks liegen Räume zu beiden Seiten eines Mittelflures, und zwölf davon in jedem Geschoß öffnen sich nach außen auf einen kleinen Park, in schmalen, langen Fensterbändern. Die anderen Ansichten sind geschlossen, in rotem Granit verkleidet und nur da unterbrochen, wo die Flure in Fensterflächen enden. Die langen durchlaufenden Fensterbänder sind auch in allen Hotelzimmern zum Hof wiederholt.

Das Verhältnis von Einzel- zu Doppelzimmern ist 5 zu 1 bei einer Gesamtzahl von 126 Betten – 6 Doppelsuiten (eine mit Sauna), 12 Doppel- und 90 Einzelzimmer, von denen 42 auch mit zwei Personen belegt werden können; die maximale Bettenzahl kommt damit auf 168. Einige Räume können als Suiten zusammengelegt werden. Neben den normalen Hotelzimmern (sämtliche mit Bad oder Dusche) wurden im Westflügel, mit eigenem Eingang 12 Dauer-Apartments geschaffen. Sie haben Kleinküchen und werden für mindestens vier Wochen vermietet. Die Raumgrößen sind klein bei einem Abstand der Trennwände von 3,00 m auf Achse. Das kleinste Apartment mißt 5,92 m in der Tiefe und kommt damit auf eine gesamte Nutzfläche von etwa 15 qm, Bad und Vorraum eingeschlossen. Daraus läßt sich ablesen, daß das Hotel überwiegend für Geschäftsreisende und für durchreisende Touristen gedacht ist. Kastenmöbel, Gepäckablagen und Schreibplatten in Hotelzimmern sind als Einheiten an die Wand gehängt, um die kleinen Räume nicht beengt erscheinen zu lassen.

Die Küchen sind ebenso differenziert wie die Raumtypen. Die Hauptküche verfügt über ein Fließbandsystem, das alle Sektionen vom Gardemanger (Koch für kalte Gerichte) bis zum Patissier (für Süßspeisen und Gebäck) verbindet. Die Frühstücksküche ist eine völlig getrennte Anlage; daneben gibt es die Festsaalküche, die auch benutzt wird, um spät abends Gerichte zu servieren, wenn die Hauptküche geschlossen ist, und die Barküche, die warme Gerichte bis in die Nachtstunden abgeben kann.

Die Gesamtform des Atrium-Hotels bringt die fast ungebrochenen Außenfronten der drei Gastgeschosse in Gegensatz zu den großflächig verglasten beiden unteren Geschossen. Deren durchgehende Höhe wird von Terrassen halbiert, die auf allen vier Seiten in wechselnder Tiefe vorspringen und unter sich schattige Promenaden schaffen. Auf zwei Seiten des Gebäudes sind Läden angelegt, ebenso im ersten Obergeschoß, wo die breite hochgelegene Terrasse als Café im Freien genutzt wird, das mit dem öffentlichen Platz durch eine Freitreppe verbunden ist.

Das Atrium ist in seinem oberen Teil auf allen Seiten von Mauerflächen und Fensterstreifen umgeben. Vorspringende Terrassen im unteren Teil wurden nicht als Zimmerterrassen ausgebildet, sondern überdecken nur einen

Teil der Atriumfläche auf der Ebene der Bar und des Restaurants (erstes Obergeschoß). Das Atrium liegt mit seinem Boden ein volles Geschoß über Straßenhöhe (auf der Dachebene des Festsaales) und erscheint dadurch weniger hoch in der Proportion als das Gebäude von außen gesehen. Im Mittelpunkt steht ein Brunnen aus einem Steinkapitell vom früheren Braunschweiger Schloß und Betonringen, umgeben von Pflanzenkästen, die mit ihren mäanderförmigen Zügen das Bild bereichern.

Das Atrium-Hotel, gebaut mit einem Aufwand von 6,4 Millionen Mark und für 1,2 Millionen Mark eingerichtet, ist die erste Phase eines größeren städtebaulichen Projektes, das in den nächsten Jahren Wirklichkeit werden soll; es umfaßt drei Wohnhochhäuser und eine Ladenpromenade für Fußgänger. Die neue Ladengruppe wird mit dem Bahnhof durch einen Fußgängersteg und Rolltreppen verbunden; Besucher gehen vorbei an der Hotelterrasse durch den Ladenbezirk weiter zur Stadt, ungestört vom Fahrverkehr.

2. Narrow bands of guest-room windows surround the atrium, which is above the ceiling of the central ballroom, and has a fountain and plant-boxes.
3. Only on the east side (right) do the bands of guest-room windows face outwards.

2. Das Atrium. Gästezimmer mit langen schmalen Fensterbändern. Ein Brunnen und angehobene Pflanzenbecken auf der Deckenplatte des zentral gelegenen Festsaals.
3. Nur auf der Ostseite (rechts) liegen hinter den Fensterbändern Gästezimmer auf der Außenseite.

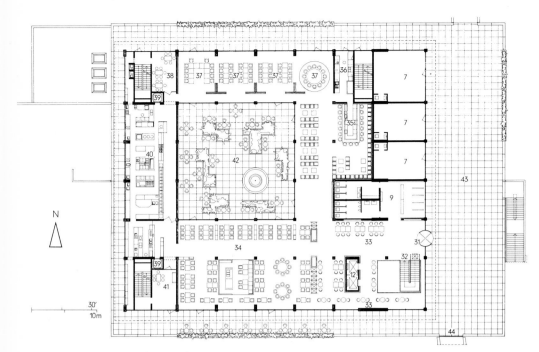

Plan, first floor / Grundriß erstes Obergeschoß.

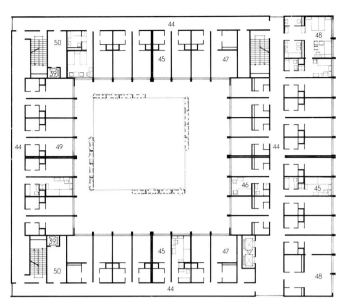

Plan, fourth floor / Grundriß viertes Obergeschoß.

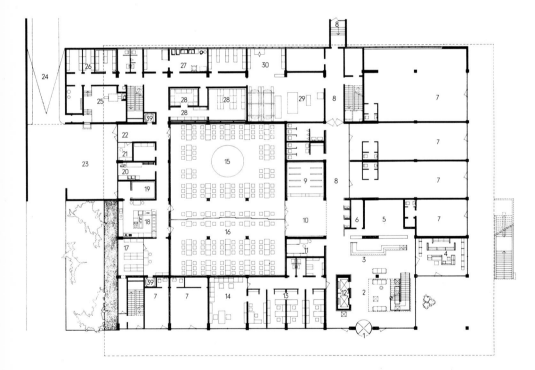

Plan, ground floor / Grundriß Erdgeschoß.

Key to plans: 1 Hotel entrance, 2 Lobby, 3 Front desk, 4 Newspapers and gift shop, 5 Desk office, 6 Telephone exchange, 7 Shops, 8 Passage to garage, 9 Coats, 10 Ballroom lobby, 11 Luggage, 12 Passenger elevators, 13 Administration and bookkeeping, 14 Manager' soffice, 15 Ballroom, 16 Small ballroom, 17 Laundry, 18 Service counter ballroom, 19 Beer cooling, 20 Meat preparation, 21 Doorkeeper, 22 Delivery, 23 Service court, 24 Access to garage, 25 Heating plant, 26 Wine storage and beverage cooling, 27 Vegetable storage and preparation, 28 Refrigeration rooms, 29 Hot water supply and fan room, 30 Workshop, 31 Entrance restaurant level, 32 Stairway to ground floor, 33 Café, 34 Restaurant, 35 Bar, 36 Bar kitchen, 37 Private dining rooms, 38 Employees' dining room, 39 Service elevator, 40 Main kitchen, 41 Waiters' office, 42 Atrium, 43 Terrace, 44 Corridor, 45 Single room, type A, 46 Single room, type B, 47 Double room, type A, 48 Double room, type B, 49 Long-stay apartment with kitchenette, 50 Room service.

Legende zu den Plänen: 1 Hoteleingang, 2 Lobby, 3 Empfang, 4 Kiosk, 5 Büro Empfangschef, 6 Telephonzentrale, 7 Läden, 8 Durchgang zur Garage, 9 Garderobe, 10 Foyer Festsaal, 11 Kofferraum, 12 Aufzüge, 13 Verwaltung und Buchhaltung, 14 Büro des Managers, 15 Großer Festsaal, 16 Kleiner Festsaal, 17 Wäscherei, 18 Anrichte Festsaalküche, 19 Bierkühlraum, 20 Fleischvorbereitung, 21 Pförtner, 22 Anlieferung, 23 Wirtschaftshof, 24 Zufahrt zur Garage, 25 Heizung, 26 Weinlager und Getränkekühlraum, 27 Gemüselager und -vorbereitung, 28 Kühlräume, 29 Warmwasserbereitung und Lüftung, 30 Werkstatt, 31 Eingang Restaurantgeschoß, 32 Treppe vom Erdgeschoß, 33 Café, 34 Restaurant, 35 Bar, 36 Barküche, 37 Konferenzräume, 38 Personal-Speiseraum, 39 Personalaufzug, 40 Hauptküche, 41 Kelneroffice, 42 Atrium, 43 Terrasse, 44 Flur, 45 Einzelzimmer Typ A, 46 Einzelzimmer Typ B, 47 Doppelzimmer Typ A, 48 Doppelzimmer Typ B, 49 Dauerapartment mit Kleinküche, 50 Etagenservice.

4. Model of proposed development adjoining the hotel.
5. The hotel lobby at street level, with the main stairway leading up to the restaurants at terrace and bridge level.
6. The reception desk is lit by a metal-sheathed lighting trough.
7. View from restaurant level down the staircase to the lobby and main entrance. The concrete wall in the restaurant vestibule (background) is decorated with the device of the Atrium Hotel in gold leaf.

8. Focal point of the atrium is the capital of a Corinthian column from Brunswick's demolished ducal palace.
9. The court, with projecting slabs over the restaurant area.

4. Modellansicht des Gesamtausbaus mit Ladenzentrum und Apartmenthäusern im Anschluß an das Hotel.
5. Die Eingangshalle des Hotels mit dem Treppenaufgang zum Restaurantgeschoß in Terrassen- und Brückenhöhe.

6. Ein metallverkleidetes Leuchtband beleuchtet den Empfangsbereich.
7. Blick von der Treppe im Restaurantgeschoß hinunter in die Lobby mit dem Haupteingang. Die Betonwand im Hintergrund des Restaurantvestibüls zeigt das Symbol des Atrium-Hotels in Blattgoldauflage.
8. Im Mittelpunkt des Atriums das Kapitell einer Säule vom Braunschweiger Schloß als Brunnenaufsatz.
9. Der Innenhof mit den Deckenvorsprüngen über dem Restaurantbereich.

10. The large ballroom on ground floor level can be connected with the smaller dining room beyond by opening a sliding wall.

11. When the sliding walls are opened, the four club-rooms on the north side of the atrium become one room.

12. The restaurant seen from the café, screened by room-height dividers.

13. Restaurant and café (beyond). In the foreground is the Swedish buffet.

14. A single room. The unbroken window band and the light, mostly wall-hung furniture have the effect of widening the room. The sofa may be used as a second bed.

15. Large double room two window units wide. A curtain separates sleeping from living areas. All furniture is crisply rectangular in form.

16. The bar forms an open bay next to the sitting area in the passage on the east side of the atrium.

17. A canopy of chromed Mero members signalizes the bar, which has a travertine top, wall paneling of walnut, paintings by Vasarely. The brown and gold carpet also covers the walls of the counter.

10. Durch Öffnen einer Schiebewand kann der große Festsaal im Erdgeschoß mit dem kleinen Saal (hinten) zu einer Raumeinheit verbunden werden.

11. Bei geöffneten Schiebewänden lassen sich die vier Klubzimmer auf der Nordseite des Atriums in einen einzigen Raum verwandeln.

12. Blick vom Cafévestibül zum Restaurant. Eine tiefe Vitrinenwand als Raumteiler.

13. Restaurant und Café (im Hintergrund). Vorn das Schwedenbuffet.

14. Einzelzimmer. Das durchgehende Fensterband und die leichten, großenteils an der Wand aufgehängten Möbelelemente gleichen die geringe Raumbreite optisch aus. Das Sofa kann als zweites Bett benutzt werden.

15. Großes, über zwei Fensterachsen reichendes Doppelzimmer. Schlaf- und Wohnteil durch Vorhang abteilbar. Alle Möbel in klaren, kubischen Formen.

16. Der Barraum schließt als offene Bucht an den Sitzbereich im Umgang auf der Ostseite des Atriums an.

17. Die Bar selbst ist durch einen Baldachin aus verchromten »Mero«-Stäben betont. Theke aus Travertin, Nußbaumvertäfelung, Bilder von Vasarely. Braungoldener Teppich an den Seiten der Theke hochgezogen.

Hotel du Mont d'Arbois, Megève, France

Architect: Bernard H. Zehrfuss

Hotel du Mont d'Arbois, Megève, Frankreich

Architekt: Bernard H. Zehrfuss

The old mountain hotel near Mont Blanc, famous for its site, its cuisine and its distinguished guests, had become obsolescent and spatially inadequate. The owners considered replacing the old building with a completely new one. In the end, however, they decided to respect the tradition of the place and to preserve the existing relationship between building and landscape. Plans for a renovation and for extensions were worked out over several years.

The exteriors of the old building were not greatly changed. A new copper roof was added, also balconies for all guest-rooms. Inside, however, the existing building was entirely reconstructed, from the reception desk to the bathrooms and the new pantries on each floor. The entrance was transferred to the north side; formerly it had taken up valuable space in the sun and disturbed guests relaxing on the balconies.

Early studies had revealed that even the entirely renovated hotel building with its extensions would not provide enough space. Zehrfuss had inserted new rooms for games and television, a sauna and a gymnasium into the existing basement, and to the west side of the old building he added an indoor swimming pool with sliding glass walls. The new kitchen, however, had to be on the same level as the dining rooms. Zehrfuss built it, logically, as a separate kitchen pavilion between the existing hotel and the clubhouse to the north.

His idea was to give the new complex a club atmosphere, by building a clubhouse overlooking the famous golf course. The space requirements were still further expanded. Today, the clubhouse contains a second restaurant planned as a grill room, two large lounges, a bar and a series of luxury apartments. It is connected with the main building and the kitchen by a two-storey gallery. On the west side an outdoor swimming pool was added; it is covered in the winter to serve as a skating and curling rink.

By adding the new structures, Zehrfuss made possible a rational reduction in the working of the hotel during the low season between summer and winter, when the main building and the clubhouse can be operated as separate units. His architecture is restrained in character: he used single-pitch roofs composed in a village-like fashion, natural wood in the façades, interiors with deep colors and richly varied lighting effects.

Das Berghotel unter dem Mont-Blanc, berühmt durch seine Lage, seine Küche und seine illustren Gästescharen, war funktionell veraltet und räumlich zu klein geworden. Man dachte an Abriß und Neubau, aber am Ende wollte man doch die Tradition des Platzes wahren, den gewohnten Rapport von Haus und Landschaft erhalten. Die Pläne für einen Umbau und Erweiterungen entstanden im Laufe mehrerer Jahre.

Von außen geschah an dem Altbau nicht viel. Er bekam ein neues Kupferdach und Balkone für alle Zimmer. Im Innern jedoch führte der Architekt einen Neubau im bestehenden Gebäude durch, vom Empfang zu den Bädern und Etagen-Anrichten. Der Eingang wurde auf die Nordseite verlegt; zuvor hatte er im Süden gut besonnten Platz weggenommen und die Ruhe auf den Balkonen gestört. Es hatte sich früh gezeigt, daß selbst das völlig umgebaute alte Hotel mit seinen Erweiterungen räumlich nicht genügen konnte. Zwar hatte Zehrfuss im Keller des Altbaues Spielraum und Fernsehzimmer, Sauna und Gymnastiksaal neu eingerichtet und nach Westen ein Hallenbad mit Schiebewänden aus Glas vor den alten Trakt gelegt. Die neue Küche aber mußte auf derselben Ebene wie die Speiseräume liegen. Zehrfuss baute sie folgerichtig als getrennten Küchenpavillon zwischen dem Altbau und dem Clubhaus im Norden.

Die Idee war, dem ganzen Komplex eine Clubatmosphäre zu geben, ein »Clubhouse« mit Blick auf den bestehenden Golfplatz zu bauen. Das Raumprogramm wurde immer weiter gesteckt. Heute enthält das Clubhaus ein zweites Restaurant, als Grill eingerichtet, zwei große Salons, eine Bar und eine Reihe von Luxuszimmern. Zur Verbindung mit Hauptgebäude und Küche dient eine zweigeschossige Galerie. Auf der Westseite wurde noch ein Schwimmbecken im Freien angelegt, das im Winter mit einer Eisbahn und Curlingpiste überdeckt wird.

Zehrfuss erreichte durch die Zuordnung der neuen Baukörper, daß das Hotel in der toten Saison zwischen Sommer und Winter sich rationell auf einen verkleinerten Betrieb im Hotel oder nur im Clubhaus beschränken kann. Gestalterisch hielt er sich an eine sachliche Formel: Pultdächer in fast dörflicher Manier übereinander gesetzt, viel Naturholz in den Fassaden, das Innere mit satten Farben und stark variierten Lichteffekten.

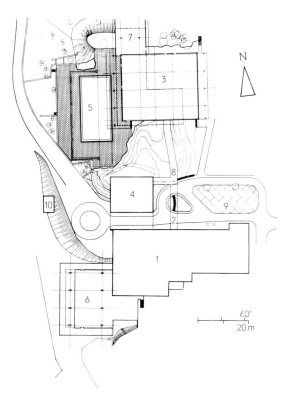

Site plan. Key: 1 Existing hotel building, 2 Main entrance, 3 Clubhouse, 4 Kitchen pavilion, 5 Outdoor swimming pool, 6 Indoor swimming pool, 7 Storage, 8 Two-storey connecting gallery for staff and guests, 9 Parking space, 10 Shed for propane gas containers.

Lageplan. Legende: 1 Bestehendes Hotelgebäude, 2 Haupteingang, 3 Clubhaus, 4 Küchenpavillon, 5 Schwimmbecken im Freien, 6 Hallenbad, 7 Abstellraum, 8 Zweigeschossige Verbindungsgalerie für Personal und Gäste, 9 Parkplätze, 10 Raum für Propangasbehälter.

1. The clubhouse and connecting gallery. Exteriors in larchwood.

1. Das Clubhaus mit Galerie. Fassaden in Lärchenholz.

2. Grill restaurant in the clubhouse. Light finishes, lively colors in flooring and fabrics.
3. The bar and lounge with fireplace. Plain wood and a great splash of color in the rug.
4. The gallery between the hotel and clubhouse (guest level). The second level is for the staff only.
5. Gymnasium in the basement of the old building.
6. The indoor swimming pool, low-ceilinged, with a wide view of the valley.

2. Grillrestaurant des Clubhauses. Lichte Flächen, lebendige Farbigkeit der Böden und Textilien.
3. Bar und Rauchzimmer mit Kamin. Schlichtes Naturholz, der Teppich als großer Farbakzent.
4. Die Galerie zwischen Hotel und Clubhaus (Gästeebene). Das zweite Galeriegeschoß ist ausschließlich dem Personal vorbehalten.
5. Gymnastikraum im Keller des Altbaues.
6. Schwimmhalle, niedrig gehalten, mit weitem Blick ins Tal.

Kurhaus Bad Mergentheim, Germany

Architects: Wilhelm Tiedje and G. Krische

Kurhaus Bad Mergentheim, Deutschland

Architekten: Wilhelm Tiedje und G. Krische

The old Kurhaus with its hundred-year-old central building no longer fulfilled the demands of modern hotel accomodation. As long ago as 1960 a new building was planned between the existing guest-room wings; it was to serve as a new gathering place for social life in this popular spa.

The lowness of the guest-room wings imposed a certain height limit on the two main floors of the new building. The architects overcame this obstacle by making the lounge and café-restaurant into two-storey spaces with surrounding galleries. The public rooms open on three sides to the Kurpark.

The kitchen and restaurant for 170 persons are on the top floor. Four reinforced concrete beams are cantilevered towards the park and frame the room and the view with their sunbreakers. A basement floor is used for treatment rooms, an indoor swimming pool and the pump room of the Karlsquelle.

The new building with its strong horizontal lines deliberately defers to the tall trees of the Kurpark. The entrance side, a largely closed facade, ties in with the old flanking wings.

Das alte Kurhaus mit seinem hundert Jahre alten Mittelteil genügte nicht mehr den Anforderungen unserer Zeit. Ein neues Gebäude wurde, seit 1960, als Mittelpunkt des gesellschaftlichen Lebens in dem vielbesuchten Kurort zwischen den bestehenden Wohnflügeln geplant.

Die geringe Höhe der Zimmerfluchten legte für die beiden Hauptgeschosse des Neubaues die Raumhöhe fest. Die Architekten nahmen dieses Hindernis, indem sie Halle und Café zweigeschossig mit umlaufenden Galerien entwickelten. Die Gesellschaftsräume öffnen sich auf drei Seiten weit zum Kurpark.

Die Küche und das Restaurant für 170 Personen liegen im obersten Stockwerk. Vier Stahlbetonträger kragen weit zum Park aus und geben mit ihren Sonnenlamellen dem Raum einen prägnanten Rahmen. Ein Sockelgeschoß nimmt Therapieräume, das Schwimmbad und die Trinkhalle der Karlsquelle auf.

Der Neubau ordnet sich mit seiner stark horizontalen Gliederung den hohen Bäumen des Kurparks unter. Die Eingangsseite, geschlossener, gleicht sich mehr den alten Flügeln an.

1. The park elevation with terraces and sitting balconies.

1. Die Parkseite mit ihren Terrassen und Sitzbalkonen.

Key to plans: 1 Main entrance, 2 Lobby, 3 Front desk, 4 Office, 5 Corridor to guest-room wings, 6 Manager, 7 Café, 8 Wine restaurant, 9 Bar, 10 Television room, 11 Coffee kitchen, 12 Hall, 13 Conference room, 14 Reading room, 15 Gallery of café, 16 Breakfast room, 17 Staff dining room, 18 Kitchen for breakfast room, 19 Lockers, 20 Terrace, 21 Restaurant, 22 Main kitchen.

Legende zu den Plänen: 1 Haupteingang, 2 Lobby, 3 Empfang, 4 Büro, 5 Verbindungsflur zu den Wohnflügeln, 6 Direktor, 7 Café, 8 Weinstube, 9 Bar, 10 Fernsehraum, 11 Kaffeeküche, 12 Halle, 13 Konferenzzimmer, 14 Lesezimmer, 15 Cafégalerie, 16 Frühstücksraum, 17 Personal-Eßraum, 18 Küche für Frühstücksraum, 19 Personalumkleideraum, 20 Terrasse, 21 Restaurant, 22 Hauptküche.

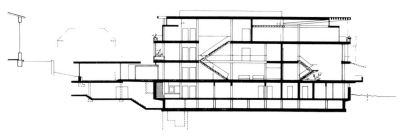

Section from north to south / Schnitt Nord-Süd.

Site plan with the new center building between the existing guest-room wings / Lageplan mit dem Neubau zwischen den bestehenden Wohnflügeln.

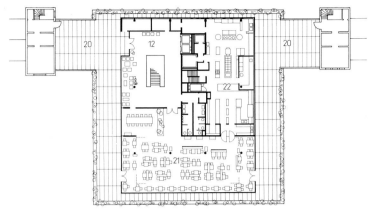

Plan, second floor / Grundriß zweites Obergeschoß.

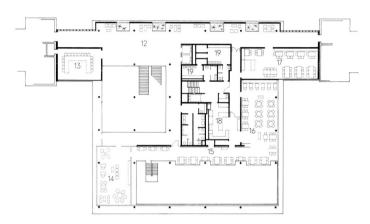

Plan, first floor / Grundriß erstes Obergeschoß.

30'
10m

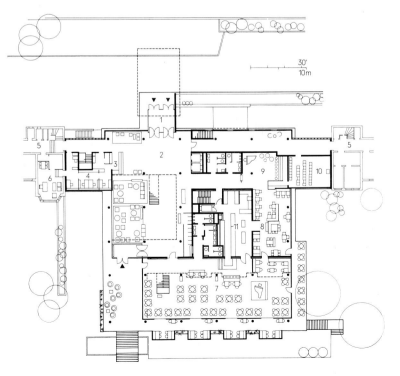

Plan, main floor (entrance level) / Grundriß Hauptgeschoß (Eingangsgeschoß).

2. The second-floor restaurant. A low roof strip below the sunbreakers emphasizes the horizontal.
3. The two-storey café, open to the Kurpark on three sides. The gallery is a breakfast room.

2. Restaurant im zweiten Obergeschoß. Ein niedriger Dachstreifen unter den Sonnenblenden soll den Raum horizontal gliedern.
3. Das doppelgeschossige Café, auf drei Seiten zum Kurpark geöffnet. Galerie als Frühstückszimmer.

Hotel Intercontinental, Dublin

Architect: William B. Tabler

The Intercontinental Hotels Corporation's three hotels in Ireland occupy a place of their own among the group's many hotels, and in the work of Tabler, who specialises in hotels. They are modest, without any hint of glamor, more Irish than international, and they do not impose themselves on their surroundings, preferring to merge into them.

The Dublin Intercontinental, like its smaller counterparts in Cork and Limerick, is basically a motor hotel. Though it has an 8-storey guest-room slab and is the biggest hotel in Dublin and the city's only convention hotel, this does not change its essential character. The low wing with the public and service rooms is entirely separate from the tall slab, being connected to it only by a glazed hallway. There are nearly 200 parking spaces in front of and behind the building. On the ground floor are the reception desk, the lounge and the lengthy dining room, which gains apparent width from a formal garden lying between it and the guest-room slab. The kitchen is about halfway along, and serves both the dining room and the ballroom, an area of almost 700 m², which can be sub-divided or can be enlarged by taking in the adjacent private dining rooms. The ballroom foyer is remarkably long and has a side entrance; the coat-room and lavatories are placed on the side nearest the main entrance, so that a single large group can serve all guests, whether they use the dining room, bar or ballroom. The upper floor of the low building accommodates the service rooms, offices, repair shops and mechanical plant. All the service functions are hidden behind a screen of slender concrete uprights. The elevations of the guest-room slab are also finished in concrete and precast stone.

The 320 guest apartments are all the same size (3,80 m by 4,45 m) and furnished, in changing sequences, as studios (with one bed and a daybed), and as twinbed apartments. There are very few units with double beds. As is customary in all the corporation's hotels, the manager lives on the premises. Guest-rooms are finished in smooth plaster and decorated in rich colors—carpets a deep red or blue, one wall in each bedroom red or canary yellow. The bedspreads and curtains are of Irish linen. Another combination of strong colors—white, black and ruby red—marks the rooftop restaurant on the ninth floor. The fortunate position of the hotel—it is at the edge of the city and near the Botanical Gardens of Trinity College—gives this room a panoramic view of Dublin, the Wicklow Hills and the bay.

The restrained yet colorful furnishings of the public rooms were the choice of an Irish group which took part in the project. Local materials and fabrics were chosen to impart an Irish atmosphere. The architect was, for the first time, commissioned to design both the building and its interiors. He worked with a talented Irish designer, Mrs. de Polo, who succeeded in bridging the all-too-frequent gap between architecture and interior design. The lobby is floored with black Irish limestone which extends through lounge and hall and out onto the sidewalk. The black sets off excellently the colorful tweed upholstery. Walls are sheathed with afrormosia, a dark, warm-toned wood; curtains are off-white, of hand-woven wool. The tables are green Connemara marble and table cloths are white or undyed tweed.
The total cost of the project was four million dollars.

1. The low reception wing. Service rooms are on the upper floor behind concrete screens.
2. Façades without ostentation, of concrete and cast stone.
3. Garden court beside the restaurant. A glazed passage leads to the guest-room slab.

1. Der flache Eingangstrakt. Hinter den Betonlamellen des Obergeschosses die Nebenräume.
2. Schlichte Fassaden in Beton und Kunststein.
3. Gartenhof vor dem Restaurant; verglaste Passage zum Hochhaus.

Hotel Intercontinental, Dublin

Architekt: William B. Tabler

Die drei irischen Häuser der Intercontinental Hotels Corporation haben einen besonderen Platz unter den vielen Projekten des Konzerns und im Schaffen des Hotelspezialisten Tabler. Sie sind bescheiden gehalten, ohne Anflüge von Glamour; sie sind mehr irisch als international; sie zwingen sich nicht dem Stadtbild auf, sondern werden Teil ihrer Umgebung.

Wie seine kleineren Gegenstücke in Cork und Limerick, basiert auch das Dublin Intercontinental auf dem Konzept des Motor-Hotels. Darüber täuscht auch der achtgeschossige Bettenblock nicht hinweg und nicht die Tatsache, daß es das größte Hotel Dublins ist und das einzige, das Kongresse aufnehmen kann. Der Flachbau mit den Gesellschafts- und Nebenräumen ist vom hohen Trakt räumlich stark abgesetzt und nur durch eine verglaste Galerie mit ihm verbunden. Fast 200 Parkplätze sind im Vorfeld und auf der Rückseite untergebracht. Im Erdgeschoß liegen Empfang und Halle und der gestreckte Speisesaal, der optisch durch einen etwas formalistisch in Rechteckfelder aufgeteilten Garten im Winkel zum Hauptbau ausgeweitet wird. Die Küche liegt fast mittig und bedient außer dem Speisesaal den großen Ballsaal von fast 700 qm, der teilbar ist, aber auch durch die anstoßenden Speiseräume für private Veranstaltungen erweitert werden kann. Bemerkenswert das sehr lange Foyer des Ballsaals mit dem Eingang von der Seite. Garderobe und Waschräume sind in Richtung Haupteingang gelegt; eine einzige großangelegte Installationsgruppe versorgt alle Gäste des Hauses in Speisesaal, Bar und Ballsaal. Das zweite Geschoß des Flachbaues nimmt die Serviceräume, Büros, Werkstätten und die technischen Anlagen auf. Alle diese untergeordneten Funktionen sind hinter einer Fassade aus feingegliederten Betongittern verborgen. Die Fassaden des Bettentrakts zeigen ebenfalls Beton und Kunststein und gehen auch formal eng mit der Gestaltung des Flachbaus zusammen.

Die 320 Gäste-Apartments, alle von einer Größe (3,80 auf 4,45 m) sind in wechselndem Rhythmus als Studios (mit einem Bett und einem Sofabett) und als Twin-Apartments mit getrennten parallelen Betten eingerichtet. Nur wenige Einheiten haben Doppelbetten. Wie in allen Hotels des Konzerns wohnt der Direktor im Hause. Die Schlafräume sind glatt verputzt und in satten Farben ausgestattet, Teppiche kräftig rot oder blau, eine Wand rot oder kanariengelb gestrichen. Bettbezüge und Vorhänge sind aus irischem Leinen. Ein starker Farbakkord, Schwarz, Weiß und Rubinrot, prägt auch das Dachrestaurant im neunten Stock. Die Lage des Hotels am Rande der City dicht an dem Botanischen Garten des Trinity College kommt hier im Rundblick über Dublin, die Wicklow Hills und die Bucht voll zur Geltung.

Die schlichte und doch lebendig farbige Ausstattung der Gesellschaftsräume ging auf den Wunsch einer irischen Gruppe zurück, die sich an dem Projekt beteiligte. Örtliche Materialien und Gewebe sollten eine irische Atmosphäre schaffen. Der Architekt hatte zum erstenmal Entwurf und Raumgestaltung in seiner Hand. Er arbeitete mit der begabten irischen Innenarchitektin Mrs. de Polo zusammen, die es verstand, die Trennung von Architektur und Dekoration bruchlos auszugleichen. Irischer schwarzer Kalkstein ist als Bodenbelag für Eingang, Halle und Flur gewählt und zieht sich draußen über Anfahrt und Gehsteig. Er bringt die farbkräftigen Tweedstoffe voll zur Geltung. Die Wände sind mit Afrormosia, einem dunklen warmgetönten Holz, verkleidet; Wollvorhänge, handgewebt, fast weiß, vor den Fenstern. Die Tische sind aus grünem irischen Marmor von Connemara gearbeitet, für die Tischtücher wurde weißer und naturfarbener Tweed verwendet.

Die Gesamtkosten betrugen vier Millionen Dollar.

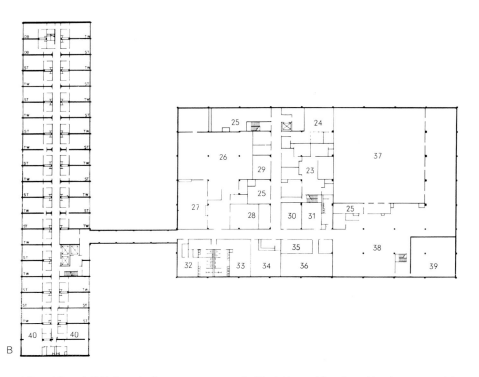

A Plan, ground floor / Grundriß Erdgeschoß.
B Plan, first floor / Grundriß erstes Obergeschoß.
C Plan, typical floor / Grundriß Normalgeschoß.
D Plan, top floor / Grundriß Dachgeschoß.

4. The lobby and fireplace. Hand-woven curtains, colorful tweed upholstery and rugs.
5. The lounge and access to the front desk. Flooring of black limestone.
6. The restaurant, a long rectangle divided by wooden screens. Irish easy chairs of afrormosia.

4. Halle mit Kamin. Handgewebte Vorhänge, farbige Tweedstoffe und Teppiche.
5. Lounge und Durchgang zum Empfang. Böden aus schwarzem Kalkstein.
6. Das Restaurant, langgestreckt, unterteilt durch Holzblenden. Irische Sessel in Afrormosia.

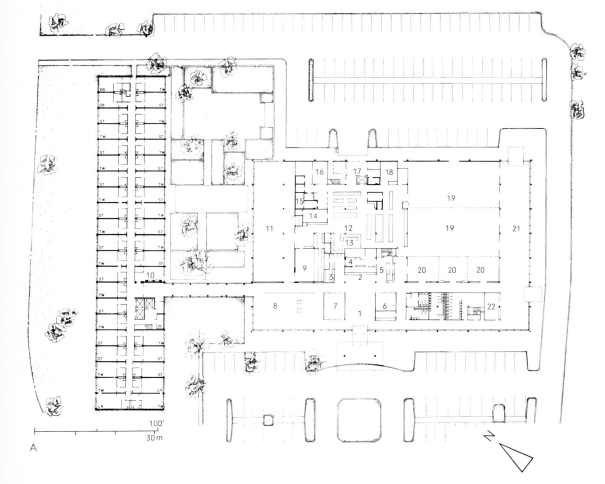

Key to plans: 1 Entrance lobby, 2 Front desk, 3 Coats, 4 Telephone switchboard, 5 News stand, 6 Bank, 7 Gift shop, 8 Lounge, 9 Bar, 10 Barber shop, 11 Dining room, 12 Kitchen, 13 Dishwashing, 14 Bakery, 15 Refrigeration rooms, 16 Storage, 17 Goods reception, 18 Room service, 19 Ballroom, 20 Private dining rooms, 21 Ballroom foyer, 22 Coats, 23 Managing staff, 24 Accounts department, 25 Storage, 26 Laundry, 27 Housekeeping, 28 Valet, 29 Print shop, 30 Carpenter's shop, 31 Upholstery and paint shop, 32 Women's lockers, 33 Men's lockers, 34 Staff dining room, 35 Senior staff dining room, 36 Electro-mechanical workshop, 37 Void above ballroom, 38 Mechanical services, 39 Boiler room, 40 Manager's suite, 41 Roof restaurant, 42 Preparation, TW Twin bedroom, ST Studio type bedroom (single bed and daybed).

Legende zu den Plänen: 1 Eingangshalle, 2 Empfang, 3 Garderobe, 4 Telephonzentrale, 5 Zeitungsstand, 6 Bank, 7 Laden für Geschenkartikel, 8 Lounge, 9 Bar, 10 Friseur, 11 Speisesaal, 12 Küche, 13 Spülküche, 14 Bäckerei, 15 Kühlräume, 16 Lagerraum, 17 Anlieferung, 18 Zimmerservice, 19 Ballsaal, 20 Speiseraum für private Veranstaltungen, 21 Foyer des Ballsaals, 22 Garderobe, 23 Direktion, 24 Buchhaltung, 25 Lagerraum, 26 Wäscherei, 27 Hausdamen, 28 Kleiderpflege, 29 Druckerei, 30 Tischlerei, 31 Polsterei und Malerwerkstatt, 32 Umkleideraum für Frauen, 33 Umkleideraum für Männer, 34 Angestellten-Speisesaal, 35 Speiseraum für leitende Angestellte, 36 Elektromechanische Werkstatt, 37 Luftraum über Ballsaal, 38 Technische Anlagen, 39 Boilerraum, 40 Wohnung des Direktors, 41 Dachrestaurant, 42 Anrichte, TW Doppelzimmer mit Betten in Twin-Anordnung, ST Studio-Schlafraum (Einzelbett und Sofabett).

7. The roof restaurant has a panoramic view and a harmonious décor of red, white and black.
8. The bar. Photographs of a rich variety of Irish faces are the only decoration.
9. The ballroom. A wooden floor on steel springs, for dancing the jig.

7. Das Dachrestaurant, Rundblick und Farbakkord in Rot, Weiß und Schwarz.
8. Die Bar. Fotos, das vielseitige Gesicht Irlands, als einzige Dekoration.
9. Der Ballsaal. Holzboden auf Stahlfedern für die irische Gigue.

10. The exterior of the guest-room slab, natural gray concrete, lightly textured.
11. A bedroom (with twin-beds). Modest dimensions, rich colors.
12. Studio-type bedroom with single bed and daybed. Furniture is unpretentious in form and crisp in line.

10. Fassade des Bettentrakts. Betongrau, wenig strukturiert.
11. Schlafraum (Twin-Anordnung). Bescheiden dimensioniert, in satten Farben.
12. Schlafraum des Studiotyps (mit Einzelbett und Sofabett). Auch die Möbel in klaren, einfachen Formen.

Hotel Intercontinental, Cork, Ireland

Architect: William B. Tabler

This hotel in Cork, on Muskerry Island, has two wings of 48 apartments each: its total cost was 1½ million dollars. It demonstrates yet again that the best results are the product of a well-planned integration of surroundings, architecture and interior design. The building itself is quite simply finished. The two-storey guest wings have exterior walls and interior partitions of exposed cement blocks. The entrance building is of precast concrete panels on steel frames. Paved walks and floors in the lobby and public rooms are plain bricks. The elevations are as simple as the materials: precise Mondrianesque sequences of vertical elements. The clean-cut façades are in vivid contrast with the luxuriant Irish landscape around them—the buildings open onto a wide garden court beside the river Lee.

The guest-room wings and the reception building are to the standard design used again in Limerick (see next item). The parking spaces for 110 cars (there are more parking stalls than guest-rooms) are in several groups along the periphery of the site, as at the Dublin Intercontinental. In keeping with the basic conception of a motor hotel, as opposed to a motel, the cars are not parked next to the guest-room doors. The shape and orientation of the site did not permit an optimum layout for the standardised design, however. A guest may walk as much as 200 m from the lobby to his apartment, passing most of the service rooms and an entire guest-room wing. The distances from the parking spaces are, of course, much shorter. The restaurant is easily reached from the entrance drive, but has no view of the river.

1. The river Lee and the flat green of the hotel garden.
2. The entrance and restaurant: a repeated pattern of vertical elements.

1. Der River Lee und das flache Geviert des Hotelgartens.
2. Eingang und Restaurant. Reihung vertikaler Elemente.

Hotel Intercontinental, Cork, Irland

Architekt: William B. Tabler

Das kleine Hotel in Cork auf Muskerry Island – zweimal 48 Apartments, Gesamtkosten sechs Millionen Mark – zeigt einmal mehr, daß ein gelungener Einklang von Umgebung, Architektur und innerer Gestaltung die besten Ergebnisse bieten kann. Der Bau selbst ist mehr als einfach ausgeführt. Die zweigeschossigen Gästeflügel haben Wände aus Zementblocks, unverputzt nach außen und im Inneren. Das Eingangsgebäude wurde aus vorgefertigten Betonscheiben auf Stahlrahmen errichtet. Schlichte Ziegel bedecken Gehsteig, Eingangshalle und die Böden in den öffentlichen Räumen. Einfach wie die Materialien sind die Aufrisse, eine mondrianhafte Präzision gereihter vertikaler Elemente. Diese klare Profilierung ist ein lebendiger Gegensatz zu der üppig grünen irischen Landschaft rings um die Gebäude, die sich mit einem weiten Gartenhof auf den River Lee öffnen.
Die Gästeflügel und der Empfangsbau sind Teile eines Standardentwurfs, der noch einmal in Limerick wiederholt wurde. Die Parkplätze für 110 Wagen (ihre Anzahl übersteigt die Zimmerzahl) sind wie in Dublin als getrennte Flächen an der Peripherie angelegt. Im Gegensatz zum Grundkonzept eines Motels stehen bei diesem Motor-Hotel die Wagen nicht vor den Zimmertüren. Der Zuschnitt des Grundstücks erlaubte für den standardisierten Entwurf kein ideales Layout. Der Weg des Gastes aus der Lobby, vorbei an allen Nebenräumen durch einen Gästeflügel zu seinem Apartment im letzten Gebäude, kann fast 200 m betragen; allerdings sind die Wege von den Parkplätzen kürzer. Das Restaurant ist von der Vorfahrt gut zu erreichen, hat aber nichts von der Aussicht auf den Fluß.

3. The restaurant, divided by sliding panels in blue and red.
4. The bar. Simple furniture in wood and leather, a country inn.
5. The gallery to the guest-room wings has large areas of linen curtain.

3. Das Restaurant, zweigeteilt durch Schiebewände in Blau und Rot.
4. Die Bar. Schlichte Möbel in Holz und Leder, ein Country Inn.
5. Galerie zu den Gästeflügeln. Leinen in großer Fläche.

Site plan and ground floor plan. Key: 1 Entrance canopy, 2 Parking spaces, 3 Lobby, 4 Front desk, 5 Bank, 6 Administration, 7 Meeting rooms, 8 Gift shop, 9 Lounge, 10 Bar, 11 Restaurant, 12 Kitchen, 13 Preparation, 14 Storage, 15 Machinery room, 16 Boiler room, 17 Transformer room, 18 Housekeeping, 19 Staff dining room, 20 Laundry, 21 Guest-room wing, TW Twin bedroom, ST Studio type bedroom (single bed and daybed).

Lageplan und Grundriß Erdgeschoß. Legende: 1 Vorfahrt mit Schutzdach, 2 Parkplätze, 3 Eingangshalle, 4 Empfang, 5 Bank, 6 Verwaltung, 7 Konferenzräume, 8 Laden für Geschenkartikel, 9 Lounge, 10 Bar, 11 Restaurant, 12 Küche, 13 Anrichte, 14 Lagerraum, 15 Technische Anlagen, 16 Boilerraum, 17 Trafostation, 18 Hausdamen, 19 Angestellten-Speisesaal, 20 Wäscherei, 21 Flügel mit Gastzimmern, TW Doppelzimmer mit Betten in Twin-Anordnung, ST Studio Schlafraum (Einzelbett und Sofabett).

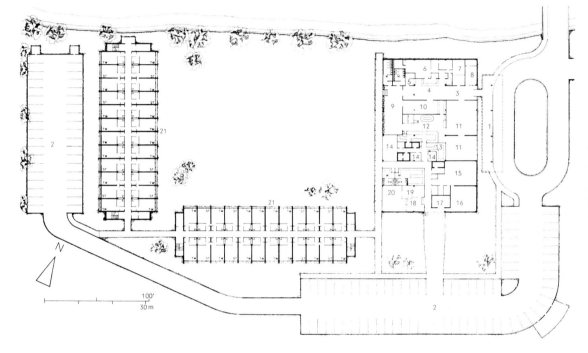

100'
30 m

Hotel Intercontinental, Limerick, Ireland

Architect: William B. Tabler

Hotel Intercontinental, Limerick, Irland

Architekt: William B. Tabler

The plan in all its parts and details is a repetition of the standard design used in Cork, the only difference being that the guest-room wings are laid out symmetrically on both sides of the reception building. The open space of the garden court is kept entirely level, with strips of gravel and meandering stone-flagged paths framing the lawn. Tall trees behind the guest-room wings give the low buildings a rich setting of greenery. The interior designer, Mrs. de Polo, tried to "keep the décor simple and almost crude, because in a sense, the building materials are crude". All furniture in Limerick, as in Cork, is of oak and solid in character. Large tapestries dominate the walls, the floors have deep-pile carpets in rich, strong colors. The two restaurants are divided by red and blue sliding panels. In the bedrooms, with their whitewashed walls of cement blocks, carpets are beige; hand-woven bedspreads cover the beds during the day. Curtains in guest and public rooms are undyed linen.
The interior designer, working closely with the architect, has achieved her aim—to create an intimate warmth of the kind found in bygone Irish country inns.

Der Plan ist in allen seinen Teilen bis in die Einzelheiten eine Wiederholung des Hauses in Cork – nur daß die Gästeflügel symmetrisch zu beiden Seiten des Empfangsgebäudes liegen. Die offene Fläche des Gartenhofes ist völlig eben gehalten, mit Streifen von Kies und verspringenden Steinwegen am Rande der Rasenfläche. Hohe Bäume hinter den Gästeflügeln geben den flachen Trakten eine lebendige Kulisse von Grün. Die Innenarchitektin de Polo versuchte, »ihre Ausstattung einfach und fast roh zu halten, da in einem gewissen Sinne auch die Baumaterialien roh sind«. Alle Möbel in Limerick, wie auch in Cork, sind daher aus Eiche und schwer im Maßstab. Breite Wandteppiche setzen die Akzente, die Böden haben Wollteppiche mit hohem Flor und reichen, satten Farben. Die beiden Restaurants werden durch Schiebewände in Blau und Rot unterteilt. In den Schlafräumen mit ihren geschlämmten Wänden aus Zementsteinen, sind die Teppiche beige; handgewebte Wolldecken dienen als Bettspreiten. Die Vorhänge in den Gäste-Apartments und in den Gesellschaftsräumen sind naturfarbenes Leinen.
Mit ihren Interieurs erreichte die Raumgestalterin, was sie wollte: eine wohlig intime Atmosphäre zu schaffen, wie man sie in irischen Country Inns der alten Zeit findet.

1. Entrance drive beneath old trees.
2. The garden court. Stone paths around a wide lawn.

1. Vorfahrt unter alten Bäumen.
2. Das Gartenquadrat. Plattenpfade um einen weiten Rasen.

3. The lounge, separated from the long gallery by steps and greenery.
4. The restaurants. Hand-woven table cloths, heavy armchairs with wooden backs, delicate greenery.
5. A bedroom. Plain walls, hand-woven bedspreads, light-colored carpeting.

3. Die Lounge, durch Stufen und Grün von der langen Galerie getrennt.
4. Die Restaurants. Tischtücher handgewebt, schwere Armsessel mit Holzlehne, feinblättriges Grün.
5. Ein Schlafraum. Nüchterne Wände, handgewebte Überzüge, heller Teppich.

Site plan and ground floor plan. Key: 1 Entrance canopy, 2 Parking spaces, 3 Lobby, 4 Front desk, 5 Bank, 6 Administration, 7 Meeting rooms, 8 Gift shop, 9 Lounge, 10 Bar, 11 Restaurant, 12 Kitchen, 13 Preparation, 14 Storage, 15 Machinery room, 16 Boiler room, 17 Transformer room, 18 Housekeeping, 19 Staff dining room, 20 Laundry, 21 Guest-room wing, TW Twin bedroom, ST Studio type bedroom (single bed and daybed).

Lageplan und Grundriß Erdgeschoß. Legende: 1 Vorfahrt mit Schutzdach, 2 Parkplätze, 3 Eingangshalle, 4 Empfang, 5 Bank, 6 Verwaltung, 7 Konferenzräume, 8 Laden für Geschenkartikel, 9 Lounge, 10 Bar, 11 Restaurant, 12 Küche, 13 Anrichte, 14 Lagerraum, 15 Technische Anlagen, 16 Boilerraum, 17 Trafostation, 18 Hausdamen, 19 Angestellten-Speisesaal, 20 Wäscherei, 21 Flügel mit Gastzimmern, TW Doppelzimmer mit Betten in Twin-Anordnung, ST Studio-Schlafraum (Einzelbett und Sofabett).

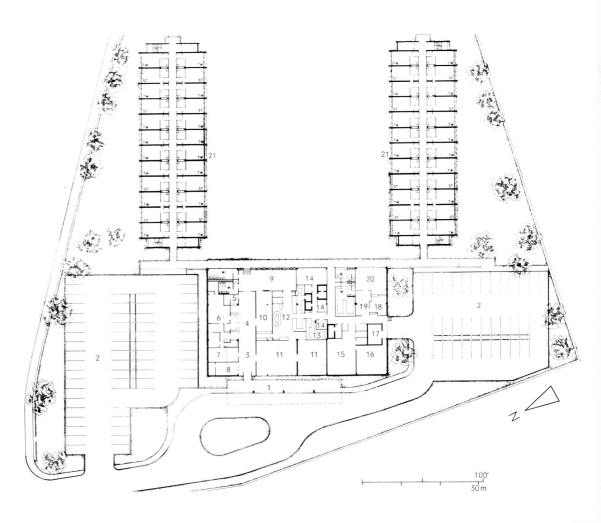

Esso Motor Hotel, Hanover

Architect: Paul Beyersdorf

This hotel is one of a chain spanning Europe from north to south. Soon motorists will be able to travel from northern Sweden to the Mediterranean via Göteborg, Copenhagen and Brescia or Courmayeur, and stop at an Esso Motor Hotel every evening. Their cars will be serviced and tanks filled at the service center during the night. The garage servicing will be of uniform quality everywhere, but the character of the hotels and of their buildings will differ according to region. Every hotel will be designed by local architects and furnished by local interior designers. Regional dishes will be served in the restaurants.

The Esso Hotel in Hanover is the German stage on the route south to Frankfurt and the Rhineland. The site was carefully chosen: 1,5 km from the Hamburg–Frankfurt autobahn, 5 from the city center, 3 along the Fair Freeway to the world's largest industrial fair, a quarter of an hour's drive from the airport and ten minutes from the Hamburg–Cologne autobahn. But the site was not chosen only for its convenient position in the road network: the hotel stands at the main gate of the Deer Garden, and is an invitation to rest and refreshment for the two million who

visit the park every year. The building is meant to be much more than accommodation for a much-needed night's sleep after a day behind the steering wheel. It aims to attract both business people and families out on vacation or weekend trips. A pause in almost rural surroundings, a leisurely meal, can become a positive experience, a pleasant part of travelling.

All guest-rooms have an open view over the woods and meadows of the Deer Garden. There are 68 units (20 double rooms, 41 studio units, very few singles or suites) and each one is extended by a loggia. Additional facilities are on a large scale. A lighted parking area holds 300 cars, free of charge; 160 persons can take part in conferences or private parties, the restaurants accommodate 350 guests and the two terraces facing the Deer Garden another 300. A surprising feature in a hotel of this size (total cost 1,2 million dollars) is that there is not just one restaurant plus a snack bar, but four specialized restaurants: the Tiergarten Restaurant for all three main meals and afternoon tea, the Sophia Room, a gourmet restaurant featuring flambé dishes, the Bristol Grill and the Hunter's Room, a luncheon, beer and wine restaurant for traditional fare.

The hotel is a three-storey building on concrete pilotis. The façade and the shaded areas of the deep loggias are carefully proportioned; so is the relief of the floor slabs and railings and the slight projection of the loggia walls. All four sides are constructed of precast panels with pebble finish. The single-storey restaurant wing is faced with contrasting dark wood and has large expanses of floor-to-ceiling glass. The guest-rooms, mechanically ventilated like the rest of the building, are finished in white plaster with a few touches of color.

1. The entrance side. Broad and narrow bands of concrete with aggregate exposed; cross-walls are thin and project slightly. Deep shadows in the loggias.

1. Die Eingangsseite. Breite und schmale Bänder in Waschbeton; dünne, knapp durchschießende Schotten. Tiefe Schatten der Loggien.

Esso-Motorhotel, Hannover

Architekt: Paul Beyersdorf

Das Haus ist Teil einer Hotelbrücke, die von Norden nach Süden über Europa geschlagen wird. Bald können Autofahrer vom nördlichen Schweden über Göteborg und Kopenhagen bis Brescia und Courmayeur reisen und jeden Abend in einem anderen Esso-Hotel übernachten. Ihr Fahrzeug wird nachts in einer Groß-Serviceanlage getankt und durchgesehen. Die Wagenpflege ist überall gleich, völlig verschieden in ihrem Charakter aber sind die Bauten und der Service in den Hotels. Jedes Haus wird von einheimischen Architekten entworfen, von örtlichen Möbelhäusern ausgestattet. Es bietet in seinen Restaurants regionale Spezialitäten.

Das Esso-Hotel in Hannover ist die deutsche Etappe auf dem Weg nach Frankfurt und nach dem Rheinland. Sein Standort wurde gründlich sondiert: 1,5 km von der Autobahn Hamburg–Frankfurt, gut 5 km zur Innenstadt, über den Messeschnellweg 3 km zur größten Industriemesse der Welt, eine Viertelstunde Weges zum Flugplatz und kaum zehn Minuten zur Autobahn Hamburg–Köln. Doch es kam der Gesellschaft nicht allein darauf an, ihr Projekt verkehrsgünstig zu plazieren. Der Bau in Hannover liegt am Haupteingang zum Tierpark, er ist ein Auftakt und ein Rastpunkt für 2 Millionen Menschen, die jedes Jahr den Park besuchen. Das Haus soll sehr viel mehr sein als eine Unterkunft für einen Zwangsstop nach einem Tag am Steuer. Es will nicht nur Geschäftsreisenden, sondern gerade Familien auf der Ferienreise und an den immer länger werdenden Wochenenden dienen. Ein kurzer Aufenthalt in fast ländlicher Stille, eine geruhsame Mahlzeit sollen zu einem Erlebnis, zu einem anregenden Teil der Reise werden.

Hotelgäste haben von allen Räumen freien Ausblick auf die Wälder und Wiesen des Tiergartens. Die 68 Einheiten (20 Doppelzimmer, 41 Studios, ganz wenige Einzelzimmer und Suiten) sind durch Loggien über die ganze Fassadenfläche erweitert. Die Einrichtungen und Außenanlagen sind großzügig geplant. Ein beleuchteter Parkplatz, gebührenfrei, hat Platz für 300 Wagen; 160 Personen können an Konferenzen oder privaten Festen teilnehmen; in den Gaststätten finden 350 Menschen Platz und auf den beiden Terrassen zum Tiergarten noch einmal 300. Erstaunlich für ein Hotel dieser Größe (Gesamtkosten 4,9 Millionen Mark): es gibt nicht nur eine große Gaststätte und eine Snackbar, sondern vier spezialisierte Restaurants: das Tiergarten-Restaurant für alle drei Mahlzeiten und den Nachmittagskaffee, das Sophienzimmer, ein Gourmetlokal, vor allem für flambierte Gerichte, den Bristol-Grill – Bristol ist die Patenstadt von Hannover – und schließlich die Jägerstube, ein Imbiß-, Bier- und Weinlokal für traditionelle Gerichte.

Das Hotel ist ein dreigeschossiger Bau auf freigeformten Stützen. Die Fassaden mit den Schattenzonen der tiefen Loggien sind in Proportion und Relief der Decken, Brüstungen und ganz knapp durchschießenden Wandscheiben fein ausgewogen. Die vier Seiten sind aus vorgefertigten Waschbetonelementen zusammengefügt. Das eingeschossige Restaurationsgebäude hat im Kontrast dazu eine Holzfassade und ist nach außen voll verglast. Die Zimmer, wie das ganze Gebäude mechanisch belüftet, zeigen große weiße Putzflächen und wenige farbige Texturen.

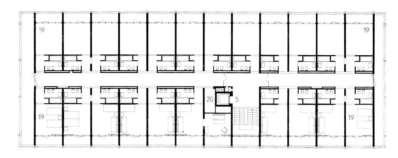

Plan, typical floor / Grundriß Normalgeschoß.

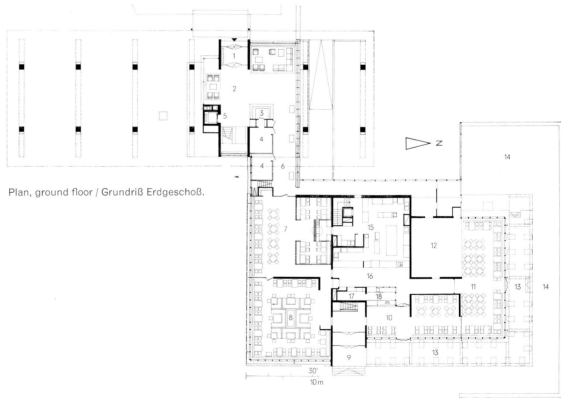

Plan, ground floor / Grundriß Erdgeschoß.

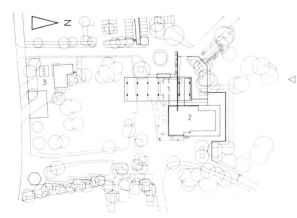

◁ Site plan / Lageplan.
Key/Legende: 1 Hotel, 2 Restaurants, 3 Gas station / Tankstelle.

Key to plans: 1 Hotel entrance, porch, 2 Lobby, 3 Front desk, 4 Office, 5 Elevator, 6 Passage to restaurant wing, 7 Bristol Grill, 8 Sophia Room, 9 Entrance restaurant wing, 10 Hunters' Room, 11 Tiergarten Restaurant, 12 Conference room, 13 Inner terrace, 14 Outer terrace, 15 Kitchen, 16 Service corridor, 17 Coffee kitchen, 18 Beverage counter, 19 Guest-room, 20 Service.

Legende zu den Plänen: 1 Hoteleingang, Windfang, 2 Lobby, 3 Empfang, 4 Büro, 5 Fahrstuhl, 6 Durchgang zum Restaurantflügel, 7 Bristol-Grill, 8 Sophienzimmer, 9 Eingang zum Restaurantflügel, 10 Jägerstube, 11 Tiergarten-Restaurant, 12 Konferenzraum, 13 Innere Terrasse, 14 Äußere Terrasse, 15 Küche, 16 Kellnergang, 17 Kaffeeküche, 18 Getränkeausschank, 19 Gastzimmer, 20 Etagenservice.

2. The end wall, finished in precast concrete and small facing bricks.
3. The restaurant wing is low, built of wood and glass, its front punctuated by verticals.

2. Giebelseite in Vorsatzbeton und feinformatigen Verblendern.
3. Der Restaurantbau flach, in Holz und Glas, senkrecht gegliedert.

4. The lobby: flagged floor, walls finished with large pebbles, white concrete structure.
5. The Tiergarten Restaurant. Polished wooden ceiling, near-transparent curtains, very light metal chairs.
6. The Bristol Grill; this hotel of under 70 rooms has four restaurants.
7. A double room. Smooth white plaster in contrast to the wood, brick and mosaic finishes in the restaurants.

4. Die Empfangshalle. Steinboden und Steinwände, weißer Beton.
5. Das Tiergarten-Restaurant. Spiegelnde Holzdecke, fast durchsichtige Vorhänge, ganz leichte Metallstühle.
6. Der Bristol-Grill. Knapp 70 Zimmer und vier verschiedene Restaurants.
7. Ein Doppelbettzimmer. Glatter, weißer Putz – Kontrast zu den Restaurants mit ihren Hölzern, Ziegel- und Mosaikflächen.

Hilton Hotel, San Francisco, California

Architect: William B. Tabler

This building is a challenge to the innumerable motels on the outskirts of American cities. It is a motor hotel—called a motor pool hotel by some—that offers the American traveler much more than a luxury hotel in the city, plus a large basement garage. He can find everything he wants under one roof—luxury and prestige, three cocktail lounges and three restaurants, and better service for his car than even a large motel could provide. Most important: he can drive his car to his doorstep and does not have to unload all his baggage. The sharpness of the transition from the bare garage with its exposed sprinkler system to the carpeted apartment—they are separated from each other only by a narrow corridor with occasional doors—must trouble him hardly at all.

This new experimental type of a downtown motor hotel was launched on a vast scale. The hotel with its 1200 guest-rooms and ballroom for 3000 is large even for U.S.-sized conventions. The ballroom has a ceiling of up to 6 m high and can be divided into nine rooms of different sizes, all of which have separate access. Instead of a deep foyer, there are corridors on all four sides of the ballroom, with vertical connections to the guest-room floors.

The broad core of the building accommodates 50 cars per floor (350 all told), next to the doors of just over 60 apartments (58 double rooms plus four corner suites). A certain number of apartments can be used by families who need more than one room. The guest-garage floors (4th–10th), therefore, are used entirely by guests who can drive up to their 'motel door' in spite of being in a high-rise building. The garage occupies more space per floor than the guest-rooms.

The garage area measures 44 ×67 m in plan. Seven slabs of this area are suspended, with their dead and live loads, from a supporting structure at the top. The trusses above the garages have a depth of more than three full storeys. Between them there is space for storage-rooms, workshops, machinery and air-conditioning plant and staff rooms. The reason for this structural tour de force is obvious. It frees of all columns the ballroom beneath the garages, and so allows for a rational use of space in the ballroom area. The apartments on the four outer sides of the massive building are, of course, exposed to street noises, but guests are not seriously disturbed. The architects have deliberately kept glass areas small, and the windows of the fully air-conditioned rooms are never opened. The skin of the building, a plane of reinforced concrete with small perforations, is structurally a huge shear panel and gives the building added security against earthquakes.

More than half the guest-rooms are at higher levels than the guest-garage floors. They are strung out round the periphery of the 11th to 13th floors and, on the 14th to 17th floors, on both sides of the corridors around a lofty penthouse patio with a swimming pool placed, like so many other things, between the trusses supporting the garage slabs. As on all other floors, the six guest elevators are concentrated in the southwest corner. This results in fairly long walking distances to the guest-rooms. For the staff, whose elevators are in the northwest corner, the situation is the same. Garage space also exists for guests whose rooms are on the top floors: nearly 400 cars are parked on three basement levels by attendants, and another 1500 parking spaces are provided in multi-level car parks across the street. This raises the capacity to nearly two parking spaces per apartment, giving the hotel ample facilities for peak hours at dinner time and for balls and conventions.

For guests who choose to stay on one of the motel floors there is a separate front desk at the main entry drive on

Ellis Street, saving them the trouble of getting out of their cars. Other hotel guests enter the building from Mason Street and reach the raised main lobby by escalators. A plaza above street level connects the west side of the 20-million dollar hotel with a high-rise office building (total cost 6 million dollars), with its own cocktail lounge on the roof. The idea of a motor pool hotel has thus been expanded to become a large-scale business and convention center.

1. Ellis Street with garage entrances and raised plaza. Behind the glass wall are the hotel lobby and main restaurant. The office tower will be built on the parking lot to the left.

1. Ellis Street mit Einfahrten und erhöhter Plaza. Hinter der Glaswand Hotelhalle und Hauptrestaurant. Auf dem Parkplatz links ist das Bürohochhaus geplant.

Hilton-Hotel, San Francisco, California

Architekt: William B. Tabler

Das Projekt ist eine Herausforderung an die unzähligen Motels in den Randzonen amerikanischer Cities. Hier ist ein Motor-Hotel – man hat es ein Motor-Pool-Hotel genannt –, das dem amerikanischen Gast sehr viel mehr bietet als ein Stadthotel der Luxusklasse mit Großgarage. Er findet alles unter einem Dach, Komfort und Prestige, drei Bars und drei Restaurants, und dazu für seinen Wagen besseren Service als selbst ein großes Motel ihm bieten kann. Was ihm das Wichtigste ist: Er fährt im Wagen bis vor seine Zimmertür und braucht nicht das ganze Gepäck auszuladen. Der optische Gegensatz zwischen der nüchternen Garage mit ihren frei liegenden Sprinklerrohren zum teppichbelegten Apartment – beides nur getrennt durch einen schmalen Gang mit Feuertüren hier und da – kann in Amerika kaum stören.

Das Experiment eines neuen Typs des Motor-Hotels im Stadtinnern wurde gleich in großem Rahmen lanciert. Das Haus ist mit fast 1200 Räumen, mit einem Ballsaal für 3000 Menschen groß genug für Kongresse von amerikanischem Ausmaß. Dieser Ballsaal – Deckenhöhe bis zu

geschoß unter den Garagen von allen Stützen, der Saal kann sich räumlich groß entfalten. Daß die Apartments auf den vier Außenseiten des massigen Blocks aufgereiht sind, setzt sie dem Straßenlärm aus, was jedoch wenig ins Gewicht fällt. Die Architekten haben die Glasflächen bewußt klein gehalten; die Fenster der voll klimatisierten Räume werden nie geöffnet. Die kaum durchbrochene Außenhaut in Betonkonstruktion wirkt statisch als geschlossene Scheibe und erhöht die Standsicherheit des Gebäudes bei Erdbeben.

Mehr als die Hälfte der Gästezimmer liegt oberhalb der Gast-Garagen-Geschosse: im 11. bis 13. Geschoß einseitig außen, im 14. bis 17. Geschoß zweihüftig um einen hochräumigen Penthouse-Patio mit Schwimmbad, das wie so vieles zwischen den Bindern über den Garagengeschossen Platz findet. Wie für alle Geschosse liegen auch hier sechs Gästefahrstühle in der Südwestecke konzentriert. Dadurch ergeben sich teilweise lange Wege zu den Zimmern. Für den Service, dessen Fahrstühle in der Nordwestecke liegen, ist es ähnlich. Auch für die

2. East entrance (Mason Street). The hotel lobby is one storey above street level.
3. The plaza, 4 m above the street, relieved by touches of greenery.

2. Osteingang (Mason Street). Die Hotelhalle liegt ein Geschoß über der Straßenebene.
3. Die Plaza, 4 m über der Straße. Sparsam gesetzte Grünakzente.

sechs Metern – ist in neun größere und kleinere Säle teilbar, die alle getrennt zu erreichen sind. Anstelle eines tiefen Foyers sind vier Korridore rings um den Ballsaal gelegt, mit vertikalen Verbindungen zu den Gastgeschossen.

Der breite Kern des Baues nimmt 350 Wagen, 50 je Geschoß, auf, vor den Türen von etwa 60 Apartments (58 Räume, dazu vier Suiten in den Gebäudeecken). Ein Teil der Wagen ist mit Familien besetzt, die mehr als ein Zimmer brauchen. Es ergibt sich eine Auslastung der Gast-Garagen-Geschosse (4. bis 10.) ausschließlich mit Gästen, die im Wagen vor ihre Moteltür im Hochhaus fahren wollen. Die Wagenhalle nimmt in jedem Geschoß mehr Platz ein als die Gäste mit ihren Räumen.

Der Garagenteil mißt 44 × 67 Meter im Plan. Sieben dieser Flächen sind mit ihren Eigen- und Verkehrslasten an einer hochgelegten Konstruktion aufgehängt. Die tragenden Binder über den Garagen nehmen die Höhe von drei vollen Geschossen ein. Sie lassen zwischen sich Raum für Lager, Werkstätten, technische Einrichtungen, Klimaanlagen und Personalräume. Der Sinn dieses konstruktiven Kraftaktes zeigt sich klar: Er befreit das Ballsaal-

Gäste der hochgelegten Geschosse sind Garagen da. Fast 400 Wagen werden in drei Kellergeschossen von Parkwärtern geparkt, und 1500 weitere Abstellplätze liegen in mehrgeschossigen Garagen an der anderen Straßenseite. Damit hat das Hotel fast zwei Abstellplätze je Gastzimmer und ist für jeden Verkehrsanfall zur Dinnerstunde, bei Bällen und Kongressen gerüstet.

Für die Gäste, die in den »Motelgeschossen« wohnen wollen, ist ein gesonderter Empfang in der Haupteinfahrt an der Ellis Street eingerichtet, was das Aussteigen erspart. Die anderen Hotelgäste betreten das Haus von der Mason Street und erreichen die höher gelegene Haupthalle über eine Rolltreppe. Eine Plaza über Straßenniveau verbindet auf der Westseite das Zwanzig-Millionen-Dollar-Hotel mit einem Bürogebäude (Baukosten sechs Millionen Dollar), das seine eigene Bar auf dem Dach hat. Damit wird das Gesamtkonzept eines Motor-Pool-Hotels erweitert zum großen Geschäfts- und Kongreßhotel amerikanischen Stils.

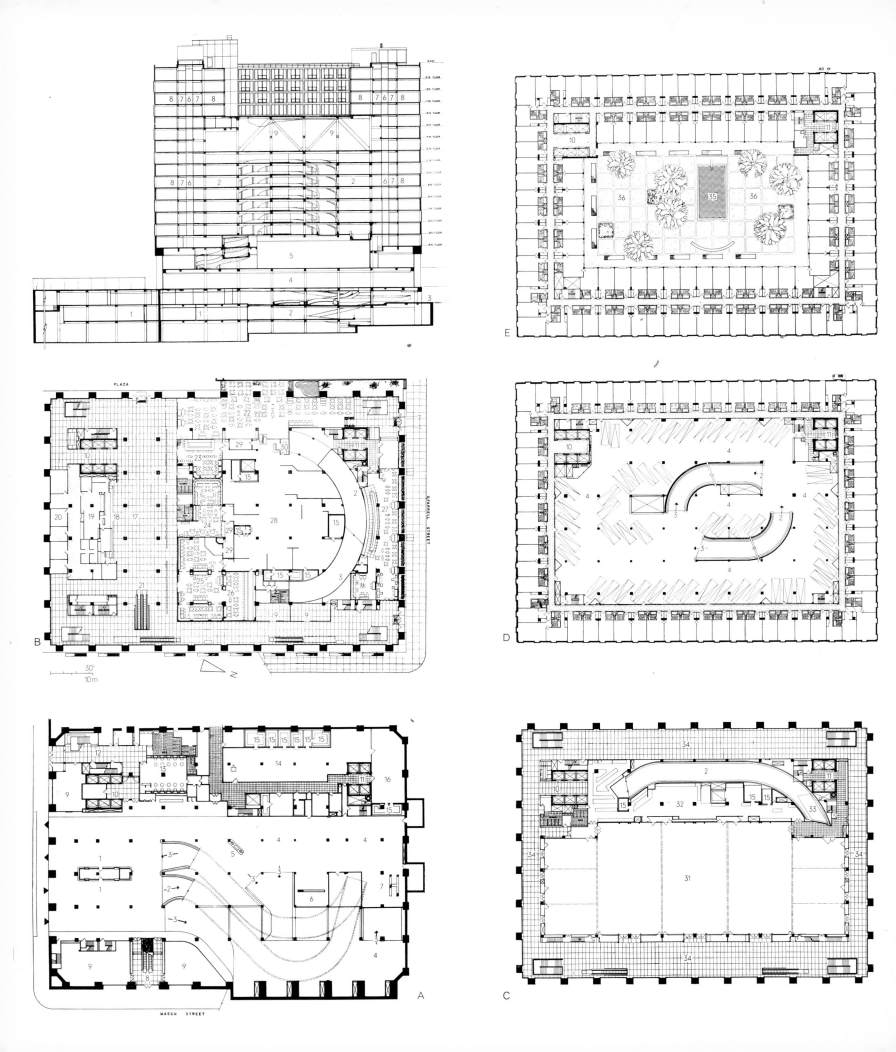

A Plan, motor entrance level / Grundriß Einfahrtgeschoß.
B Plan, lobby level / Grundriß Empfangs- und Restaurantgeschoß.
C Plan, ballroom level / Grundriß Ballsaal-Geschoß.
D Plan, 7th, 9th, 11th floors / Grundriß 7., 9., 11. Geschoß.
E Plan, 16th floor / Grundriß 16. Geschoß.

East-west section. Key: 1 Service, 2 Parking, 3 Motor entrance, 4 Lobby, 5 Ballroom, 6 Corridor, 7 Bathroom, 8 Guest-room, 9 Mechanical equipment.

Schnitt in Ost-West-Richtung. Legende: 1 Serviceräume und technische Installation, 2 Parkfläche, 3 Wageneinfahrt, 4 Lobby, 5 Ballsaal, 6 Korridor, 7 Bad, 8 Gastzimmer, 9 Installationsgeschosse.

Key to plans: 1 Motor entrance and registration, 2 Ramp up, 3 Ramp down, 4 Parking, 5 Gas pumps, 6 Wash area, 7 Car lift, 8 Lobby, Mason Street entrance, 9 Rentable area, 10 Passenger elevators, 11 Service elevators, 12 Lower lobby Ellis Street, 13 Barbershop, 14 Food and beverage storage, 15 Refrigeration rooms, 16 Wine storage, 17 Lobby, 18 Front desk, 19 Front office, 20 Administration rooms, 21 Escalators from motor entrance level, 22 Main dining room, 23 Theater bar, 24 Sea food room, 25 Steam room, 26 Men's bar, 27 Cocktail lounge, 28 Main kitchen, 29 Rotisserie, 30 Room service, 31 Ballrooms with sliding partition walls, 32 Ballroom kitchen, 33 Auto lift, 34 Corridor, 35 Swimming pool, 36 Roof garden.

Legende zu den Plänen: 1 Wageneinfahrt und Kontrolle, 2 Auffahrtrampe, 3 Abfahrtrampe, 4 Parkfläche, 5 Zapfsäulen, 6 Wagenwäsche, 7 Wagenpflege, 8 Eingangshalle Mason Street, 9 Vermietbare Fläche, 10 Gästefahrstühle, 11 Personalfahrstühle, 12 Untere Lobby Ellis Street, 13 Herrenfriseur, 14 Lebensmittel- und Getränkelager, 15 Kühlräume, 16 Weinlager, 17 Lobby, 18 Empfang, 19 Büroräume am Empfang, 20 Räume der Verwaltung, 21 Rolltreppe vom Einfahrtsgeschoß, 22 Hauptrestaurant, 23 Theaterbar, 24 Fischrestaurant, 25 Grillrestaurant, 26 Men's Bar, 27 Cocktail-Lounge, 28 Hauptküche, 29 Rotisserie, 30 Zimmer-Service, 31 Ballsäle mit Schiebewänden, 32 Ballsaalküche, 33 Autolift, 34 Korridor, 35 Schwimmbecken, 36 Dachgarten.

4. The penthouse patio on the 16th floor, surrounded by four-storey guest-room wings.
5. The main ballroom. The sliding partitions are out of sight in wall recesses.
6. Guest-room on one of the guest-garage levels. The cars are just across the hallway.

4. Der Penthouse-Patio im 16. Geschoß, umgeben von vierstöckigen Gästeflügeln.
5. Der große Ballsaal. Die teilenden Schiebewände bleiben unsichtbar in Nischen.
6. Gastzimmer im Hochgaragengeschoß. Über den Korridor Zugang zum Wagen.

Motel Warm Mineral Springs Inn, Venice, Florida

Architect: Victor A. Lundy

It is in the late hours of the day that life comes to a motel. It has to attract guests after sundown, and few motels are more strikingly presented to potential guests traveling on the highway than this design of Lundy's, on the Tamiami trail between Sarasota and Miami. Seventy-five white concrete parasols, at two heights, are arranged in a long L-shape (a third wing is to be added later to round out a U-shape) and three more parasols on very tall stems form a display against the night sky.

The motel is no less striking in daytime. Lundy strove for flowing plastic forms, which would evoke the slender growing shapes of palm-trees, and allowed himself to be inspired by the legend that the "Fountains of Youth" of Ponce de León were found in this region on the west coast of Florida. Though this motivation may sound romantic, the architect has also managed to produce a strictly economical solution. His project of 19 fairly large motel units with kitchenettes was built for 160 000 dollars, including the reception lobby and the owner's living quarters.

The construction job was done mainly by unskilled workers. First, the 22,9 cm square prestressed stems were anchored in the foundations and stabilized by the slab of poured concrete. The shells, hyperbolic paraboloids 5 cm thick, were cast on the site in plywood forms. They were then hoisted up and placed with their inner steel sleeves on the protruding drainpipes in the stems, and connected and weather-sealed by welding. A coat of plastic paint replaces the roof skin. All partitions are nonbearing and were put up after the erection of the roof parasols.

The shells measure 4,40 m square—the modular width of a motel unit plus overlaps. Lundy arranged them in a checkerboard pattern, at two heights differing by 61 cm, thus enlivening the roofline and giving each apartment unit a ceiling composed of six half-shells. The lower ceiling zones are over the entrance, the sleeping area, and the dining corner, while the higher half-shells, washed by bright daylight, crown the kitchen recess, bathroom and living area. Only the dividing partitions to the neighboring units—constructed of mahogany plywood and centered on the concrete supports—touch the roof shells.

The glass walls facing the lawn and the masonry screens on the entrance side (cars are kept out of sight along the outer perimeter) are limited to door height, which is equal to the stem height of the lower shells. The space above is closed with clear plastic sheets. The shells seem to float, and guests can look up at night to the sky and see the stars.

The air-conditioning unit in every room is suspended and has fluorescent light fixtures on top and below; the condensed water drips into a plant-box cut out of the floor. Details like these make Lundy's motel equally interesting for overnight guests and for families who stay on for an extended vacation at the mineral springs.

The outer rows of concrete parasols have their columns outside, clear of the glass or screen walls. Their wide overhangs give shelter from the rain and sun, and cast lively shadow patterns on the ground. This "forest of white palm-trees" (Lundy) with its rich roof shapes of alternating height, creates both a human scale and an impression of airy lightness.

1. The motel by night. Concrete parasols as structure and sculpture.
2. Checkerboard roof pattern shows clearly from the air.
3. Screen walls reach to door height on the entrance side. Concrete blocks, up-ended, stress the verticality of the structure.
4. The reception area. Staggered shells seem to float in floodlighting.
5. Wide roof overhangs on the garden side.
6. Covered space between the apartment wings. Not a car is visible.

1. Das Motel bei Nacht. Betonschirme als Struktur und Skulptur.
2. Die schachbrettartige Dachstruktur tritt in der Luftaufnahme deutlich hervor.
3. Auf der Anfahrtseite türhohe Wände. Betonsteine, hochkant gesetzt, betonen das vertikale Aufstreben der Konstruktion.
4. Der Empfang. Schwebend versetzte Schalen im Flutlicht.
5. Weite Überstände auf der Gartenseite.
6. Überdeckter Platz zwischen den Apartmentflügeln, Wagen sind nirgends im Blick.

Motel Warm Mineral Springs Inn, Venice, Florida

Architekt: Victor A. Lundy

Es sind die späten Stunden des Tages, die Leben bringen in ein Motel. Abends vor allem muß es um Gäste werben, und selten hat ein Motel sich wirksamer dem Gast von der Fernstraße präsentiert als Lundys Hotel am Tamiami Trail zwischen Sarasota und Miami. 75 weiße Betonschirme, in zwei Höhen gestaffelt, reihen sich zu einer langen L-Form (ein dritter Flügel soll später das U schließen) und drei hochgestelzte Schalen formen ein Wahrzeichen am nächtlichen Himmel.
Das Motel in seiner Taggestalt ist nicht weniger frappierend. Lundy suchte in seinen fließend aufgehenden Formen dem schlanken Bau der Palmen nachzuspüren, ließ sich inspirieren von der Sage, die »Quellen der Jugend« des Ponce de León hätten in diesem Winkel an der Westküste Floridas gelegen. So romantisch motiviert das klingt, ging der Architekt doch nüchtern wirtschaftlich vor. Sein Projekt für 19 größere Moteleinheiten mit Kleinküchen kostete einschließlich Empfang und Wohnung des Besitzers nur $ 160 000,–.

Der Bau wurde überwiegend mit ungelernten Arbeitern ausgeführt. Zuerst verankerte man die vorgespannten Stiele 22,9 cm stark) in den Fundamenten und steifte sie durch die Bodenplatte in gegossenem Beton aus. Die Schalen, hyperbolische Paraboloide von 5 cm Stärke, entstanden am Bau in Formen aus Sperrholz. Sie wurden mit ihren Stahlmanschetten im Zentrum auf herausstehende Entwässerungsrohre in den Stützen gesetzt und durch Schweißen verbunden und abgedichtet. Ein Kunststoffanstrich ersetzte die Dachhaut. Trennwände, sämtlich nichttragend, kamen zum Schluß.
Die Schalen messen 4,40 m im Quadrat: die modulare Breite einer Moteleinheit mit den Überständen dazu. Lundy setzte sie im Schachbrettmuster 61 cm höher oder tiefer, brachte damit Leben in seine Dachlinie und gab jedem Apartment eine bewegte Deckenzone aus sechs Halbschalen. Niedere Deckenpartien ergeben sich über dem Eingang, dem Schlafteil und der Eßecke; die höheren Halbschalen, von intensivem Tageslicht heraus-

gehoben, markieren Kochecke, Bad und Wohnbereich. Nur die Wände zu den Nachbarn – in Mahagoni-Sperrholz, auf der Achse der Stützen – berühren die Dachschalen. Die Glaswände zum Rasenplatz und die gemauerten Blenden zur Anfahrt (die Wagen bleiben auf den Außenseiten, unsichtbar) gehen nur bis zur Türhöhe, das heißt bis zum Ansatz der unteren Schalen. Der Raum darüber ist mit klaren Plastikscheiben geschlossen; die Schalen scheinen zu schweben, der Gast sieht nachts ein Stück Sternenhimmel. Die äußeren Reihen der Betonschirme stehen mit ihren Stützen vor den Längsfronten. Ihre weiten Überstände schützen vor Regen und Sonne und bringen Schattenmuster auf den Boden.
Das Klimagerät in jedem Raum ist hochgehängt und gibt aus Leuchtröhren Licht nach oben und nach unten. Kondenswasser tropft in ein Pflanzenbecken am Boden. Lundy macht mit diesen Details sein Motel gleich attraktiv für Durchreisende und für Familien, die längere Zeit zur Kur bei den warmen Quellen bleiben.

7. An apartment. Clear plastic sheets above door height.
8. Living-sleeping area. There is a fascinating play of light and dark on the roof shells.

7. Ein Apartment. Über Türhöhe klare Plastikscheiben.
8. Wohn- und Schlafteil, in den Deckenschalen ein fesselndes Spiel von Hell und Dunkel.

1. The guest can see the flora of the region outside his ▷ room. There are light screens between the divided columns.
2. A bedroom pavilion. Thin-edged sunbreakers supported by slim planks.

1. Für den Gast die Pflanzenwelt der Region. Leichte ▷ Blenden zwischen geteilten Stützen.
2. Ein Wohnpavillon. Sonnenblenden mit schmalen Stirnflächen, Stützen aus brettdünnen Laschen.

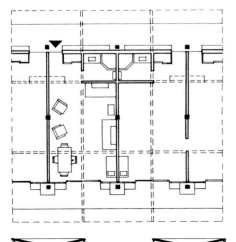

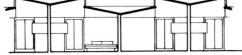

Plan and section of an apartment unit / Grundriß und Schnitt einer Zimmereinheit.

Hilton Inn, Seattle, Washington

Architects: Skidmore, Owings & Merrill

This airport motel, near the Seattle-Tacoma International Airport, invites air travelers to spend a few hours or days relaxing in beautiful surroundings. The architects did not wish to build "just another big motel" supplying mass accommodation, but to provide quiet rooms in carefully landscaped grounds. Though built for guests traveling by air, the Hilton Inn has large parking areas holding 233 cars for a total of 150 rooms. The parking areas are distributed on all four sides, round the periphery of the site. 150 parking stalls altogether (equaling the number of rooms) are provided by the three areas to the north, east and south. The other large parking area near the main entrance is kept free to serve the restaurant, coffee bar and conference rooms.

The guest-rooms are in four pavilions, all two storeys high, but varied in plan, with rooms on one side or on both sides of the hallway and with interior stairways or, in the south pavilion, exposed exterior staircases. The buildings are connected with each other and with the lounge by covered walks. They enclose the large garden court and the swimming pool, which is in front of the glass wall of the upper restaurant level. The main restaurant with

the bar is down a few steps. In the reception building, single-storeyed and almost square in plan, the kitchen and service rooms were kept fairly small to fit the character of a motor inn.

The exteriors display trim surfaces of stone, glass and wood. The west and south exposures of the pavilions are shaded by neat horizontal blinds; there are no massive balcony slabs. The wooden structural members of the pavilions—the beams and especially the divided columns—are slim. In contrast, the timber structural frame of the restaurant and lounge pavilion appears more solid. It is neatly separated from the ceiling plane and projects on the outside of the west and east façades, ending in thin divided columns.

In the interiors and the landscaping, the architects have tried to bring the guests into contact with the rocks, woods and plants of the American northwest; and with works of art showing first hints of a regional style.

Hilton Inn, Seattle, Washington

Architekten: Skidmore, Owings & Merrill

Dieses Flughafen-Motel, nicht weit vom internationalen Seattle-Tacoma Airport gelegen, ist eine offene Einladung an Flugreisende, in landschaftlich schöner Umgebung Stunden oder Tage der Entspannung zu verbringen.

Die Architekten wollten deshalb jeden Anklang an »Groß-Motel« und nüchterne »Unterbringung« vermeiden und allen Gästen ruhige Räume inmitten gärtnerisch gepflegter Anlagen bieten. Obschon für Fluggäste bestimmt, hat das Hilton Inn reichlich Parkplätze, bei 150 Zimmern können 233 Wagen abgestellt werden. Die Parkflächen sind auf allen vier Seiten des Geländes über die Außenzone verteilt. Auf der Nord- und Ostseite und nach Süden wird bereits die Zahl von 150 Stellplätzen (gleich der Zimmerzahl) erreicht. Der große Parkplatz vor dem Empfangsbau bleibt für Besucher von Restaurant und Cafébar und für Konferenzteilnehmer frei.

Die Gastzimmer sind in vier Wohnpavillons angeordnet, durchgehend zwei Geschosse hoch, aber variiert in einhüftiger oder zweihüftiger Anlage, mit Innentreppen oder, nach Süden, mit herausgestellten Treppenhäusern. Die Gebäude sind durch gedeckte Gänge untereinander und mit der Empfangshalle verbunden. Sie umschließen einen weiten Gartenhof mit dem Schwimmbad, das sich vor die Glasfront des oberen Restaurants legt. Das Hauptrestaurant mit der Bar liegt einige Stufen tiefer. In dem eingeschossigen, fast quadratischen Empfangsbau konnten die Küchen- und Serviceflächen entsprechend dem Charakter eines Motor-Inns ziemlich knapp gehalten werden.

Die Fassaden sind flächig in Stein, Glas und Holz ausgeführt, auf den West- und Südseiten der Pavillons werden sie durch fein profilierte waagerechte Blenden beschattet (massive Balkonplatten fehlen). An den Wohnflügeln sind auch die Holzbalken und mehr noch die zweigeteilten Stützen betont feingliedrig dimensioniert. Im Restaurant und Empfangsgebäude ist die Holzkonstruktion kräftiger. Sie entfaltet sich abgesetzt von der Deckenebene und schießt auf der West- und Ostseite nach außen durch, gefaßt von den wiederum zweigeteilten Stützen.

In der Ausstattung der Räume, wie in der Gartengestaltung versuchten die Architekten den Gästen das Wesen des amerikanischen Nordwestens – seine Steine, Hölzer und Pflanzen, seine Ansätze heimischer Kunst – nahezubringen.

Plan ground floor. Key: 1 Parking area, 2 Lobby, 3 Café bar, 4 Conference room, 5 Kitchen, 6 Restaurant, 7 Coats, 8 Gift shop, 9 Office and reception, 10 Guest-rooms, 11 Swimming pool.

Grundriß Erdgeschoß. Legende: 1 Parkplätze, 2 Lobby, 3 Cafébar, 4 Konferenzraum, 5 Küche, 6 Restaurant, 7 Garderobe, 8 Laden für Geschenkartikel, 9 Büros und Empfang, 10 Gästezimmer, 11 Schwimmbecken.

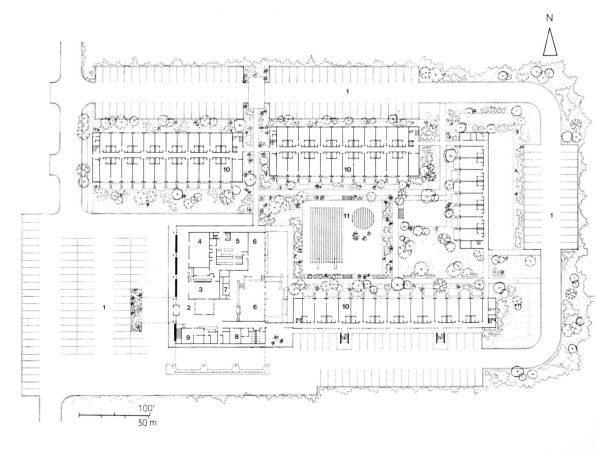

N

100'
30 m

3. Two-storey covered walks connect the buildings.
4. Lobby outside the café and conference room. Local stone and heavy timber in the tradition of the northwest.
5. The bar between the two restaurant levels; the east terrace.
6. View from the upper restaurant level of the garden court with swimming pool.

3. Zweigeschossige gedeckte Gänge verbinden die Gebäude.
4. Blick von der Lobby in die Halle vor Café und Konferenzraum. Örtlicher Stein und kräftige Hölzer in der Tradition des Nordwestens.
5. Bar zwischen den beiden Ebenen des Restaurants mit Blick auf die Ostterrasse.
6. Vom höher gelegenen Restaurantteil geht der Blick über den Gartenhof mit dem Schwimmbecken.

BP-Motel, Haderslev, Denmark

Architect: Bent Moudt

This luxury motel for motorists and anglers is beside Euroway E 3, on the shore of Haderslev Dam. An existing gas station, at some distance from the motel building, was expanded to form a complete service center for passing cars. In addition to the 45 parking stalls of the motel, there are another 70 on a public lot to the south. The explicitly linear character of the main building appears again in the service station and utility annex. There is nothing on the exteriors to draw attention to the BP trade name.

The motel, which might very well have been called a motor hotel, has 30 rooms, all with a view over the river and the historic town of Haderslev. The living-bedroom units are all the same size and virtually square (3,80 m by 3,86 m). They have a closed lobby with a large recess for luggage and rather sparse cupboard space (travelers on E 3 do not unpack much for one night) and a terrace. Furniture consists of two beds and a daybed that can sleep a child or two. Access to the rooms is on the south side through open corridors that extend on both floors as continuous terraces, and as balconies on all four sides of the restaurant and reception block. The owners wished to offer Danish architecture and Danish furniture, neat detailing, lively colors and lighting effects.

The restaurant building is a pure cube of glass; its box-like shape is played down by long narrow fascias. The neat precision of all details is typified by the fine-drawn vertical metal members on the face of the balcony terraces. The railings are of thin square steel tubes and toughened glass panels, which are entirely transparent. They also extend along the two fronts of the long bedroom wing and are repeated, with slight variations, in the two-storey lobby.

The restaurants, among them Denmark's largest grill unit, are upstairs on three sides of the service core. There are further reception and party rooms for 15 to 100 persons. The kitchen is down on the ground level; it sends food to an upstairs service buffet via 6 kitchen elevators. The two restaurants and the large snack bar are hardly separated at all, and the fireplace corner is a wide open, quiet bay of the grill room. It is not made fully apparent that the restaurant is one and a half storeys high: the upper windows, as the roof does not overhang, admit ample daylight to the tops of the public rooms; the light is diffused downwards through a gridded wooden false ceiling, stained a pale color, at the height of the projecting balcony.

1. The restaurant and motel wing from the southeast. Cars on the sunken parking lot are mostly out of sight.

1. Restaurant und Motelflügel von Südosten. Die Wagen sind auf den tiefer liegenden Parkplätzen fast dem Blick entzogen.

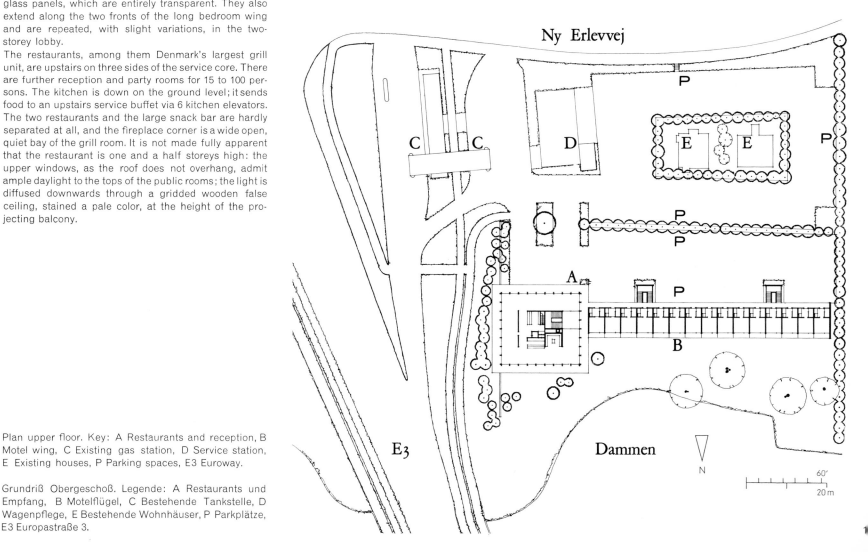

Plan upper floor. Key: A Restaurants and reception, B Motel wing, C Existing gas station, D Service station, E Existing houses, P Parking spaces, E3 Euroway.

Grundriß Obergeschoß. Legende: A Restaurants und Empfang, B Motelflügel, C Bestehende Tankstelle, D Wagenpflege, E Bestehende Wohnhäuser, P Parkplätze, E3 Europastraße 3.

BP-Motel, Haderslev, Dänemark

Architekt: Bent Moudt

An der Europastraße E 3 entstand am Ufer des Haderslev Dam ein Luxusmotel für Durchreisende und Sportangler. Eine bestehende Tankstelle wurde durch eine Großanlage für Wagenpflege, weit abgesetzt vom Motel, ergänzt. Neben den 45 Parkplätzen des Hauses stehen noch 70 weitere Abstellplätze auf einem öffentlichen, nach Süden gelegenen Platz zur Verfügung. Die klare, lineare Struktur des Hauptkubus wurde auch auf das Nebengebäude und die Tankstelle übertragen. Nichts an den Gebäuden wirbt laut um Aufmerksamkeit für den Markennamen.

Das Motel, das fast zu Unrecht auf die Bezeichnung Motor-Hotel verzichtet, hat 30 Zimmer mit Sicht auf den breiten Wasserlauf und auf die historische Stadt Haderslev. Die Wohn-Schlaf-Räume sind alle gleich groß, fast quadratisch 3,80 × 3,86 m, haben einen abgeschlossenen Vorraum mit großer Gepäcknische und wenig Schrankraum (Gäste auf der Europastraße packen für eine Nacht nicht viel aus) und eine Terrasse. Sie sind mit zwei Betten und einer Tagescouch ausgestattet, die für Kinder zum zusätzlichen Bett wird. Die Räume werden auf der Südseite über offene Gänge erreicht, die sich in beiden Geschossen als umlaufende Terrasse oder als

vierseitig vorgelegter Balkon um den Block der Restaurant- und Empfangsräume fortsetzen. Die Auftraggeber wünschten dänische Architektur und dänische Möbelkunst zu zeigen, sauberes leichtes Detail, lebendige Farben und Beleuchtungen.

Der Restaurantbau ist ein reiner Glaswürfel, dem durch knappe horizontale Gesimse, das obere zurückspringend, die Kastenstruktur genommen ist. In der Senkrechten betonen strichartig feine Metallstäbe am Rand der Balkons die knappe Präzision aller Details. Die Brüstungen aus dünnem Vierkantstahl mit Glasfeldern sind völlig durchsichtig gehalten; sie laufen auch über die beiden Fronten des langen Zimmerflügels und kehren in der zweigeschossigen Halle leicht variiert wieder.

Die Restaurants, darunter Dänemarks größter Grill, liegen oben auf drei Seiten des Servicekerns. Weitere Gesellschafts- und Partyräume können 15 bis 100 Personen aufnehmen. Die Küche ist nicht auf der gleichen Ebene untergebracht, sondern im Erdgeschoß; sie liefert die Gerichte über 6 Speiseaufzüge an ein Kellnerbuffet. Die beiden Restaurants und die große Snackbar sind gegeneinander kaum unterteilt, auch die Kaminecke ist nur

eine offene ruhige Bucht am Grillraum. Die Höhe der 1½ geschossigen Restaurants tritt nicht voll in Erscheinung. Das obere Fensterband, ohne Dachüberstand, bringt viel Licht in die Deckenzone. Eine kassettierte Decke in hellem Holz auf der Höhe des vorspringenden Balkondaches filtert dieses Licht und wirkt selbst schwebend leicht.

2, 3. The long silhouette seen from the river. In summer a busy café terrace, in winter a single plane of ice and snow-covered meadows.

2, 3. Die lange Silhouette vom Fluß her. Im Sommer belebte Caféterrasse, im Winter eine Fläche aus Eis und verschneiten Uferwiesen.

4. The corridors on the south side, continued in the balcony terrace of the restaurant building. Bathrooms and lobbies are lit and ventilated through louvered strips.
5. The full height of the staircase. The false ceiling is a suspended wooden grid, filtering the light from the upper windows.

4. Laubengang auf der Südseite, fortgesetzt in den Balkons des Restaurantbaus. Nebenräume der Zimmer durch Jalousiestreifen belichtet und belüftet.
5. Die Treppenhalle in voller Höhe gesehen. Doppelschichtige Decke in gestäbtem Holz und untergehängten Kassetten. Weiches Licht aus dem obersten Fensterband.

6. The grill room. Light-colored wood and wicker-work. A fireplace corner with dark paneling and a copper hood.
7. The stairs to the restaurants. Light steps over shallow dark water.
8. Open corridors to rooms, but enclosed stairways, glazed in narrow strips.
9. An apartment with a view of Haderslev. Whitewashed walls, restrained Danish furniture.

6. Der Grillroom. Helles Holz und Korbgeflecht. Dunkel getäfelter Kaminwinkel mit kupferner Rauchabzughaube.
7. Die Treppe zu den Restaurants. Helle Stufen über flachem, dunklem Wasserbecken.
8. Offene Verbindungsgänge zu den Zimmern, doch regengeschützte Treppenläufe, in schmalen Vertikalstreifen verglast.
9. Eine Zimmereinheit mit Blick auf Haderslev. Weißgetünchte Wände, dänisch-sachliche Möbel.

San Pedro Community Hotel, San Pedro, California

Architects: Richard J. Neutra and Robert E. Alexander

1. The horizontal rows of the guest-room wings.
2. The main building from the south: the cocktail lounge is at the center.

1. Die stark horizontalen Zeilen der Wohnflügel.
2. Das Hauptgebäude von Süden. In Bildmitte die Cocktailbar.

The harbor city of San Pedro, half an hour's drive from Los Angeles, needed a modern hotel. A group of citizens duly formed and financed an association to build this hotel, with large rooms for social events, a swimming club and a golf course. It soon became a focal point of community life. Travelers in Southern California are motorized, driving their own or rented cars, so a motor hotel was a natural choice. It had to attract traveling businessmen and motoring tourists and to offer, at the same time, the comfort of a resort motel for extended holidays. The Community Hotel on its hilly 20 hectare site has a panoramic view over the largest harbor on the Pacific and a country club atmosphere. It attracts many visitors from Los Angeles for Sunday brunch and is a meeting point for golfers from the nearby course, which surrounds the buildings with acres of well-trimmed greenery and so obviates the need for costly landscaping. Above the entrance, Neutra has formed a kind of abstract sculpture from a pointed projecting canopy, a column, metal channel and folded steel plate, and a lighting fixture; otherwise he keeps firmly to his rectangular idiom. The lobby and lounge area and the cocktail lounge with its low bar have open transitions from room to room to compensate for a certain lack of width. The dining and banquet room is screened off by an oyster bar and an

aquarium forming the rear wall of the cocktail lounge. The dining room can be divided by four folding partitions. No interior hallway is needed for guests attending receptions, conferences or exhibitions; the large overhanging roof of the viewing terrace to the southeast offers protection enough. The full depth of the dining room (about 13,50 m without columns) is spanned by welded steel beams, which carry and conceal fluorescent tubes on their flanges.
The guest-room wings are placed in several tiers on the gentle slope. Every guest has his car at his doorstep, a wall-to-wall window to enjoy the sea view visible over the low buildings downhill, and his own sun terrace. The small apartments (3,05 m by 6,40 m or 20 m², two thirds of which are in the main area) are used as living rooms in daytime. There are a few larger apartments of 25 m². chambermaids with service carts move along ramps. No guest is bothered by over-service proffered by a host of tip-hungry staff, but service is available when he wants it. The single-storey guest-room wings are fairly far apart, as required for fire safety. "The free grouping, the careful landscaping, the informal air of the entire establishment, as well as the utilization of all the features of natural beauty, which the site has to offer" (Neutra) make this hotel a hill resting-place of unusual charm.

Key to plan, which was modified in some details when actually executed: 1 Main entrance, 2 Lobby, 3 Manager, accounting, 4 W.C., 5 Check room, 6 Ramp, 7 Lounge, 8 Bar, 9 Guest-rooms, 10 Linen storage, 11 Dining and banquet rooms, 12 Movable platform, 13 Booths, 14 Sea Food bar, 15 Service corridor, 16 Chair and table storage, 17 Kitchen, 18 Dishwashing, 19 Pantry, 20 Refrigeration rooms, 21 Food storage, 22 Staff lockers and dining facilities, 23 Loading platform, 24 Workshop.

Legende zum Grundriß, der in einigen Details von der Ausführung abweicht: 1 Haupteingang, 2 Lobby, 3 Verwaltung und Buchhaltung, 4 WC, 5 Prüfraum, 6 Rampe, 7 Lounge, 8 Bar, 9 Gästezimmer, 10 Wäsche, 11 Speise- und Bankettsäle, 12 Bewegliche Plattform, 13 Nischen, 14 »Sea food«-Bar, 15 Kellnergang, 16 Lagerraum für Tische und Stühle, 17 Küche, 18 Spülküche, 19 Anrichte, 20 Kühlräume, 21 Lagerraum für Lebensmittel, 22 Kleiderablage und Eßraum für Angestellte, 23 Anfahrt für Lieferanten, 24 Werkstatt.

San Pedro Community Hotel, San Pedro, California

Architekten: Richard J. Neutra und Robert E. Alexander

In der Hafenstadt San Pedro, eine halbe Autostunde von Los Angeles entfernt, fehlte seit langem ein modernes Hotel. Eine größere Gruppe von Einwohnern tat sich zu einer Gesellschaft zusammen, stellte die Finanzierung sicher und baute ein Hotel, das mit seinen Gesellschaftsräumen, seinem Schwimmclub und Golfplatz ein echter Sammelpunkt des kommunalen Lebens wurde. Wer in Südkalifornien reist, ist motorisiert, im eigenen oder gemieteten Wagen. Das Konzept eines Motor-Hotels bot sich an. Es mußte attraktiv sein für Geschäftsreisende und umherfahrende Touristen und zugleich mußte es die Züge eines Resort-Motels für längeren Aufenthalt in den Ferien haben. Das Community Hotel bekam auf seinem Hügelgelände von 20 Hektar einen Panoramablick auf den größten Seehafen am Pazifik und den Charakter eines Country-Clubs. Es zieht viele Besucher aus Los Angeles zum sonntäglichen »Brunch« an und ist ein Treffpunkt der Golfspieler vom nahen Gelände, das mit seinen wohlgetrimmten Flächen kostspielige Grünanlagen des Hotels überflüssig macht.

Über dem Eingang formte Neutra aus dem spitz vorschießenden Dach, aus Metallstäben, Stütze, Lasche und Leuchte eine Art abstrakter Plastik; sonst bleibt er streng beim rechtwinkligen Duktus. Halle und Lounge, die Bar mit ihrem niedrigen Tresen, lassen durch fließende Übergänge von Raum zu Raum die fehlende Breite nicht spürbar werden. Der Speise- und Bankettsaal ist durch eine Austernbar und ein Aquarium hinter der Cocktail-Lounge abgeschirmt. Er läßt sich vierfach durch Faltwände unterteilen. Ein innerer Korridor für Gäste der einzelnen Empfänge, Konferenzen oder Ausstellungen fällt weg; der breite Dachüberstand der Aussichtsterrasse nach Südosten bietet Schutz genug. Konstruktiv ist die stützenfreie Spannweite des Saals (rund 13,50 m) mit geschweißten Stahlträgern bewältigt. Sie werden durch Leuchtstoffröhren auf den Flanschen zu Lichtvouten.

Die Wohnflügel stufen sich in mehreren Rängen den flachen Hang hinunter. Jeder Gast hat den Wagen vor seinem Eingang, ein raumbreites Fenster mit dem Blick aufs Meer, hinweg über die Dächer der Nachbargebäude weiter unten, und seine eigene Sonnenterrasse. Die kleinen Apartments (3,05 auf 6,40 m oder knapp 20 qm, davon zwei Drittel der Fläche als Wohn-Schlaf-Teil) sind tagsüber Wohnräume. Daneben gibt es eine Minderzahl größerer Apartments von 25 qm. Die Zimmermädchen bewegen sich mit ihren Servicewagen auf Rampen. Kein Gast wird durch »Over-Service« von einer Fülle allzu dienstbereiter Geister geplagt, aber er kann Bedienung haben, wann er will.

Die eingeschossigen Wohnflügel sind, schon wegen der Feuersicherheit, in ziemlich großem Abstand gesetzt. »Die freie Gruppierung, die sorgfältige Gartengestaltung, der zwanglose Eindruck der ganzen Anlage, wie der Einsatz aller Mittel natürlicher Schönheit, die das Gelände bieten kann« (Neutra), machen aus diesem Hotel eine Hügel-Karawanserei besonderer Art.

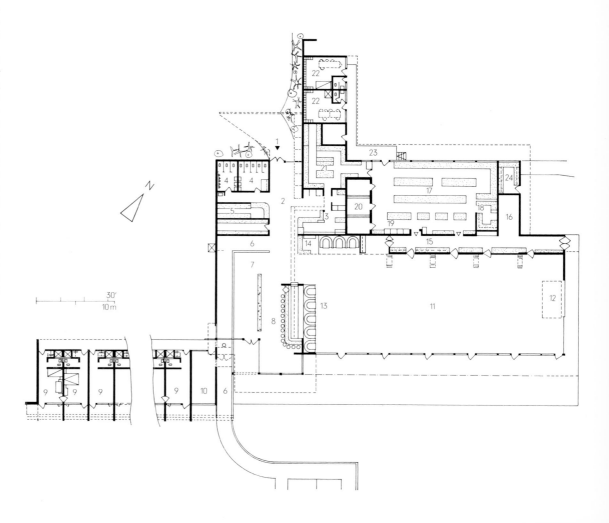

Floor plan, main building / Grundriß Hauptgebäude.
Key see page 126 / Legende siehe Seite 126.

3. The entrance canopy, a sculptural composition uninhibited by the conventions of rectangularity.
4. Viewing terrace outside the restaurant.
5. Stairs to the viewing terrace, flanked by tall ground cover plants.
6. Concrete terraces, wide roof overhangs sheathed in wood, and a spidery strut to net the distant view.
7. An apartment, small but with a grand view.
8. The lounge's open fireplace.
9. The dining room. Sliding partitions are half-closed.
10. The front lobby: the ceiling is relieved by a striplight and one lowered area.

3. Die Vorfahrt, plastische Komposition in freiem Taktmaß.
4. Aussichtsterrasse vor dem Restaurant.
5. Zwischen hohem Bodenbewuchs die Treppe zur Aussichtsterrasse.
6. Betonterrassen, weite Überstände in Holz verschalt, ein »Spinnenbein« rahmt die Fernsicht.
7. Ein Wohn-Schlafraum, klein in den Maßen, mit weitem Blick.
8. Die Lounge mit offenem Kamin.
9. Der Speisesaal, Schiebewände halb geschlossen.
10. Der Empfang. Lichtstreifen und niedere Deckenzone als knappe Akzente.

Holiday House, Malibu Beach, California

Architect: Richard J. Neutra

1. The hotel on the bluff, seen from the east.

1. Das Haus auf der Klippe, von Osten gesehen.

A hotel is to Neutra "a home for those who have left home —it can inspire ideas for home living, regenerate its modes. Resort hotels have often served as a paradisal, if brief supplement to an otherwise humdrum existence." For this stimulating experience, he has provided an architectural context which clearly bears his signature, and makes no concessions to the taste of the tourists and film-makers from Malibu who often come to this small 17-apartment beach hotel.

Neutra liked the site, a bluff above Escondido Beach facing the sea to the south. He put two parallel rows of apartments on the steep slope, the lower row far enough down to keep its white gravel roof almost out of sight of the top row. The space between the two groups, an open corridor with small garden, is spanned by a wooden pergola that will gradually be overgrown with bougainvillea. The tall block of the reception building closes the garden court to the east. The two-storey spider-leg struts —one of Neutra's trademarks—relate to the scale of the tall olive tree at the entrance.

The two rows, of 8 and 9 apartments respectively, directly face the sea. Their rooms are equal in size, and yet the two groups are quite diverse in design. The lower apartments have white ceilings and roof overhangs, and their sunbreakers are narrow planks attached to tapering cantilevered beams. The end walls and most of the wall panels between the terraces are sheathed in redwood. On the upper group the shielding wall panels are white, and they project beyond the roof overhang which has a dark wood soffit. While the lower slope is covered with plain grass and succulents, guests on top of the hill will enjoy a view of the Pacific heightened by a deep purple carpet of bougainvillea covering the pergola of the garden court. Neutra has not limited his color scheme to white and natural browns. There are lively contrasts between of redwood, pale yellow plaster, rust-colored railings, and the silvery green foliage of the olive trees.

The apartments have daybeds, usually placed at right angles, bath tubs and tiny kitchen corners. The end suites are large and have a fireplace, cocktail bar, and separate sleeping quarters. The southwest suite with the lawn terrace is occupied by the owners.

The Holiday House really is a seaside hotel. Cars are not parked on the doorsteps, as they would be at a motel, and in fact are not very noticeable. The buildings are compactly grouped and their structures are related to each other. An intimate restaurant, halfway between the sea and the brow of the bluff, a beach and a barbecue area, changing cabins as well as riding stables complete the project.

Holiday House, Malibu Beach, California

Architekt: Richard J. Neutra

Ein Hotel ist für Neutra »ein Haus fern dem eigenen Haus – es kann zu Ideen für das eigene Heim inspirieren, den herrschenden Modus erneuern. Ferienhotels haben oft als paradiesische, wenngleich kurze Ergänzungen eines sonst eintönigen Daseins gedient.« Er sah es als seine Aufgabe, ein befreiendes Erlebnis zu vermitteln, im Rahmen einer Architektur, die eindeutig seine Handschrift trägt, ohne Kompromiß an den Geschmack der Touristen und der Filmleute von Malibu, die häufig dieses kleine Strandhotel von 17 Apartments aufsuchen.

Der Platz kam Neutra gelegen, ein Stück Steilküste über Escondido Beach mit dem Meer im Süden. Er legte zwei parallele Zeilen an den stark fallenden Hang, die untere tief genug, daß ihr weiß bekiestes Dach den Ausblick von oben nicht stören kann. Den Raum zwischen den beiden Flügeln, Gang und Grünfläche, überspannte er mit einer Pergola aus Holzlatten, die mit der Zeit von Bougainvillea-Ranken überwachsen wird. Der hohe Riegel des Empfangsbaues schließt den Gartenhof nach Osten ab. Seine zweigeschossig durchgehenden »Spinnenbeine« – ein für Neutras Architektur typisches Motiv – nehmen den Maßstab des mächtigen Olivenstammes am Eingang auf.

Die Zeilen mit 8 und 9 Apartments sind beide ganz auf das Meer gerichtet, in den Räumen einheitlich groß. Und doch sind sie recht verschieden gestaltet. Die unteren Apartments haben weiße Decken und Dachüberstände, vorgesetzte Stirnbretter auf schmal zulaufenden Kragbalken; die Giebel und die Mehrzahl der Blenden zwischen den Terrassen sind in Rotholz verkleidet. In der oberen Reihe sind die Blenden weiß, und sie springen weiter vor als der Dachüberstand mit seiner dunklen Untersicht in Holz. Ist der untere Hang mit schlichtem Gras und Fettpflanzen bedeckt, so erleben die Gäste der oberen Gruppe den Blick auf den Pazifik gesteigert durch eine scharlachrote Blütendecke von Bougainvillea, die sich über die Pergola des Gartenhofs breitet. Neutra hat seine Farben am Bau durchaus nicht auf Weiß und Naturbraun beschränkt. Es gibt lebhafte Kontraste von Rotholz, blaßgelbem Putz, rostroten Geländern und silbrig grünem Olivenlaub.

Die Apartments haben Tagescouchen, großenteils übereck gestellt, Wannenbäder und winzige Kochecken. Die Endsuiten sind großräumig, mit Kamin, Cocktailbar und getrenntem Schlafteil ausgestattet. Die Südwestsuite mit der Rasenterrasse wird von den Besitzern selbst bewohnt.

Das Holiday House nennt sich mit Recht ein Hotel am Meer. Wagen stehen nicht, wie bei einem Motel, vor allen Türen, treten überhaupt kaum ins Bild, und die Baugruppe als Ganzes ist strukturell stark verklammert. Ein intimes Restaurant auf halber Höhe zwischen dem Rand der Klippe und dem Meer, ein Strand mit Barbecue, Badehütten und Reitstall runden die Anlage ab.

2. The entrance, flanked by olive trees.

2. Der Eingang flankiert von Olivenstämmen.

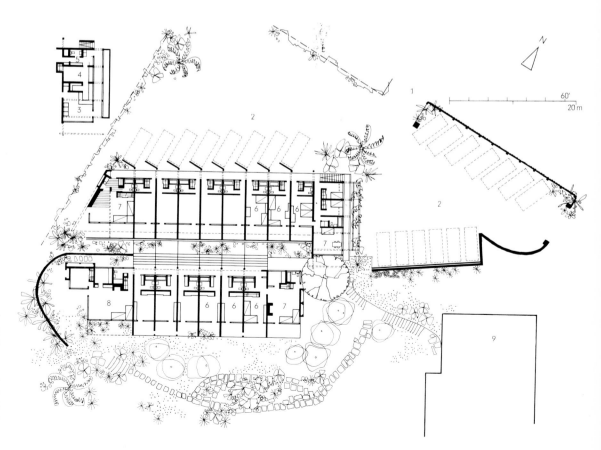

Plans, main floor and above left lower floor of the reception building. Key: 1 Entrance, 2 Parking area, 3 Lobby, 4 Office, 5 Service, 6 Smaller apartments, 7 End suites, 8 Owners' suite, 9 Restaurant on lower level.

Grundrisse Hauptgeschoß und Untergeschoß des Empfangsgebäudes (links oben). Legende: 1 Einfahrt, 2 Parkplätze, 3 Lobby, 4 Büro, 5 Etagenservice, 6 Kleinere Apartments, 7 Ecksuiten, 8 Suite des Besitzers, 9 Niedriger gelegenes Restaurant.

3. The gate to the garden court. White screens and a slim pergola.
4. The owners' apartment. Fixed glass windows, ventilation louvres below.

3. Das Tor zum Gartenhof. Weiße Blenden, leichte Rahmen der Pergola.
4. Wohnung des Besitzers. Feste Glasflächen, Lüftungsjalousie in der Brüstung.

5. The west suite. Dark projecting roof sheathed in wood: large areas of glass.
6. Wood and brick. No concessions to tourist taste.

5. Die Westsuite. Dunkler Dachvorsprung in Holz, viel Glas.
6. Holz und Ziegel. Kein Zugeständnis an das touristische Genre.

Pavilion Hotel Les Tourelles, Ste. Maxime, France

Architects: Herbert Weisskamp (Neue Heimat International) and Richard Heil with Henri and René Audineau

The Château des Tourelles above the bay of St. Tropez was for many years the property of a French movie producer, and its palm-studded park and pine forest made a natural backdrop and shooting stage for countless Riviera films. In 1964, the property was bought by the German Construction Workers' Union as one of a chain of vacation centers. The château was renovated and painted white inside and out, and its stuccoed interiors were furnished in an up-to-date manner. Today it accommodates a brasserie-restaurant, cocktail lounge and reading room, plus five apartments, the manager's flat, kitchens and a conference room with roof garden.

80 bungalows and apartment units were built on the wooded site behind the château, leaving untouched the subtropical garden toward the sea. The architects developed their site plan with great care, to make the fairly high density less obvious. They grouped 30 apartments in two-storey L-shaped buildings around a small square, built single-storey houses on the flat part of the site and put 30 houses on the steep slope, where they form cascading groups shaded by the gnarled boughs of the cork oaks, and have the best view of the sea to the west. All units are parallel, with a north-south orientation. The architects tried to save every tree, big or small, but the time-consuming effort of fitting the buildings in under the trees was all but wasted. Before planning was finished, the maritime pines were attacked by pests and had to be felled and burned.

The built area spreads out from the side entrance, where the former gardener's house serves as a reception and administration building. A single loop of road with well-distributed parking lots makes all groups of houses accessible. The hillside types (H) are reached by short staggered runs of stairways and ramps. All hillside houses are built to the same plan, overlapping the lower unit halfway (the living room of the upper unit over the neighbor's bedrooms) and staggered to both sides in plan. By this simple means a very intricate massing has been achieved. All hillside houses have roof terraces and most of them another patio at ground level, partly roofed by the sidestepping of the house above. Flat roofs, rare in the Provençal style which to this day predominates in the Var, made this possible.

The single-storey buildings on the northern and eastern part of the site are developed from one basic plan—two bedrooms with bath, cooking area and dining bar, and a living room of 28 m². To the west there is either a covered patio (in type S) or another bedroom (in type SL). The S-type houses have pergolas spanning the entire length of the living room and patio, supported only by thin columns of square steel tubing. Long patio walls over the full height or stepped down to head height are used to give a broad restful effect.

The two-storey apartment houses have 3 units on each floor with individual balconies, and a common terrace shaded by pergolas. The strong horizontals of the pergolas and their projecting plant-boxes diminish the mass of the buildings and give them a human scale appropriate for vacationers. The pergolas will soon be covered with such flowering vines as bougainvillea. In the small units which have a sleeping alcove, the kitchens with their dining bars open into the living room (dining bars instead of closed kitchen units are used in almost two-thirds of the houses).

Guests at Les Tourelles, all of whom will be workers and employees of the German construction industry, may choose to live in the seclusion of their houses and do their own cooking or may take their meals in the restaurant and participate in the social activities of the vacation center.

T-type houses form a transition between the new structures and the château. Their low silhouettes effectively set off the turreted mass of the old building.

The new houses are painted in one color, a pure white, on their smooth surfaces and are thus both in unison and in contrast with the playful elevations of the fin-de-siècle château. Only the flooring of beige and pale yellow broken marble, and the natural-stained wood, add muted touches of color.

The landscaping by H. Weisskamp seeks to counter the impression of density by stressing the cohesion, rather than the fragmentation of the whole site. There is no attempt to mimic the classical park in front of the château, where there are palm-trees, yuccas, century plants, bamboo groves and tall spreading cedars, and no attempt to provide a quick substitute for the perished pines by replacing them with groups of fast-growing trees. The emphasis is on dense ground cover: lavender, succulents and gazonia with deep green or silvery foliage; and a few groups of tall trees. The peaceful expanses of ground cover complement the old cork oaks and the newly-planted groups of umbrella pines and blue cypresses.

The relationship between buildings and open spaces is further defined by plantings of oleander and erect mimosa. Flowering creepers (bougainvillea, virginia creeper and wistaria) provide colorful detail. They will completely cover some walls and pergolas. The steep slope on the west side will keep its natural covering of cork oaks and wild mimosas. Placed between the flights of steps are cypresses and blue cedars tall enough to increase the apparent space.

1. A cascade of hillside houses (type H), staggered on plan to give variety.
2. Group of three-bedroom houses (type SL) screened by cork oaks.

1. Eine Kaskade von Hanghäusern (Typ H), seitlich versetzt in lockerer Gruppierung.
2. Eine Gruppe von Häusern mit vier Räumen (Typ SL), abgeschirmt durch die Stämme von Korkeichen.

Pavillonhotel Les Tourelles, Ste. Maxime, Frankreich

Architekten: Herbert Weisskamp (Neue Heimat International) und Richard Heil mit Henry und René Audineau

Das Château des Tourelles war viele Jahre Sitz eines französischen Filmmagnaten und mit seinem Palmenpark, seinem Pinienhain über der Bucht von St. Tropez Hintergrund und Schauplatz ungezählter Rivierafilme. Im Jahre 1964 kaufte die deutsche Gewerkschaft Bau, Steine, Erden den Besitz für ihr Erholungswerk. Das Schloß wurde umgebaut, innen und außen weiß gestrichen, seine gestuckten Räume mit Möbeln unserer Zeit ausgestattet. Es enthält heute Brasserie, Restaurant, Bar und Bibliothek, fünf Apartments, Verwalterwohnung, Küchenanlagen und einen Konferenzraum mit Dachgarten.

Auf dem waldigen Gelände hinter dem Schloß – der subtropische Garten zum Meer blieb unberührt – entstanden 80 Bungalows und Ferienwohnungen. Die Architekten planten ihr Layout mit großer Sorgfalt, um die Dichte der Einheiten optisch aufzulockern. Sie faßten 30 Apartments in zweigeschossige Winkelbauten um einen knappen Platz zusammen, bauten auf dem flachen Teil des Geländes eingeschossige Bungalows und legten 30 Terrassenhäuser in kleinen Kaskaden an den Steilhang, wo sie ungestört im Astwerk der Korkeichen aufgehen und den besten Ausblick nach Westen aufs Meer haben. Alle Häuser sind parallel zueinander in Nord-Süd-Richtung gebaut. Die Architekten suchten alle großen und kleinen Bäume zu erhalten, doch die zeitraubende Arbeit der Einpassung war fast vergeblich. Noch während der Planungsperiode wurden die Pins Maritimes, wie ganze Pinienwälder im Gebiet des Var, von Schädlingen befallen und mußten abgeholzt und verbrannt werden.

Das neue Gelände wurde von der Seiteneinfahrt aus erschlossen; das alte Gärtnerhaus dient als Empfang und Verwaltung. Eine einzige Straßenschleife mit gut verteilten Parkplätzen macht alle Hausgruppen zugänglich. Die Hangtypen (H) werden über kurze verspringende Treppen und Rampen erreicht. Alle Hanghäuser sind einheitlich geplant, sie setzen sich jeweils halb übereinander (der Wohnraum der oberen Einheit über die Schlafzimmer des unteren Nachbarn) und versetzen sich nach beiden Seiten im Plan. Allein durch dieses Mittel entsteht die große kubische Vielfalt in der Erscheinung. Alle Häuser am Steilhang haben Dachterrassen, die meisten außerdem einen Patio zu ebener Erde, der vom seitlich verschobenen Haus darüber überdeckt wird. Flachdächer, eine Seltenheit in der Domäne des provenzalischen Stils, die das Var heute noch ist, machten diese Lösung möglich.

Die Bungalows im Norden und Osten des Geländes sind aus einem Grundtyp entwickelt: zwei Schlafräume mit Bad, Kochecke und Eßbar, ein Wohnraum von 28 qm. Nach Westen schließt ein überdeckter Patio an (Typ S) oder ein zusätzliches Schlafzimmer (Typ SL). Bei den Häusern des Typs S überspannt eine Pergola die ganze Breite des Wohnraums und des Patios, die vier Hölzer ruhen auf einer dünnen Stütze aus Vierkant-Stahlrohr. Lange Patiowände in voller Höhe oder fast auf Augenhöhe herabgestuft, sind als abschirmende Elemente eingeplant.

Die zweigeschossigen Apartmenthäuser haben oben und unten je drei Wohnungen mit Einzelbalkons und einer gemeinsamen Terrasse im Schatten von Pergolen. Die starken horizontalen Akzente dieser Pergolen mit den vorspringenden Pflanzenboxen überspielen die Masse der Häuser und bringen sie auf ein menschliches, feriengerechtes Maß. Sie werden in kurzer Zeit von blühenden Ranken wie Bougainvillea überwachsen sein. In den kleinen Einheiten mit Schlafnische gehen die Küchen mit ihren Eßbars frei in den Wohnraum über. (Eßbars statt geschlossener Küche sind in fast zwei Drittel aller Wohnungen eingebaut.)

Die Gäste im Pavillonhotel Les Tourelles, sämtlich Beschäftigte der Bauindustrie, haben die Wahl, ganz zurückgezogen in ihren Häusern zu leben und zu wirtschaften oder an den Mahlzeiten im Restaurant und am geselligen Leben teilzunehmen.

Den Übergang zum Schloß bilden Häuser vom Typ T. Ihre flach geschichteten Silhouetten lassen die turmgekrönte Masse des Schloßbaues wirkungsvoll zur Geltung kommen.

Die neuen Häuser sind in einer einzigen Farbe gestrichen, weiß in glatten Flächen, zugleich im Einklang und im Kontrast mit den spielerisch profilierten Schloßfassaden des Fin-de-siècle. Farblich abgesetzt sind nur die Böden in beigem oder gelblichen Bruchmarmor und die naturgebeizten Hölzer. Dachsimse und Pergolen in rotem Zedernholz bringen einen warmen Ton ins Bild.

Die Gartengestaltung von H. Weisskamp sucht dem Eindruck gesteigerter Wohndichte durch betonte Kohäsion zu begegnen, nicht durch Fragmentierung. Sie vermeidet Anklänge an den klassischen Park vor dem Schloß mit seinen Palmen, Cicas, Yuccas, Agaven und Bambusgehölzen, seinen breitgewachsenen hohen Zedern und sie versucht nicht, die zugrunde gegangenen Pinien durch schnell aufschießende Baumgruppen zu ersetzen. Die Betonung liegt auf dichten Bodendecken – Lavendel, Dickblattpflanzen (Ficoïden) und Gazania in grünen und silbrigen Arten und auf wenigen Gruppen hoher Bäume. In seiner Großflächigkeit bringt der niedrige Bodenbewuchs die alten Korkeichen und die neugesetzten Gruppen von Schirmpinien und blauen Zypressen gut zur Geltung.

Die räumlichen Zusammenhänge der Häuser und Freiflächen sind durch Oleander und hochwachsende Mimosen definiert. Blühende Ranken – Bougainvillea, Vignes Vièrges, Glyzinen – sorgen für farbenfrohes Detail. Sie werden einzelne Wände und Pergolen ganz überwachsen. Der Steilhang nach Westen bleibt in seinem natürlichen Bewuchs von Korkeichen und wilden Mimosen. Zwischen den Läufen der Freitreppen stehen einzelne Zypressen und Blauzedern, die durch ihre hohe Form den Eindruck größerer Räumlichkeit geben.

Key to site plan: 1 Main access, 2 Reception, administration, 3 Château des Tourelles, 4 Two-storey apartment house, 5 Single-storey house, T-Type, 6 Hillside house, H-Type, 7 Single-storey house, S-Type, 8 Single-storey house, SL-Type.

Legende zum Lageplan: 1 Haupteinfahrt, 2 Anmeldung, Verwaltung, 3 Château des Tourelles, 4 Zweigeschossiges Apartmenthaus, 5 Bungalow, T-Typ, 6 Hanghaus, H-Typ, 7 Bungalow, S-Typ, 8 Bungalow, SL-Typ.

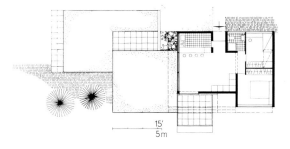

3, 4. Hillside houses seen from the top, white cubes and
screen walls, patches of greenery, a gnarled tree; a play
of changing levels.
5. S-type house with patio to the left. A long pergola supported by the slenderest of steel columns.

3, 4. Hanghäuser von oben. Weiße Kuben und Sicht-
wände, Matten von Grün, ein knorriger Stamm; ein Spiel
wechselnder Niveaus.
5. Haus Typ S mit Patio zur Linken. Eine langgezogene
Pergola gestützt auf einen dünnen Metallstab.

15'
5m

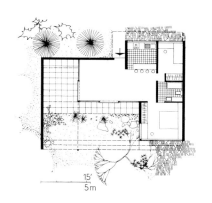

15'
5m

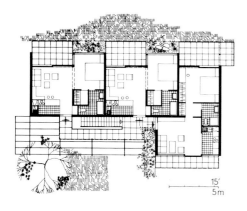

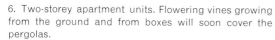

6. Two-storey apartment units. Flowering vines growing from the ground and from boxes will soon cover the pergolas.

7. A group of two-storey and lower T-type houses seen toward the sea. The castle with its turrets is in the background.

6. Zweigeschossige Apartments. Blühende Ranken vom Boden und aus Pflanzenkästen werden bald die Pergolen übergrünen.

7. Eine Gruppe zweigeschossiger und flacher Häuser vom Typ T gegen das Mittelmeer gesehen. Das Schloß mit seinen Türmchen im Hintergrund.

Youth Hotel, Nikko, Japan

Architect: Yoshinobu Ashihara

This small building of 450 m² floor area, beside the Daiya river, has rigidly horizontal lines and a butterfly-winged hood on its flat roof, and manages to dominate a wide hilly landscape. It marks a new trend in building for young travelers, a trend towards a youth hotel which offers more space and comfort in its public rooms than the old youth hostel.

The two wings, for girls and young men, run parallel with the contours of the slope and are staggered in plan. The central block houses the baths and service rooms, as well as the front desk and the two kitchens, in one of which young people may do their own cooking. The lounge is raised one floor on stilts and has large bays of glass; it has balcony terraces on three sides. There is a tremendous free-standing chimney with fireplace; the chimney continues down to serve an outdoor fireplace on the lower terrace.

The center section of the building is of reinforced concrete; the wings have walls of hollow-block masonry. Thousands of pebbles collected from the riverside are a major feature of the building and its landscaping. The strong horizontals of the concrete facias and railings are further stressed by the horizontal lines of the wood shading slats. They are easily adjustable to accord with the position of the sun, and cast lively shadow patterns on the narrow strip of gravel outside the bedrooms. The hotel can accommodate from 50 to 80 young people at a time.

1. General view. The hotel is between the river and the woods.
2. The lounge seen from the entrance.

1. Gesamtansicht. Das Haus zwischen Fluß und Wald.
2. Die Halle vom Eingang gesehen.

Longitudinal section / Längsschnitt.

Key to the main floor plan: 1 Entrance, 2 Front desk 3 Lounge, 4 Fireplace, 5 Kitchen, 6 W.C., 7 Washroom, 8 Bathroom, 9 Storage, 10 Machinery room, 11 Gymnasium, 12 Women's dormitories, 13 Men's dormitories.

Legende zum Grundriß: 1 Eingang, 2 Empfang, 3 Halle, 4 Offener Kamin, 5 Küche, 6 Toilette, 7 Waschraum, 8 Bad, 9 Abstellraum, 10 Maschinenraum, 11 Gymnastikraum, 12 Mädchen Schlafräume, 13 Männer Schlafräume.

Plan, main floor / Grundriß Hauptgeschoß.

Jugendhotel, Nikko, Japan

Architekt: Yoshinobu Ashihara

Der kleine Bau von 450 qm behauptet sich in einer weiten Hanglandschaft am Daiya-Fluß durch seine straffen Horizontalen und den aufschwingenden Akzent seines hochgesetzten Dachteils. Er weist auf einen neuen Trend im Bauen für die reisende Jugend, den Trend zum Jugendhotel. Der Begriff der Herberge paßt kaum noch auf ein Haus dieser Art.

Die beiden Flügel für Mädchen und junge Männer sind parallel zum Hang angelegt und im Plan diagonal versetzt. Der mittlere Block nimmt die Bäder, Wasch- und Nebenräume auf, den Empfang und zwei Küchen. In einer davon können die jungen Leute selbst kochen. Die Halle, großzügig verglast und auf Stützen gestellt, ist auf drei Seiten von Balkon-Terrassen umgeben. Ein mächtiger Kaminblock wurde in den Raum gestellt; er setzt sich auf der unteren Terrasse als Außenkamin fort. Der Mittelteil ist in Stahlbeton ausgeführt, die Seitenflügel als Mauerwerksbau in Hohlsteinen. Vom nahen Fluß wurden Tausende von Kieselsteinen herangeschafft. Sie sind ein bestimmender Akzent für das Bauwerk und die Gartenanlage. Die horizontale Schichtung der Betontraufen und Brüstungsstreifen wird unterstrichen durch die waagerechten Linien der weitmaschigen Sonnengitter aus Holz. Sie sind nach dem Sonnenstand mit wenigen Handgriffen verstellbar und beleben den schmalen Kiesgarten vor den Schlafräumen mit ihren Schattenschlägen. Das Haus kann fünfzig bis achtzig junge Menschen aufnehmen.

3. The porch. Concrete parapets are molded to form benches.
4. Entrance and lobby. Emphatic horizontal fascias of concrete.
5. Night view from the south.

3. Veranda. Brüstung als Betonbank.
4. Eingang und Halle. Horizontale Bänder in Beton.
5. Nachtansicht von Süden.

Hotel Prisank, Kranjska Gora, Yugoslavia

Architect: Janez Lajovic

The hotel is sited in the heart of the village of Kranjska Gora which with its deep winter snows and its sheltered southerly aspect, is fast becoming Yugoslavia's first skiing resort. To the south, the valley is dominated by Mount Prisank. To give the best possible view of the mountains, the bedroom wing (120—140 beds, on three floors) is set at an angle to the other wing, and is split and cranked near the middle. The small scale of its hipped roof relates it to a modest old shingled peasant house on the edge of the village green, which acts as a service annex. The roofline of the shorter central section, which contains bedrooms as well as the reception area and the raised lounge, dips down towards the low restaurant building. The long sloping planes of the roof define a sheltered area at the entrance. This protected zone extends as a café terrace facing some mighty beech trees and the village's former court-house. The three sections of the hotel building form an arc between the existing houses, and are well integrated with the pattern of the village, closing it off from the open meadows.

The restaurant section is single-storeyed but large in plan. There are four restaurants, a café and a snack bar (320 seats all told) surrounding a central kitchen. The main restaurant and snack bar to the north and east, with their terrace under the beech trees, have given new life to the village street and square, where their entrance is.

The restaurants which face south-west and the café at the junction with the bedroom wing, are graded in size and are mainly used by hotel guests. From here one has the best view up the valley to the high mountains, and can enjoy long hours of sunshine. For longer-staying guests there is a loggia above the café, next to the second floor lounge. A night club for fifty persons is in the basement and is easily accessible from both the hotel and the street.

The restaurant building has an exposed concrete structure with bush-hammered surfaces; ceilings and roofs are wood. The guest-room wings have ceilings of prefabricated slabs, and hollow block walls, plastered and whitewashed; exteriors are faced with pine boards. All woodwork is in selected timber, finished with clear matt varnish. Floors are oak parquet with sisal carpets.

The building with its particular roofline and all its furnishings, also designed by Lajovic, "is made to reflect the character of a sporting hotel and the form and rhythm of the village and its surroundings."

Plan, ground floor. Key: 1 Main restaurant, 2 Snack bar, 3 Terrace, 4 Stairs to W.C.s, 5 Café, 6 South restaurants, 7 Kitchen, 8 Service entrance with goods lift, service and staff rooms, 9 Stairs to bar, 10 Hotel entrance, 11 Reception with office and telephone switchboard, 12 Hall, 13 Single bedroom, 14 Chambermaid's room, 15 Double bedroom, 16 Suite.

Grundriß Erdgeschoß. Legende: 1 Hauptrestaurant, 2 Snackbar, 3 Terrasse, 4 Treppe zu den Toiletten, 5 Café, 6 Restaurants auf der Südseite, 7 Küche, 8 Nebeneingang mit Warenlift, Wirtschafts- und Personalräumen, 9 Treppe zur Bar, 10 Hoteleingang, 11 Empfang mit Büro und Telephonzentrale, 12 Halle, 13 Einzelzimmer, 14 Zimmermädchen, 15 Doppelzimmer, 16 Suite.

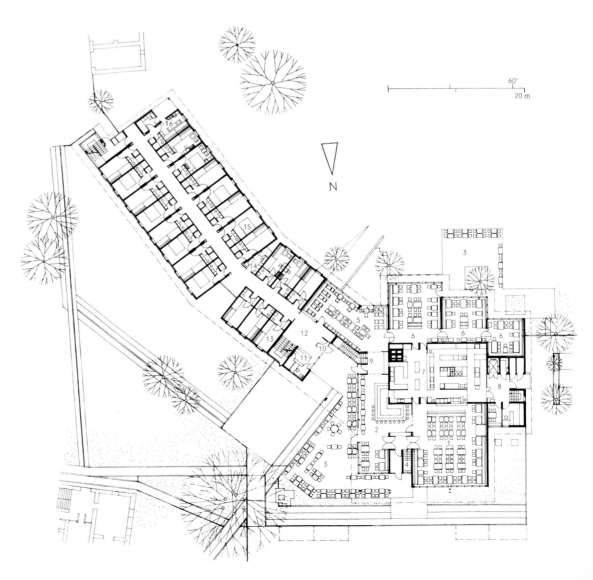

Hotel Prisank, Kranjska Gora, Jugoslawien

Architekt: Janez Lajovic

Das Hotel liegt im Kern des Dorfes Kranjska Gora, das mit seinen schneereichen Wintern und seiner nach Süden orientierten, windgeschützten Lage zum ersten Wintersportzentrum Jugoslawiens wird. Der Berg Prisank im Süden beherrscht das Tal. Um die Aussicht auf die Berge so wenig wie möglich zu blockieren, wurde die Baumasse geteilt. Der Zimmerflügel – 120 bis 140 Betten in drei Geschossen – ist in sich abgewinkelt und aufgespalten. Er schließt sich an ein Bauernhaus am Rand der Dorfwiese an und nimmt mit seiner abgewalmt ausklingenden Dachform Bezug auf das kleine schindelgedeckte Haus, das zu einer Dependance werden soll. Der kürzere zentrale Wohntrakt mit dem Empfang und der hochgelegten Lounge fällt stark gegen das niedrige Restaurant; die lang abgleitenden Dachflächen bilden vor dem Eingang eine niedrige, geschützte Zone. Sie setzt sich in einer Caféterrasse zu den mächtigen Buchen und dem früheren Gerichtsgebäude fort. Die drei Komponenten des Hotelbaus formen einen Bogen zwischen den erhalten gebliebenen Häusern, eine harmonische Einheit, die sich leicht in die Dorfstruktur einfügt und den Ort zu den Wiesen hin abschließt.

Der Restaurantteil ist eingeschossig flach, aber groß in der Fläche. Vier Restaurants, Café und Snackbar mit zusammen 320 Plätzen legen sich um eine zentrale Küche. Hauptrestaurant und Snackbar nach Norden und Osten – mit der Terrasse unter den Buchen – tragen zum Leben auf der Dorfstraße und dem Marktplatz bei, wo sie auch ihren Eingang haben.
Die Südwest-Restaurants und das Café im Winkel zum Hauptbau, in der Größe gestaffelt und mehr für Hotelgäste bestimmt, haben die schönste Aussicht talaufwärts auf die Alpengipfel und sind reichlich besonnt. Für die Wohngäste ist über dem Café noch eine Loggia neben der Lounge angelegt. Im Keller liegt eine Bar, vom Hotel und von draußen gleich gut zu erreichen.
Der Restaurantbau ist in gestocktem Sichtbeton ausgeführt, Decken und Dach sind in Holz konstruiert. Die Wohnflügel haben Fertigteildecken und Wände aus Hohlsteinen, verputzt und weiß gestrichen, die Außenflächen sind mit Holzdielen verschalt. Alle Zimmerarbeiten in ausgesuchtem Fichtenholz, matt lackiert. Für die Fußböden wurden Eichenparkett und Sisalteppiche verwendet.

Der plastisch bewegte Bau und die gesamte Einrichtung, ebenfalls von Lajovic entworfen, »sind auf den Charakter eines Sporthotels zugeschnitten und auf Form und Rhythmus des Dorfes und seiner Umgebung«.

1. View from the north. A variety of dipping rooflines against the backdrop of the Prisank mountains.
2. Snack bar terrace on the east side. The guest-room wing is set at an angle to make it appear less weighty.

1. Nordansicht. Wechselnde Dachschrägen vor dem Hintergrund des Prisank-Massivs.
2. Terrasse der Snackbar nach Osten. Der abgeknickte Wohnflügel verliert optisch an Masse.

3. Guest-room wing facing south, fitted into the curving line of the village houses.
4. Guest-room wing from the south.
5. The smooth roofline of the guest-room wing, low at the entrance.

3. Wohnflügel nach Süden, eingefügt in den Bogen der Dorfhäuser.
4. Der Wohnflügel von Süden.
5. Gleitende Dachlinie über dem Wohnflügel, niedrige Eingangszone.

6. The south restaurant, brightly sunlit and facing the village green.
7. Stairs of simply-detailed woodwork; there is a lighting trough in the lower bar of the railing.
8. The simplest of materials: ceilings sheathed with pine, for a sporting hotel.
9. The bar in the basement: dark-stained wood, simple lines.
10. Café with south terrace for hotel guests.

6. Das Südrestaurant, hell besonnt am Dorfanger.
7. Treppe in rustikalen Hölzern. Leuchtkehlen im unteren Holm des Geländers.
8. Einfachstes Material, Decken in Kiefer verschalt: ein Sporthotel.
9. Die Bar für 50 Personen im Keller. Tief getöntes Holz, einfache Linien.
10. Café für Hotelgäste mit Südterrasse.

Motel Xenia, Paliouri, Greece

Architect: Aris Konstantinidis

The Greek Tourist Association commissioned Konstantinidis to design a chain of Xenia Motels. They are found north in Meteora and far to the south in the islands of Poros, Andros and Mykonos. Konstantinidis' idiom is simple to the point of austerity: everything redundant has been eliminated. Even its constructivism does not seem out of place in the Greek landscape.

Paliouri is on Chalkidike, at the western tip of the peninsula (see site plan). The motel (1), five pavilions against the low green backdrop of the hills, is the core of a large tourist development along the bay. Bungalows (2) and a major hotel (7) will supplement the motel's capacity of 144 beds. Sports grounds (3), beach facilities (4), a camping area (5) and a restaurant (6) are to follow, and vacation houses (8) on the two promontories will complete this beach development.

The four guest-room pavilions of the motel are in a straight row, and behind them is the parking lot, a large undivided ribbon. Each pavilion has two levels of 9 rooms each, all with shower baths; they are served by open staircases. The restaurant pavilion is more striking in form, but its plain square columns maintain the sober character of the rest of the scheme. The largest areas are the covered hall and the covered terrace surrounding the indoor restaurant. The openness of the building is emphasized by the garden patio at the entrance.

The contrast between the restaurant wing with its rising roofs and the low two-storeyed guest-room pavilions is carried through in scale and detail. The wide fascias of the restaurant recur in the pavilions, but the strong concrete columns at the edge of the restaurant's roof have no counterpart in the pavilions, where columns are flush with the walls. Only slender steel profiles mark the rhythm of the structural frames; the reinforced concrete ceilings are clearly articulated as slabs and beams. Wide roof overhangs shade the rooms, and sliding wood panels form changing patterns.

Structural frames are gray exposed concrete, filled with red and near-black brickwork. All flooring is of red terracotta tiles; wood panels and railings are dark green, iron parts painted with red lead.

A striking feature is the high slanted ceiling of the open hall—raw concrete with form marks, flooded with light in the evenings.

1. The restaurant and the four guest-room pavilions line the wide curving bay.

1. Das Restaurant und die vier Wohnpavillons in geradem Zuge an der weit ausschwingenden Bucht.

Key to the restaurant wing plan: 1 Entrance, 2 Garden court, 3 Bar, 4 Coats, W.C., 5 Covered hall, 6 Restaurant, 7 Restaurant terrace, 8 Preparation, 9 Kitchen, 10 Truck loading.

Legende zum Grundriß des Restaurantflügels: 1 Eingang, 2 Gartenhof, 3 Bar, 4 Garderobe, WC, 5 Gedeckte Halle, 6 Restaurant, 7 Restaurantterrasse, 8 Anrichte, 9 Küche, 10 Anlieferung.

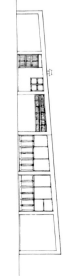

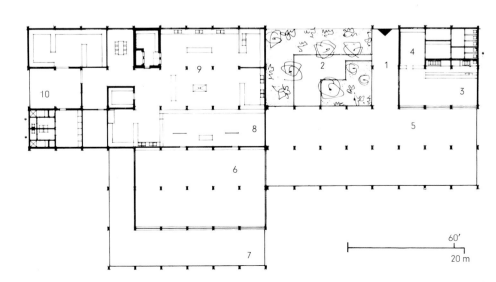

60'
20 m

Plan, restaurant wing / Grundriß Restaurantflügel.

Motel Xenia, Paliouri, Griechenland

Architekt: Aris Konstantinidis

Die Griechische Zentrale für Fremdenverkehr gab bei dem Architekten eine Kette von Xenia-Motels in Auftrag. Man findet sie von Meteora im Norden bis in die Inselwelt von Poros, Andros und Mykonos. Konstantinidis' Formensprache ist einfach bis zur Spröde, vom letzten Überflüssigen befreit. Selbst in ihren streng konstruktivistischen Tendenzen steht sie niemals fremd in den Landschaften Griechenlands.

Paliouri liegt auf Chalkidike, an der Spitze des westlichen Fingers der Halbinsel (siehe Lageplan). Das Motel (1), fünf Pavillons vor der flachen, grünen Kulisse der Hügel, ist Kern eines ganzen Touristenzentrums rings um die Bucht. Bungalows (2) und ein Großhotel (7) werden die Kapazität des Motels von 144 Betten ergänzen. Sportplätze (3), Strandbad (4), ein Campingplatz (5) und ein Restaurant (6) folgen, und Ferienhäuser (8) auf den beiden Landspitzen sollen die strandnahe Anlage abschließen. Die vier Wohnpavillons des Motels liegen in einer Reihe, auf ihrer Rückseite als breites, ungegliedertes Band der Parkplatz. Die Häuser haben zweimal neun Zimmer mit Duschbad; sie werden paarweise von offenen Treppenhäusern erschlossen. Der Restaurantpavillon ist in den Massen stärker durchgeformt, wirkt aber ruhig durch schlichte Säulenstellungen. Die größten Flächen sind die gedeckte Halle und die gedeckte Terrasse um das Restaurant. Die Offenheit des Ganzen wird durch den Gartenpatio am Eingang noch betont.

Der Kontrast des Restaurantbaues mit seinen hoch ansteigenden Dächern und den Wohnpavillons aus zwei niedrigen Geschossen ist im Maßstab und Detail gut herausgearbeitet. Die starken Gesimse sind wieder aufgenommen, doch die straffen Betonstützen am Dachrand treten bei den Wohnflügeln ganz zurück in die Wand. Feine Stahlprofile nehmen den Rhythmus der statischen Achsen auf, die Geschoßdecke zeigt sich deutlich in Platten und Balken gegliedert. Weite Überstände geben Schatten und hölzerne Schiebewände bringen Wechsel in die Fassade.

Grauer Sichtbeton für das Skelett, ausgefacht mit rotem, teils schwärzlichem Backstein. Alle Fußböden in roten Terracottaplatten, Fensterläden und Brüstungen dunkelgrün, Eisen mennigrot gestrichen.

Ein großer Effekt ist die hohe schräge Decke der offenen Halle: schalungsrauher Beton, abends angestrahlt.

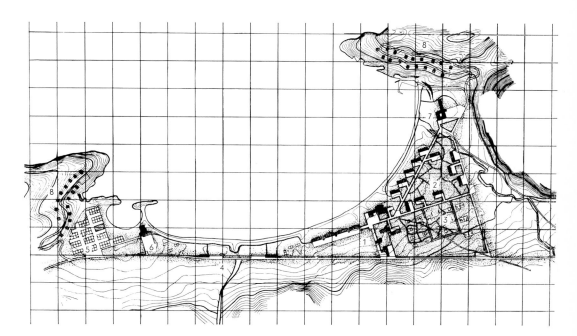

Site plan of projected tourist development (Key see page 144) / Lageplan des geplanten Touristenzentrums (Legende im nebenstehenden Text).

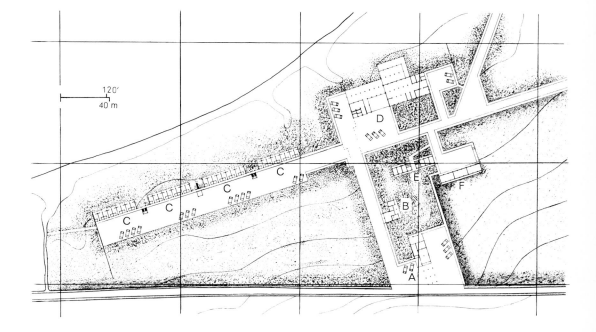

Site plan of Motel. Key: A Gas station (not built), B Reception building, C Guest room pavilion, D Restaurant wing, E Employees' room, F Mechanical room, laundry.

Lageplan des Motels. Legende: A Tankstelle (nicht ausgeführt), B Empfangsgebäude, C Wohnpavillons, D Restaurantflügel, E Personalwohnungen, F Maschinenraum, Wäscherei.

2. The concrete colonnade of the restaurant building and the tall open lounge; beyond, the delicately-detailed exteriors of the guest pavilions.

3. Their wedge-shaped section gives the lounge and terrace a lofty ceiling. The restaurant is a large space glazed on three sides.

4. The garden court of the restaurant building, wide open to the sun and sea breeze.

5. The concrete ceiling of the open-air lounge, floodlit at night.

6. Access to the restaurant is through the covered lounge. The bar is to the left, the garden court to the right.

2. Die Betonkolonnaden des Restaurantbaues, hohe offene Hallen, und die fein profilierten Fronten der Wohnpavillons.

3. Der keilförmige Querschnitt läßt die Dächer der gedeckten Halle und Terrasse hoch aufschießen. Großer verglaster Luftraum des Restaurants.

4. Der Gartenhof des Restaurantbaues, weit offen zur Sonne und Seebrise.

5. Die Betondecke der offenen Halle im Muster schmaler Schalbretter, nachts angestrahlt.

6. Zugang zum Restaurant über die gedeckte Halle. Links die Bar, zur Rechten der Gartenhof.

7. The guest pavilions with their detached staircases. A grove of young trees will screen the long parking lot.
8. Broad concrete fascias, floors clearly expressing the slab-and-beam pattern, thin metal bars, sliding wood screens, many colors.

7. Die Wohnpavillons mit ihren herausgesetzten Treppenhauskuben. Ein Hain junger Bäume wird den langen Parkplatz verbergen.
8. Breite Betonsimse, Geschoßdecken in Platte und Balken gegliedert, Metallstäbe wie dünne Striche, Holzblenden zum Schieben, Polychromie.

9. Entrance side of a guest pavilion. Rough concrete and brick flooring, enlivened by the shadows of screens and railings.

10. A double room, Spartan in its furnishing, but cheerfully colored: gray concrete, red terracotta flooring, a blue wall, steel angles painted with red lead, furniture dark green and white.

9. Eingangsseite eines Wohnpavillons. Rauher Beton und Ziegelboden, nur belebt durch Schattenschläge der Blenden und Brüstungen.

10. Ein Doppelzimmer, spartanisch ausgestattet, lebendig in den Farben: Beton grau, Boden in roter Terracotta, blaue Wand, Winkelstähle mennigrot, Möbel dunkelgrün und weiß.

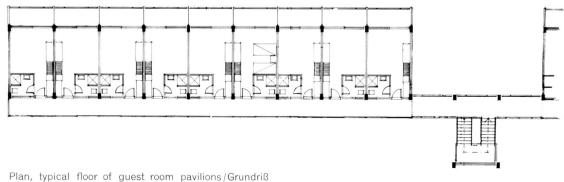

Plan, typical floor of guest room pavilions / Grundriß Normalgeschoß der Wohnpavillons.

Motel Xenia, Poros, Greece

Architect: Aris Konstantinidis

This building has little of the solid severity that usually marks Konstantinidis's work. The elevations and rooflines have an airy lightness reminiscent of masts and sails, and are curiously well suited to the island setting. The structural system used in other Xenia motels, however, has been kept. There are the same reinforced concrete frames on a 4×6 m grid, and guest-room wings are staggered and standardized to a length of two 9-room units per floor; for tourist service a chambermaid can manage more than 15 bedrooms. The architect's favorite colors are repeated: gray concrete and marble, floors of hard-burnt red bricks, a little dark green and white in doors and windows.

At the Xenia Poros all rooms have showers and balconies overlooking the sea. The guest-room wings are close to the water and face south-east, while the administration and service rooms are further up the slope towards the road. Guests approach from the top (third floor) level and have an immediate view of the sail-shaded terraces and the sea. The bedrooms are on the two lower levels. The small restaurant (just over 40 places) has dining terraces on three sides. The kitchen wing stretches over an open garden court laid out behind the guest-room wings. This space is two storeys high: air flows constantly through an opening in the roof which also admits light and rain—it is always a cool spot, even at the height of the hot season. Guests who prefer the sun and the wide view of the bay and the old town may choose the roof terrace on the north-east wing.

1. The guest-room wings from the east. White and grey rectangles crowned by the striped and chequered patterns of the awnings.

1. Die Bettentrakte von Osten. Weiße und graue Kuben, überlagert vom Streifen- und Schachbrettmuster der Sonnensegel.

2. The building from the south-west. Deep shadows mark the cool cave of the roofed garden.

2. Der Bau von Südwesten. Tiefe Schatten markieren die kühle Höhle des gedeckten Gartens.

Motel Xenia, Poros, Griechenland

Architekt: Aris Konstantinidis

Dieser Bau hat wenig von der schweren Strenge, die sonst Konstantinidis' Arbeiten kennzeichnet. Seine Fronten und Dachzonen sind wie feines Mastwerk und Segel gestaltet und passen auf selbstverständliche Weise in das Inselland. Dabei ist das konstruktive System anderer Xenia-Motels, die massiven Stahlbetonrahmen auf dem Raster 4×6 m, geblieben, die Bettenflügel sind versetzt, mit Standardlängen von zweimal 9 Zimmern je Geschoß. (Bei einfacherem Service kann ein Zimmermädchen mehr als 15 Räume betreuen.) Die Lieblingsfarben des Architekten fehlen nicht: grauer Beton und Marmor, rote Klinkerböden, dunkelgrüne und weiße Akzente an Türen und Fenstern.

Im Xenia Poros haben alle Zimmer Balkone zum Meer hinaus und Duschbäder. Die Bettentrakte liegen nach Südosten, dicht am Wasser. Betriebsräume und Verwaltung sind höher am Hang, auf der Landseite, untergebracht. Gäste fahren auf der obersten Ebene, im dritten Stock, an das Haus heran und haben gleich die segelüberdeckten Terrassen zum Meer vor sich; die Zimmer liegen eine oder zwei Treppen tiefer. Das kleine Restaurant (gut 40 Plätze) ist auf drei Seiten von Speiseterrassen umgeben. Der Küchentrakt spannt sich über einen offenen Gartenraum hinter dem vorderen Wohnflügel. Dieser Garten mit seinem zweistöckigen Volumen, seiner ständigen Luftbewegung durch eine Licht und Regen spendende Öffnung im Dach, ist kühl in der heißesten Jahreszeit. Wer die Sonne liebt und den Blick über Bucht und Altstadt, sucht die Dachterrasse des Nordostflügels auf.

Key to plans: 1 Entrance, 2 Parking area, 3 Front desk, 4 Lounge, 5 Bar, 6 Restaurant, 7 Restaurant terraces, 8 Kitchen, 9 Administration, 10 Coats, W.C., 11 Staircase, 12 Main roof terrace, 13 Open corridor to the rooms, 14 Guest-room, 15 Preparation, 16 Storage, 17 Laundry, 18 Boiler room, 19 Lockers, 20 Open garden court.

Legende zu den Plänen: 1 Eingang, 2 Parkplatz, 3 Empfang, 4 Lounge, 5 Bar, 6 Restaurant, 7 Restaurantterrassen, 8 Küche, 9 Verwaltung, 10 Garderobe, WC, 11 Treppenhaus, 12 Große Dachterrasse, 13 Gang zu den Zimmern, 14 Gastzimmer, 15 Anrichte, 16 Lagerraum, 17 Waschküche, 18 Heizraum, 19 Umkleideraum, 20 Offener Gartenhof.

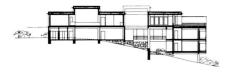

Section, service wing, garden court, guest-room wing / Schnitt durch Betriebsräume, Gartenhof und Wohnflügel.

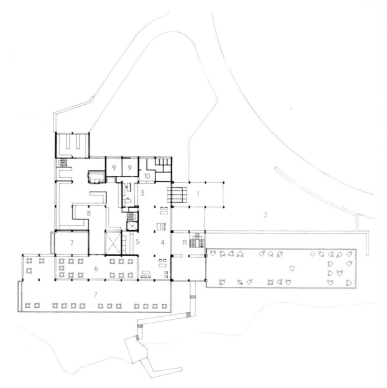

Plan, roof floor / Grundriß Dachgeschoß.

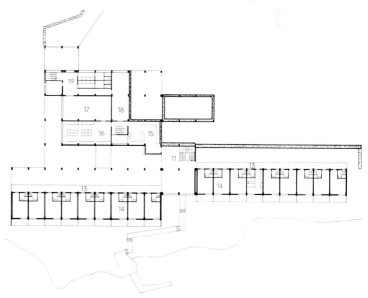

Plan, intermediate floor / Grundriß mittleres Geschoß.

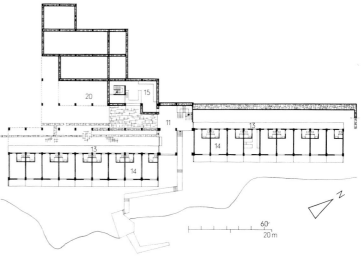

Plan, lower floor / Grundriß unterstes Geschoß.

3. The drive-way and entrance, on the roof of the guest-room wings. The raised roofs ventilate the lobby and kitchen.

3. Anfahrt und Eingang auf der Dachebene der Wohn-flügel. Die überhöhten Dachteile belüften Halle und Küche.

4. The covered garden with open corridors and stairs. Constructivist details in steel and concrete, rough broken stone.
5. Roof terrace outside the restaurant. Slender steel frames, reed mats, uniform green hills.

4. Der gedeckte Garten mit Laubengängen und Treppen-haus. Konstruktivistische Details in Stahl und Beton, grob gebrochene Steine.
5. Dachterrasse des Restaurants. Schmale Stahlrahmen, Schilfmatten, einförmig grüne Hänge.

6. The sun terrace on the east wing, a large surface checkered with the shadows of the sun screens.
7. A room with luggage and wardrobe corner. Basic furniture only, matt red brick flooring.
8. View of the water from the roofed garden between guest corridors and service rooms. There is a constant flow of air through this tall empty space.

9. Details of the south-east (sea-facing) elevations: narrow red steel angles contrast with frames of exposed concrete.

6. Die Sonnenterrasse auf dem Ostflügel. Auf großer Fläche die Schachbrettschatten der Sonnenblenden.
7. Ein Zimmer mit Gepäck- und Kleiderecke. Einfachste Ausstattung, mattroter Klinkerboden.

8. Blick zum Wasser aus dem gedeckten Garten zwischen den offenen Gängen vor den Gästezimmern, Zimmergängen und den Betriebsräumen. In dem hohen leeren Raum ständig bewegte Luft.
9. Details der Südostfassaden (Seeseite). Kontrast schlanker Winkelstähle in Rot und massiver Rahmen in grauem Sichtbeton.

Hotel La Corte dei Butteri, Orbetello, Italy

Architects: Studio 'La Ruota' di Ico e Luisa Parisi
Assistant: Lamberto Marsili

The name Shepherd's Hall—butteri is the name for the shepherds of the Tuscan maremma—was deliberately chosen. This cluster of red-walled, red-roofed buildings seems to have grown rather than have been designed. It fits as naturally as any manor-house into this landscape 156 km from Rome along the Via Aurelia. In Parisi's own words "the aim of the architecture is to provide a link between the uncommonly horizontal local landscape, the hills of the Ucellina and the curve of the bay of Argentario, at the northern tip of which the hotel stands." The linking has gone beyond the mere shaping of buildings rooted in the regional tradition. The basic element, the beach, has been framed by low groups of brick cabins, the pine forest enriched with new plantings of juniper, oleander, yucca and bougainvillea. Parisi has also formed a small salt lake to help drain a marsh. A curving path around the lake leads to a chapel that he designed as part of the resort.

On an 8 hectare site, the hotel has 70 rooms (140 beds), arranged on two levels to the east, south and west of a large interior court. The two levels are linked by shallow ramps in alternate directions; there is a tiny stairway for the staff only. Balcony terraces on the upper floors form a continuous ring above the patio. The public rooms unite in the north wing to form a single large space, the various zones of which are marked only by changes of floor level. From here, the main patio is entered through sliding glass doors shielded by bamboo curtains. With its covered walks it offers the guests a chance to rest in the shade but out of doors, among flowers and fountains, in surroundings that are a pleasant change from the overwhelming brilliance of the landscape outside. The only room isolated from the central patio and the main lounge is the dining room: it is octagonal and extends onto a square restaurant patio in the west, facing the garden and the sea. A special attraction is the television corner in the main public area. Red easy chairs are placed on steeply ascending steps. Guests have a choice between two channels, which they select by pressing a button on the armrest. Programmes appear on two screens in opposite corners of the room and are heard over miniature loudspeakers in the headrests of the chairs. The television corner is the quietest of rooms.

The apartments have small bedrooms and large baths. On the ground floor, steps lead down from the hallway into the room, and there are steps between the terraces and the beach.

La Corte dei Butteri, planned in 1962, built in 1963—65, is certainly not intended to please the champions of an exclusively modern architectural idiom. The building has elements of the International Style, of Art Nouveau, of Italian Neoliberty—but it is not a revivalist building. It has flowing lines here, abrupt angles there, but as a whole it possesses a spontaneity proper to the wild region it is in, where there is a continuous building tradition stretching back from Romantic architecture, as far as the Etruscan period. The naturalness of the building befits its nearness to sand, sea and marsh.

1. The hotel from the north; a low organic shape with monopitch roofs alternating with ridged and sometimes hipped roofs.

1. Das Hotel von Norden. Eine niedrige Silhouette; Pultdächer, Walmdächer, Satteldächer im Wechsel, eine »gewachsene« Architektur.

Site plan / Lageplan.

Hotel La Corte dei Butteri, Orbetello, Italien

Architekten: Studio »La Ruota« di Ico e Luisa Parisi
Mitarbeiter: Lamberto Marsili

Der Name Hirtenhof – butteri heißen die Hirten der tos-
kanischen Maremma – kam nicht von ungefähr. Der Komplex mit seinen rötlichen Wänden und Dächern scheint
eher gewachsen als entworfen zu sein. Er paßt in die
Landschaft an der Via Aurelia, 156 km von Rom, wie ein
Gutshof.
In Parisis Worten: »Das architektonische Thema stellt
sich dar als Mediation zwischen einer Landschaft, die
außergewöhnlich ist in ihrem horizontalen Profil, zwischen den Hügeln der Ucellina und dem Bogen des Golfs
von Argentario, an dessen Nordspitze das Hotel liegt.«
Die vermittelnde Geste ging über die reinen Bauformen
hinaus, die im Maßstab und Aufriß der regionalen Über-
lieferung verhaftet sind. Das Grundelement, der Strand,
wurde durch flache Gruppen von Ziegelkabinen einge-
faßt, der Pinienwald durch neu gepflanztes Gesträuch
von Wacholder, Oleander, Agaven und Bougainvillea
verdichtet. Weiter schuf Parisi einen kleinen Salzsee, der
eine Sumpfstelle austrocknen hilft. Ein gewundener Pfad
rings um den See führt zu einer Kapelle, die Parisi als
Teil des Ferienhotels entwarf.
Auf einem Gelände von acht Hektar hat das Hotel 70 Zimmer (140 Betten), in zwei Geschossen, angeordnet nach
Osten, Süden und Westen um einen großen quadratischen Innenhof. Die beiden Ebenen sind durch flache
alternierende Rampen verbunden, nur für die Bedienung
gibt es eine kleine Treppe. Im oberen Stock bilden Balkonterrassen einen geschlossenen Ring über dem Patio.
Die Gesellschaftsräume sind im Nordflügel zusammengefaßt zu einem einzigen Großraum, in dem die verschiedenen Zonen nur durch abgestufte Bodenebenen
markiert sind. Von diesen Räumen geht man durch Glas-
schiebetüren, geschützt durch Vorhänge aus Bambus,
in den Hauptpatio. Er gibt mit seinen gedeckten Gängen
den Gästen die Möglichkeit, in freier Luft im Schatten zu
ruhen, zwischen Blumen und Wasserspielen, in einer
Umgebung, die in angenehmem Gegensatz steht zu der
überwältigenden Helligkeit der Landschaft draußen.
Isoliert von dem zentralen Patio und dem großen Gesellschaftsraum ist nur der Speisesaal, achteckig im Plan
und erweitert durch einen wiederum quadratischen Re-
staurant-Patio nach Westen, zu den Gärten und zum
Strand. Eine besondere Attraktion ist die Fernsehecke im
großen Gesellschaftsraum. Rote Sessel sind auf hohen
Stufen steigend angeordnet. Man wählt durch Schalter
in der Armlehne eines von zwei Programmen, die auf
Bildschirmen in den beiden Raumecken laufen, und hört
über Miniatur-Lautsprecher in den Kopfstützen. Die
Fernsehnische ist der ruhigste unter allen Räumen.
Die Apartments haben kleine Schlafzimmer und große
Bäder; im Erdgeschoß führen Stufen vom Vorraum hinab,
auch die Terrassen vor den Zimmern leiten über kurze
Treppen zum Strand.
La Corte dei Butteri, geplant 1962, gebaut von 1963–65, ist
sicher nicht geschaffen für Verfechter der reinen modernen Linie. Elemente des Modern Style, des Art Nouveau,
der italienischen Richtung der Neo-Liberty klingen an,
leben aber nicht wirklich auf. Die Gebäude unter dem
bald fließenden, bald abrupten Schwung der Ziegel-
dächer haben eine spontane Qualität, spontan aus dem
Erlebnis eines wilden Landstrichs, der die Brücke von
den Etruskern zur Romantik schlägt, spontan aus dem
Erlebnis von Sonne, Sand und Sumpf.

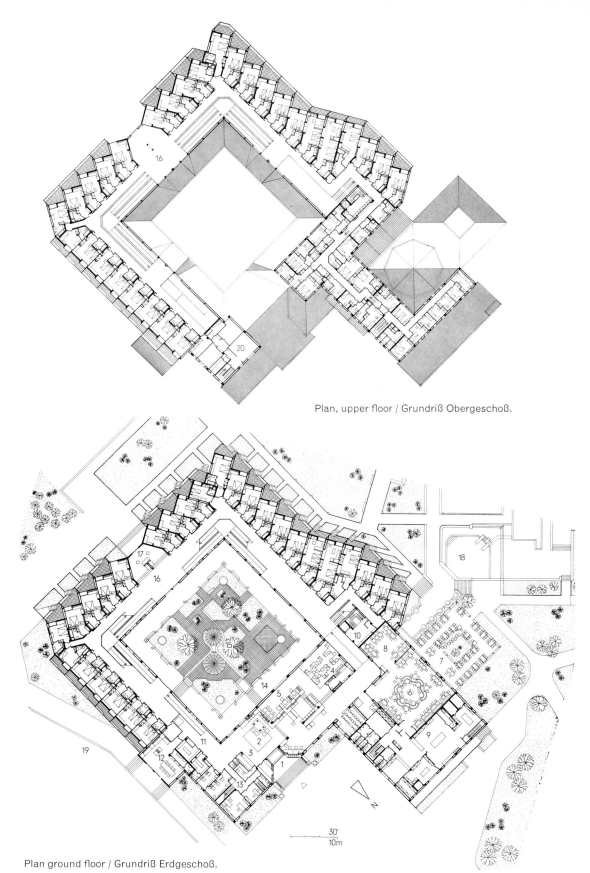

Plan, upper floor / Grundriß Obergeschoß.

Plan ground floor / Grundriß Erdgeschoß.

Key to plans: 1 Main entrance, 2 Lobby, 3 Front desk,
4 Bar, 5 Lounge with card tables, 6 Dining room, 7 Outdoor dining room, 8 Breakfast room, 9 Kitchen, 10 Coats,
11 Shops, 12 Children's playroom, 13 Administration and
management, 14 Covered walk, 15 Garden court, 16 Corridor with ramps to upper floor, 17 Entrance from the beach,
18 Swimming pool, 19 Salt lake, 20 Manager's suite.

Legende zu den Plänen: 1 Haupteingang, 2 Lobby,
3 Empfang, 4 Bar, 5 Lounge mit Spieltischen, 6 Speisesaal, 7 Offener Restaurantvorbau, 8 Frühstückszimmer,
9 Küche, 10 Garderobe, 11 Läden, 12 Kinderspielzimmer,
13 Verwaltung und Direktion, 14 Überdeckte Passage,
15 Gartenhof, 16 Innengang mit Rampen zum Obergeschoß, 17 Eingang vom Strand, 18 Schwimmbecken,
19 Salzsee, 20 Wohnung des Direktors.

2. Air view from the northwest. Shallow-roofed buildings surround a square patio.
3. The cranked west elevation: in the foreground are swimming and paddling pools between severely rectilinear brick walls.

2. Luftansicht von Nordwesten. Unter schwach geneigten Dächern eine niedrige, ineinandergeschachtelte Baumasse um einen quadratischen Innenhof.
3. Die abgeknickte Westfassade. Davor zwischen streng rechtwinkligen Ziegelmauern Schwimm- und Planschbecken.

4. The beach from an upper floor loggia. The view is enlivened by round brick cabins, set against a green background.
5. Beach cabins have brick walls, concrete roofs, and built-in showers.

4. Von einer Loggia des Obergeschosses Blick auf Bucht und Strand, gegen das Grün artikuliert durch runde Badekabinen.
5. Badekabinen am Strand aus Ziegelmauerwerk und Betondecken; eingebaute Duschen.

6. Brick terraces lead from the beach to the restaurant. The deeply-shaded area in the background is the outdoor dining room.
7. The central patio with its balcony terraces, flowers, pines, shade and fountains.
8. The strongly-modeled shape of the copper-roofed chapel, seen among trees on the far side of the lake.

6. Ziegelterrassen auf dem Weg vom Strand zum Restaurant. Die tiefe Schattenzone im Hintergrund ist der Speisesaal im Freien.
7. Der zentrale Patio mit den Balkonterrassen, Blumen, Pinien, Schatten und Wasserspielen.
8. Die Kapelle auf dem anderen Ufer des Salzsees, ein plastisches Kupferdach in den Kronen der Pinien.

9. Card tables and black easy chairs in the main lounge. To the rear left is the television corner, stilled into near-silence by the use of miniature loudspeakers in the head-rests of the chairs.
10. The broad covered walk around the garden court, deep in shade. Ramps connect the two levels.
11. The umbrella-shaped roof over the octagonal dining room. White-lacquered and uncolored wood.

9. Spieltische und schwarze Sessel im großen Gesellschaftsraum. Links hinten die Fernsehecke, lautlos durch Miniatur-Lautsprecher in den Kopfstützen der Sessel.
10. Die weit überdeckte, schattige Passage um den Gartenhof. Rampen verbinden die beiden Geschosse.
11. Das schirmförmige Dach über dem achteckigen Speisesaal. Weiß lackiertes und naturfarbiges Holz.

Hotel Lakolk, Rømø, Denmark

Architects: Knud Friis and Elmar Moltke Nielsen

An essay in exposed concrete, in rough Brutalist cubes and large, textured surfaces—that is the impression given by the new hotel on the site of the former Hotel Lakolk, which burnt down several years ago. The architects drew their inspiration from the dunes, which "let no refined detail survive." The natural curves of these same dunes reach in among the buildings, dying away in the inner court. On the south side of the site, the sand is entirely level and covered with scanty grass; a curved concrete hides neighbors. There is no tree, no shrub, to temper the harshness of the scene: the only touch of natural softness is the turf on the low-pitched roofs, though even this is as coarse in texture as the gray concrete.

The architects, as if they feared the massive structure would be unable to hold its own in the wilderness of the dunes, have further emphasized it by piercing it with small openings and painting round them with patches of strong color. Windows are distributed at random along the corridors, and their frames and the surrounding areas of wall are painted in primary colors—lemon yellow, signal red, copper green, white, and orange. "The exterior of the hotel is a concrete carapace capped with turf: the interiors are equally robust, but are painted white and almost refined in their furnishings."

The lobby, however, is as austere as the exterior walls. On the west side it has large areas of glass which face partly-closed courts and the sea beyond. Everything but this glass and the metal boxes of the light fixtures is of coarse concrete: walls, ceilings, floors and steps.

In the restaurant wing the kitchen is, surprisingly, larger than the dining room. Meals are taken quickly, as everybody lives on the beach and in the dunes.

The main building has a lounge with a bar and fireplace corner on the upper floor. Columns, beams and ceilings are of concrete left entirely untreated; only the roof overhang above the balcony, and parts of the ceiling, are painted white to reflect the sunlight. Near the fireplace the walls are white concrete, but all other walls are paneled with boards painted to match the tone of the concrete. Carpets are blue, chairs and couches have red woolen upholstery and wooden frames painted red.

Concrete ceilings and masonry walls in all the 58 rooms are whitewashed. Some softness is conferred by carpeted floors and colorful bedspreads. There are three types of guest-room: the south wing and the U-shaped northern

tract have apartments with private baths; the L-shaped wings to the west, stepped up with the slope of the dunes, have double rooms without bath or, in the outer wings, rooms for four with double-tiered beds and shared bathrooms. Guests can enter the ends of the corridors or leave for the beach without crossing the lobby area.

A building of exposed concrete like this one will certainly have its acoustic problems and, more in a northern climate than any other, it will have to stand the test of time, for it will be weathering but acquiring no patina. But its sweeping lines, its strongly articulated beams and crosswalls, will at least ensure that it preserves one quality so easily lost in conventional buildings: the beauty of a raw structure.

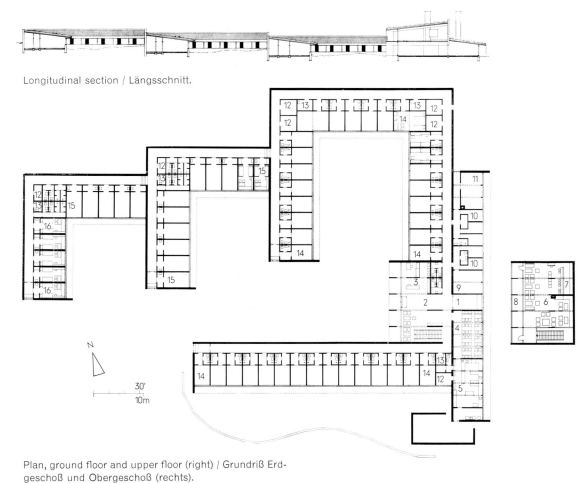

Longitudinal section / Längsschnitt.

Plan, ground floor and upper floor (right) / Grundriß Erdgeschoß und Obergeschoß (rechts).

Hotel Lakolk, Rømø, Dänemark

Architekten: Knud Friis und Elmar Moltke Nielsen

Ein Experiment in Sichtbeton, Brutalismus grober Kuben und großer rauher Flächen, so steht der Neubau auf dem Platz des alten Hotels Lakolk, das vor Jahren abbrannte. Die Architekten ließen sich von der Dünenlandschaft inspirieren, die »kein verfeinertes Detail überleben läßt«. Die natürlichen Formen der Dünen ziehen sich zwischen die Gebäude, verflachen im innersten Hof. Auf der Südseite ist das Sandgelände völlig eben; eine geschwungene Betonwand sperrt die Nachbarn ab. Nirgends aber mildert ein Baum die harten Linien. Das einzige Element, das zum béton brut tritt, ist nicht weniger herb als die schalungsrauhe graue Struktur: Grasdächer in flacher Neigung. Als könnte sich der Beton mit seiner Schwere noch nicht genug durchsetzen in der wilden Umgebung, wurde er von den Architekten in kleinen Öffnungen durchbrochen und starkfarbig pointiert. Die Fenster in den Fluren sind regellos verteilt, ihre Rahmen und Ränder auf der Wand in Primärfarben gestrichen – Zitronengelb, Signalrot, Kupfergrün, Weiß und Orange. »Außen ist das Hotel eine Betonhülle, bedeckt mit Gras, innen ist es immer noch robust, doch weiß gestrichen und fast verfeinert, was die Ausstattung angeht.«

Die Eingangshalle allerdings ist karg wie die Außenwände. Sie hat große Glasflächen nach Westen zu den Innenhöfen und zum Strand, sonst ist alles aus unbehandeltem Beton – Wände, Decken, Böden und Treppenstufen –, nur die matt polierten Metallkästen der Lampen und die Aalto-Stühle beleben das Bild.
Im Restaurantflügel fällt auf, daß die Küche größer ist als der Speiseraum; die Mahlzeiten werden schnell eingenommen, da alles Leben sich am Strand und in den Dünen abspielt.
Im Hauptgebäude, oben, befindet sich eine Lounge mit Bar und Kaminecke. Stützen, Träger und Decken sind in rauhem Beton belassen, nur der Dachüberstand über dem Balkon und ein Teil der inneren Deckenzonen sind weiß gestrichen, um das Sonnenlicht zu reflektieren. Um den Kaminplatz weiße Betonwände; alle anderen Wandflächen sind mit Brettern verschalt, die farblich genau dem Beton angepaßt sind. Teppich in Blau; Stühle und Sofabänke haben rote Wollbezüge und rot gestrichene Holzrahmen.
Die 58 Zimmer zeigen weiß gestrichene Betondecken und Ziegelwände; teppichbelegte Böden und stark far-

bige Bettspreiten und Vorhänge lockern die Strenge auf. Es gibt Gastzimmer in drei Kategorien – Zimmer mit Bad im Südflügel und in dem hufeisenförmigen Trakt nach Norden; westlich, mit dem Profil der Dünen höhergestaffelt, schließen sich zwei Winkelbauten an, die Doppelzimmer ohne Bad haben, oder, ganz nach Westen, Räume für 4 Personen mit übereinander liegenden Betten, ebenfalls nur mit gemeinsamen Bädern. An den Enden der Korridore können die Gäste ein- und ausgehen, ohne auf dem Weg zum Strand durch die Halle zu kommen.
Ein Gebäude, ganz in Sichtbeton – sicher nicht ohne akustische Probleme – hat im nördlichen Klima, mehr als ein anderes, den Test der Zeit zu bestehen. Es verwittert, aber es setzt nicht gerade eine Patina an. Durch die großgestalteten Proportionen, die stark gegliederten Schotten und Unterzüge, wird ihm etwas bleiben, das sich bei konventionellen Bauten so schnell verliert: die Schönheit eines Rohbaues.

1. East side with main entrance. The doors and the removable window shutters are painted in strong colors, as are the small windows. Roof structure and outer walls are of untreated concrete with the pattern of the formwork clearly visible. Roofs are turfed over.
2. South of the south wing the ground is entirely flat; a curved wall gives concealment from nearby houses.
3. The main building is the only two-storey part of the hotel. The deep concrete piers serve as screens for seats outside the ground floor lobby, and on the balcony outside the lounge above.

1. Ostseite mit Haupteingang. Türen und Fensterläden sind ebenso wie die kleinen Fenster in der Betonwand in starken Farben gehalten. Decken und Außenwände in schalungsrauhem Beton, Dächer mit Strandgras bewachsen.
2. Auf der Südseite des Südflügels schirmen gekurvte Betonwände den flachen Grashof gegen die Nachbarbauten ab.
3. Der Hauptbau ist der einzige zweigeschossige Teil des Hotels. Tiefe scheibenförmige Stützen unterteilen die Sitzplätze vor der Lobby im Erdgeschoß und auf dem Balkon im Obergeschoß.

◁ Key to plans: 1 Porch, 2 Lobby, 3 Front desk, telephone switchboard, office, 4 Restaurant, 5 Kitchen, 6 Lounge, 7 Bar, 8 Balcony, 9 Private sitting room, 10 Staff rooms, 11 Boiler room, 12 Storage, 13 Cleaning, 14 Single or double rooms with bath, 15 Double rooms without bath, 16 Family rooms with bunks for four persons, and no bath.

◁ Legende zu den Grundrissen: 1 Eingang (Windfang), 2 Lobby, 3 Empfang, Telephonzentrale, Büro, 4 Restaurant, 5 Küche, 6 Lounge, 7 Bar, 8 Balkon, 9 Privater Aufenthaltsraum, 10 Personalzimmer, 11 Heizraum, 12 Abstellraum, 13 Putzraum, 14 Einzel- oder Doppelzimmer mit Bad, 15 Doppelzimmer ohne Bad, 16 Familienzimmer mit Doppelstockbetten für 4 Personen, ohne Bad.

4. View from the balcony outside the lounge. Dunes and sea can be seen across the low roofs of the bedroom wings.
5. Deep concrete piers subdivide balconies into bays.

4. View from the balcony outside the lounge. Dunes and sea can be seen across the low roofs of the bedroom wings.
5. Deep concrete piers subdivide balconies into bays.

4. Blick von der oberen Lounge auf Dünen, Meer und Grasdächer.
5. Breite Stützen trennen auf dem Balkon einzelne Sitzplätze ab.

6. Wiry grass covers the undulating dunes and the low-pitched roofs.
7. The lobby. Walls, ceiling and flagged floor are of untreated concrete. Chairs designed by Alvar Aalto.
8. The stairs leading to the upper floor are of concrete cast in steel forms, contrasting with the rougher concrete of the walls.

6. Strandgräser auf flach bewegtem Dünengelände und auf leicht ansteigenden Pultdächern.
7. Die Eingangshalle. Decken, Wände und Bodenplatten in béton brut. Stühle von Alvar Aalto.
8. Das Treppenhaus zum Obergeschoß. Kontrast zwischen glattem und schalungsrauhem Beton.

9. Lobby on the ground floor. The large box-like light fittings are of dull-polished aluminium with white acrylic panels.

10. Bar next to first-floor lounge. Black ventilation pipes from the lavatories on the lower floor serve as room dividers.

11. A guest-room. Concrete ceiling and brick walls painted white; carpeting and fabrics in warm colors. Rooms without bathrooms have space for a sitting corner at the window.

9. Die Lobby im Erdgeschoß. Große kastenförmige Lampen aus matt poliertem Aluminium mit weißen Scheiben aus Acrylglas.

10. Die Bar bei der oberen Lounge. Ventilationsrohre aus den Toiletten des Erdgeschosses, dunkel gestrichen, als Raumteiler.

11. Ein Gastzimmer. Weiße Betondecke, weiß getünchte Ziegelwände, warme Farbtöne in Teppichen und Geweben. Die Zimmer ohne Bad haben Platz für eine Sitzecke am Fenster.

12. Comfort in a concrete house. Parts of the ceiling are painted white to reflect the sunlight.

13. Upper floor lounge. Concrete walls show the form marks of planed boards; other walls are covered with boards stained the same gray as the concrete. Furniture is colorful, with red frames and covers.

12. Wohnliche Atmosphäre in einem Betonhaus. Weiß gestrichene Deckenflächen reflektieren das Licht weiter in den Raum.

13. Die obere Lounge. Beton mit der Streifenstruktur der Schalbretter; Wände mit Holzbrettern verschalt, in betongrauem Ton gestrichen. Farbenfrohe Möbel, Bezüge und Rahmen rot, Ton in Ton.

Strathspey Hotel, Aviemore, Scotland

Architects: J. G. L. Poulson and Partners

Aviemore is in the Highlands of Scotland, not far from Inverness, in the valley of the River Spey, which supplies the water for much of the best whisky. The hotel is part of the Aviemore Center, a complex costing three million pounds and developed in an ambitious effort to open up the district as an all-year holiday resort. Sunshine in this Highland area is fairly rare; there are certain parts where skiing is possible, but is liable to be disrupted by storms. The usual holiday activities in the Highlands—climbing, fishing, golf, riding and sailing, were therefore complemented by ample indoor facilities, such as an ice rink for skating and curling, a swimming pool, a plastic ski practice slope floodlit at night, and an air-conditioned theater for films and concerts, seating 700. With its beautiful site under the Cairngorm Mountains, not too far from the densely populated belt between Edinburgh and Glasgow, and its wide range of first class and cheaper accommodation, the Aviemore Center seems to achieve its aim of attracting holiday guests in growing numbers. In the first eight months of operation it was visited by more than half a million people.

The Strathspey is a first class hotel of moderate size (54 double rooms, each with private bathroom) opened in late 1966 and operated independently of the Center.

There are six bedroom floors with 9 rooms each, around a central stairway. Rooms face south, west and east, and room sizes are 3,50 m by 4 m for the bedroom, plus entrance hall and bathroom. Spacious plumbing ducts are provided for easy maintenance. An extension of the bedroom area is being planned, to increase the number of rooms per floor to 15 doubles. Rooms will be added to the north, utilising the existing corridor to the emergency stair and service lift, and thereby creating a fairly complicated circulation pattern.

The ground floor plan shows multiple entrances; one foyer for the reception and the cocktail bar, one for the restaurant and Cluny Room (both have another separate entrance), one for the residents' lounge, located on the south-east side at a distance from the reception area, and the tea lounge, which interconnects with the restaurant. There are no large flowing spaces, but tightly defined rooms, and no attempt has been made to eliminate interior columns except in the restaurant, an uninterrupted space of about 12 by 20 m, divided by a folding partition.

Though designed by the same group of architects, the Aviemore Center as a whole seems to lack a compelling sense of unity, both in layout and in architectural value. This impression is emphasized rather than played down by the mountain background. In contrast with the neutral façades of the hotel, the interiors are warm and light, with honey-colored pinewood, natural stone, and tartan. Bedroom interiors are neat and well-planned with large areas of white plaster and dark wood paneling.

1. Aviemore Centre from the northeast.

1. Das Aviemore-Zentrum von Nordosten gesehen.

Hotel Strathspey Aviemore, Schottland

Architekten: J. G. L. Poulson and Partners

Aviemore liegt im schottischen Hochland, nicht weit von Inverness, im Tale (Strath) des Spey-Flusses, aus dessen Wasser viele gute Whiskies gemacht werden. Das Hotel ist Teil des Aviemore-Zentrums, eines Komplexes im Wert von 3 Millionen englischen Pfund, der aufgebaut wurde in einem kühnen Versuch, das Gebiet für den ganzjährigen Tourismus zu erschließen. Sonnenschein ist in den Highlands ziemlich selten; es gibt einige Gebiete, wo man Ski laufen kann, doch der Wintersport kommt oft durch schwere Stürme zum Erliegen. Die üblichen Feriensportarten in den Highlands – Bergsteigen, Fischen, Reiten, Segeln und Golf – wurden darum durch umfangreiche Sportanlagen in der Halle ergänzt. Aviemore hat eine Eisbahn für Curling und Kunstlauf, ein Hallenschwimmbad, einen künstlichen Übungshang mit Flutlicht für Skifahrer und einen Theaterraum mit 700 Plätzen für Filmvorführungen und Konzerte. Mit seiner schönen Lage unter den Cairngorm-Bergen, nicht zu weit von dem dichtbesiedelten Streifen zwischen Edinburgh und Glasgow, und seiner breiten Streuung von erstklassigen und weniger teuren Unterkünften scheint das Aviemore Centre seinem Ziel nahezukommen, immer größere Zahlen von Touristen anzuziehen. In den ersten acht Betriebsmonaten wurden mehr als eine halbe Million Besucher gezählt.

Das Strathspey ist ein erstklassiges Hotel mäßiger Größe (54 Doppelzimmer, alle mit eigenen Bädern); es wurde Ende 1966 eröffnet und wird unabhängig vom Centre bewirtschaftet.

Es umfaßt sechs Schlafgeschosse mit je neun Einheiten um ein zentrales Treppenhaus. Die Räume gehen nach Süden, Westen und Osten und sind im Schlafteil, ohne Eingang und Bad, 3,50 auf 4 m groß. Breite Rohrleitungsschächte machen Reparaturarbeiten leicht. Eine Erweiterung des Bettenhauses auf eine Zahl von 15 Doppelzimmern je Geschoß ist geplant. Die neuen Räume sollen nördlich über den bestehenden Korridor zur Nottreppe und zum Servicefahrstuhl angefügt werden; dabei wird ein recht kompliziertes Verkehrsschema entstehen.

Der Erdgeschoßgrundriß zeigt eine Reihe von Eingängen; ein Foyer für den Empfang und die Cocktailbar, eines für das Restaurant und den Cluny Room (beide haben noch einen separaten Zugang), ein weiteres für die Lounge der Hotelgäste (nach Südosten, abseits vom Empfang gelegen) und den Teeraum, der mit dem Restaurant verbunden ist. Große ineinandergehende Raumverbindungen gibt es nicht, sondern streng definierte Räume; es wurde auch nicht versucht, Innenstützen zu vermeiden, außer im Restaurant, das einen durchgehenden Raum von über 12 auf 20 m darstellt und durch eine Faltwand teilbar ist.

Obwohl das gesamte Aviemore-Zentrum vom gleichen Architekten entworfen wurde, scheint eine überzeugende Einheit der Komposition in der Anordnung des Ganzen und in der architektonischen Gestaltung zu fehlen. Dieser Eindruck wird durch die umgebenden Berge eher verstärkt als abgeschwächt. Anders als die neutralen Fassaden des Hotels sind die Innenräume hell und warmgetönt mit Akzenten von honigfarbenem Kiefernholz, Naturstein, Schottenkaros und Tartans. Die Schlafräume sind sauber und sorgfältig geplant; sie haben Weiß in großen Putzflächen und dunkle Holztäfelungen.

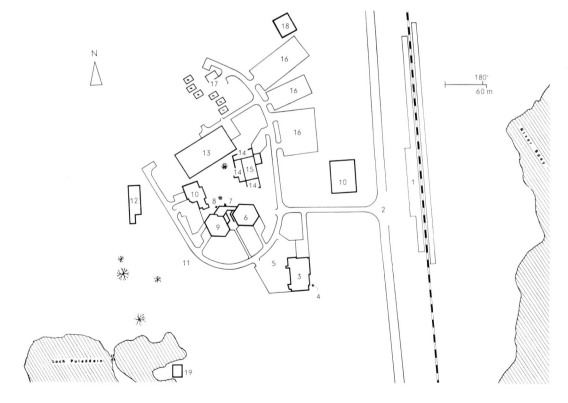

2. Strathspey Hotel from the east. The bedroom tower will be extended on the north side.

2. Das Strathspey-Hotel von Osten gesehen. Das Bettenhaus wird in nördlicher Richtung erweitert.

Site plan. Key: 1 Aviemore railway station, 2 A9 road, 3 Strathspey Hotel, 4 Sauna bath and bowling alley, 5 Hotel car park, 6 Osprey room with bar and restaurant, 7 Wild life exhibition, 8 Information centre, 9 Speyside theater, 10 Other hotels, 11 Children's playground, 12 Drambuie ski slope, 13 Ice rink, 14 Shops, 15 Swimming pool, 16 Car parks, 17 Chalets, 18 District heating plant, 19 Fishing school.

Lageplan. Legende: 1 Bahnstation Aviemore, 2 Fernverkehrsstraße A9, 3 Hotel Strathspey, 4 Sauna und Kegelbahn, 5 Hotelparkplatz, 6 »Osprey« – Raum mit Bar und Restaurant, 7 Ausstellung über die Tierwelt der Region, 8 Informationszentrum, 9 Theater, 10 Weitere Hotels, 11 Kinderspielplatz, 12 Skihang am Drambuie, 13 Eislaufhalle, 14 Läden, 15 Hallenbad, 16 Parkplätze, 17 Vermietbare Ferienhäuser, 18 Heizzentrale, 19 Fischerschule.

Plan, typical floor / Grundriß Normalgeschoß.

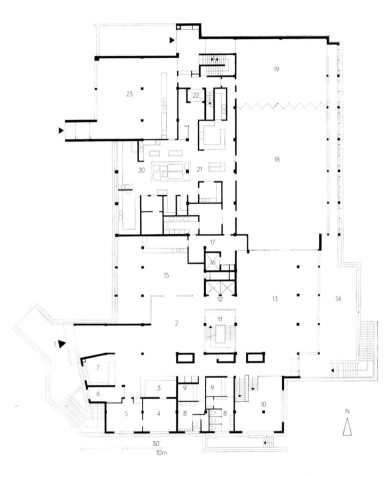

3. Reception area and central stairway.
4. The lounge area. Quiet spaces marked by interior columns, and oriented towards the view.

3. Empfang und zentrales Treppenhaus.
4. Hotel-Lounge. Ein ruhiger Raum mit Innenstützen, ausgerichtet auf die Aussicht.

Plan, ground floor / Grundriß Erdgeschoß.

Key to plans: 1 Hotel entrance, 2 Lobby, 3 Front desk, 4 Accounting, 5 Manager, 6 Porter, 7 Shop, 8 W.C.s, 9 Coats, 10 Residents' lounge, 11 Main staircase, 12 Passenger lifts, 13 Tea lounge, 14 Terrace, 15 Bar, 16 Service lift, 17 Service area, 18 Restaurant, 19 Dining room, 20 Kitchen, 21 Service, 22 Goods lift, 23 Dancing bar, 24 Bedroom. 25 Floor service, 26 Emergency stair, 27 Plumbing duct, 28 Electrical duct, 29 Duct with access panels, 30 Heating duct.

Legende zu den Plänen: 1 Hoteleingang, 2 Lobby, 3 Empfang, 4 Buchhaltung, 5 Direktion, 6 Hoteldiener, 7 Laden, 8 Toiletten, 9 Garderobe, 10 Lounge für Hotelgäste, 11 Haupttreppe, 12 Gästefahrstühle, 13 Tee-Lounge, 14 Terrasse, 15 Bar, 16 Personalfahrstuhl, 17 Kellnergang, 18 Restaurant, 19 Speisesaal, 20 Küche, 21 Anrichte, 22 Lastenaufzug, 23 Tanzbar, 24 Gästezimmer, 25 Etagenservice, 26 Nottreppe, 27 Installationsschacht, 28 Elt-Schacht, 29 Leitungsschacht, durch abnehmbare Wandtafeln zugänglich, 30 Heizungsschacht.

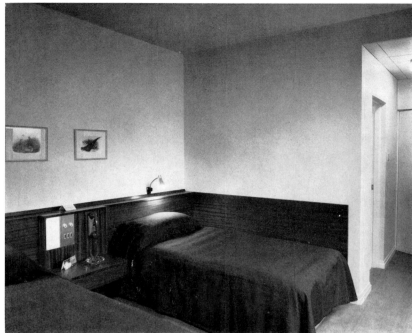

5, 6. A typical bedroom,. White plaster and deep-toned wood paneling.

7. The bar. Warm wood paneling, stone walls, modern and traditional fabrics.

8. One of the indoor features—a three-lane bowling alley.

9. The restaurant with a view of the Cairngorm Mountains.

5, 6. Ein Standard-Zimmer. Weißer Putz und tiefgetönte Holzverkleidung.

7. Der Barraum. Warmgetöntes Holz, Steinwände, moderne und traditionelle Stoffe.

8. Die Kegelbahn – Sport und Zeitvertreib in der Halle.

9. Das Restaurant mit Blick auf die Cairngorm-Berge.

Pacific Hotel, Chigasaki, Kanagawa Prefecture, Japan

Architects: Kiyonori Kikutake & Associates

The hotel with its wide flat beach attracts tourists of several kinds on their way to the Pacific from the megalopolis of Tokyo. It draws hotel guests for prolonged stays, or passing visitors who come for an afternoon on the beach or a short meal, taken if necessary behind the steering wheel of their cars. This complex of buildings — in the center of the resort area of Kanagawa prefecture, and with Fujiyama in the distance—offers a wide variety of amenities and can be regarded as a milestone on the highway of Japanese tourism's rapid growth.

Kikutake has not allowed the pure cone of nearby Mount Fuji to influence him into making his beach hotel hug the ground: on the contrary, he has given a decidedly vertical character to its rather bulky form, and was quite prepared to emphasize its verticality to an even greater degree than appears in the finished building. In the original design the service and elevator towers rose high above the main mass of the building, to cater for the future addition of more bedroom floors. The proposal, for economic reasons, was not carried through: the clear separation of the bedroom stack from the podium also had to be sacrificed. The open space which the first plan provided here was filled with public rooms—a Chinese restaurant and a salon for wedding receptions.

There can be few hotels in the world which display so striking a preponderance of public rooms, sport and entertainment facilities as the Pacific Hotel. A huge playdeck above the level of the drive-in restaurant provides several pools, rectangular for serious swimming and irregularly shaped for more casual use. Guests are divided into three streams: drive-in guests at the main entrance, hotel guests, and casual visitors who find on the raised playdeck level a bowling alley with twelve lanes, various restaurants, shopping arcades and a lozenge-shaped indoor pool filled with tropical plants. Hotel guests are led up a spiral ramp to the upper floor where they find the reception desk, main lobby and dining hall.

Above the rather conventional lower zones, Kikutake's tour de force begins with a seven-sided bedroom block that looks like a tower in spite of its limited height of five levels and its large floor area. The seven exterior faces are irregular in plan, each having elements of two different widths. Guest-rooms are cantilevered from a thick-walled septangular structural tube which like the façades has irregular wall sections, and whose corners approach the center of each of the exterior walls.

The wall of the tube screens off the bedrooms and carries the winding ramp which spirals up through the hollow core to the rooftop restaurant and panorama bar on the eleventh floor. Each floor has no less than four different types of bedroom—four rather compact double rooms, two larger living-bedroom units, a suite with separate bedroom, and two apartments that offer a Western sleeping alcove and a Japanese room with shoji (sliding paper doors) and tatami (straw mats). The reduced depth of the apartments—they at first seem shallow when compared with the circulation core—emphasizes, like the broad windows, the wide views characteristic of the hotel.

The modeling of the tower is accentuated by the bathrooms, prefabricated units cantilevering singly or in pairs from the bedrooms. These bathrooms are composed of two pvc shells joined together in various ways around a 3,8 cm thick steel tube. A problem of our fast-moving time—ever-changing bathroom fashions and grooming habits—is here solved once and for all. The podlike elements can easily be replaced with newer models.

As bold and rich in expression as the exteriors are the room color schemes by Ikko Tanaka. He felt he had reason to override purely economic considerations of mass production and easy maintenance and make use of all the colors of the rainbow, in an effort to give this unusual building strongly varied sequences of color. "I attempted to create color spaces totally unlike the ones we daily experience in our homes, our offices, and our means of transport." In other words, he did not want to subordinate his color schemes to the dictates of architecture. Tanaka thinks that the strident colors of publicity media and mass-produced goods have prompted a reaction that causes people to equate subdued colors with higher culture and calm. He considers that this has produced numerous insipid mixtures of gray, beige and green.

Tanaka's colors follow the ascending spiral of the ramp, starting on each floor with red, followed by violet, blue, green, yellow and orange, then switching to red again. Fixed elements like wall sections were made red, violet, blue, green and brown, and all other parts of the interiors strongly varied in color, to avoid the monotonous predominance of any one hue. The colors for the light furniture and the fabrics were chosen in such a way that they can be moved from one room to another, leading to yet more variations. Only the charcoal blades of the sunblinds are of one color throughout the building.

1. The sturdy shape of the tower rising above a barren beach. Mount Fuji in the background.
2. The playdeck, drive-in, and public room section topped by the bedroom tower—a vast array of sports and amusement facilities.

1. Die gedrungene Form des Turmes über einem kahlen Strand. Im Hintergrund der Fujiyama.
2. Spieldeck, Drive-in Restaurant und Unterbau mit den Publikumsräumen: ein großes Aufgebot von Anlagen für Sport und Unterhaltung.

Pacific Hotel, Chigasaki, Präfektur Kanagawa, Japan

Architekten: Kiyonori Kikutake & Associates

Das Hotel mit seinem flachen breiten Strand ist eine Attraktion für Touristen ganz verschiedener Art, die aus der Megalopolis Tokio den Weg zum Pazifik nehmen. Es zieht Wohngäste für längere Aufenthalte an und Passanten, die nur für einen Nachmittag am Strand oder für eine kurze Mahlzeit kommen, wenn nötig im Schnellverfahren hinter dem Lenkrad ihres eigenen Wagens. Der Baukomplex, mitten im Urlaubsgebiet der Präfektur Kanagawa errichtet, mit dem Fujiyama im Hintergrund, kann mit der breiten Streuung seiner Anlagen als ein Wahrzeichen des neuen Tourismus in Japan gelten.

Der Architekt ließ sich nicht von der reinen Form des Bergkegels bewegen, ein langgestrecktes Strandhotel zu planen. Im Gegenteil, er gab seiner etwas massigen Konstruktion eine deutlich aufstrebende Tendenz. Kikutake wollte in diesem Höhenstreben weitergehen, als es das fertige Bauwerk zeigt. Die Turmschächte der Fahrstuhl- und Servicegruppen sollten ursprünglich hoch über die Baumasse geführt werden, damit sich später weitere Bettengeschosse aufstocken ließen. Wirtschaftliche Gründe sprachen dagegen; sie ließen es auch nicht zu, den Turmblock der fünf Bettengeschosse stark von den Unterbauten abzusetzen. Der freie Zwischenraum der ersten Planung wurde mit zusätzlichen Räumen für das Publikum – einem chinesischen Restaurant und einem Saal für Hochzeitsfeiern – ausgefüllt.

Es gibt sicher wenige Hotels in der Welt, bei denen das Übergewicht so eindeutig auf seiten der öffentlichen Räume, der Sportanlagen und Vergnügungsstätten liegt wie bei diesem. Ein riesenhaftes Spieldeck über dem Niveau des Drive-In-Restaurants bietet mehrere Schwimmbecken, rechteckig für sportliche Gäste und spielerisch geformt zum Planschen.

Die Masse der Besucher wird in drei Ströme geteilt – Drive-In-Gäste an der Zufahrt, Hotelgäste und schließlich Badegäste, die auf dem Niveau des Spieldecks eine Kegelbahn mit zwölf Bahnen, verschiedene Restaurants, Ladenarkaden und ein rautenförmiges Hallenbad mit exotischen Pflanzen finden. Für Hotelgäste führt eine Wendelrampe zum ersten Obergeschoß, zu Empfang, Halle und Speisesaal.

Der Tour de force Kikutakes beginnt über diesen konventionell geformten Trakten mit dem siebeneckigen Bettenblock, der trotz seiner mächtigen Breite als Turm wirkt. Die sieben Außenflächen sind unregelmäßig in zwei Breitenmaßen angelegt. Die Gästezimmer kragen von einem dickwandigen konstruktiven Gehäuse aus (auch hier sind die Wandabschnitte unregelmäßig), dessen stumpfwinklige Vorsprünge durchweg nahe der Mitte der äußeren Fassadenflächen liegen.

Die Wand schirmt die Gästezimmer ab und trägt die geschwungene Rampe, die rings um die hohle Kernzone bis zum Dachrestaurant und der Aussichtsbar im elften Geschoß führt. Jedes Bettengeschoß hat nicht weniger als vier Typen von Apartments – vier kompakt bemessene Doppelzimmer, zwei größere Wohnschlafräume, eine Suite mit getrenntem Schlafraum und zwei Zimmer, die neben ihrer westlich möblierten Schlafecke einen kleinen japanischen Wohnraum mit Shoji (Papierschiebetüren) und Tatami (Strohmatten) bieten. Die geringe Tiefe der Apartments, die auf den ersten Blick im Vergleich zum Verkehrskern geradezu knapp in der Fläche wirken, betont im Verein mit den langgezogenen Fensterbändern den panoramischen Charakter des Gästeturms. Der Turm ist in hohem Grade plastisch geprägt durch die Badezimmer, die einzeln oder in Zweiergruppen als vorfabrizierte Elemente von den Schlafräumen auskragen. Sie sind zusammengesetzt aus zwei PVC-Schalen, die in einer Reihe von Varianten mit dünnen Stahlrohren (Durchmesser 3,8 cm) aneinandergefügt werden kön-

nen. Ein Problem unserer schnellebigen Zeit – der ständige Wechsel in den Badezimmermoden und -gewohnheiten – ist hier a priori gelöst. Die Elemente können leicht gegen neue Modelle ausgewechselt werden.

Kühn und vielgestaltig wie das Äußere des Baues ist die Farbgebung in den Räumen, komponiert von Ikko Tanaka. Er setzt sich über die wirtschaftlichen Aspekte der Serienherstellung und des einfachen Austausches genau gleichartiger Ausstattungsstücke hinweg und spielte alle Töne des Regenbogens aus, mit der Idee, diesem formal so ungewöhnlichen Hotel auch stark variierte Farbsequenzen zu geben. »Ich versuchte, Farbräume zu schaffen, die sich völlig unterscheiden von dem, was wir jeden Tag in unseren Häusern, unseren Büros und Verkehrsmitteln erleben.« Mit anderen Worten, seine Farben konnten sich nicht dem Zwang der Architektur unterwerfen. Nach Tanaka haben die lauten Farben der Werbung und der Massenfabrikation die Gegenreaktion ausgelöst, die in matten Farbtönen Zeichen höherer Kultur und Ansätze zur Entspannung sieht. Das Ergebnis ist in seinen Augen ein müder Dreiklang aus den Farben Grau, Beige und Grün.

Tanaka folgt mit seinen Farben der aufsteigenden Spiralform der Rampe und ließ von Geschoß zu Geschoß und von Raum zu Raum auf Rot Violett, Blau, Grün, Gelb und Orange folgen, um wieder mit Rot zu beginnen. Feste Elemente wie Wandpartien wurden in Rot, Violett, Blau, Grün und Braun gehalten und alle Dinge der Einrichtung in den Farben so variiert, daß die Hauptfarbe nie bis zur Monotonie dominiert. Die Farben der leichten Möbel und Textilien wurden so gewählt, daß sie von Raum zu Raum gewechselt werden können und zu neuen Variationen führen. Nur die Sonnenstores mit ihren graphitgrauen Lamellen sind im ganzen Gebäude von einer einzigen Farbe.

3. The base and tower building seen across the playdeck: there are swimming pools, restaurants, and a deep indoor pool.

3. Unterbau und Turmgebäude über das Spieldeck gesehen. Schwimmbecken, Restaurants und eine hohe Schwimmhalle.

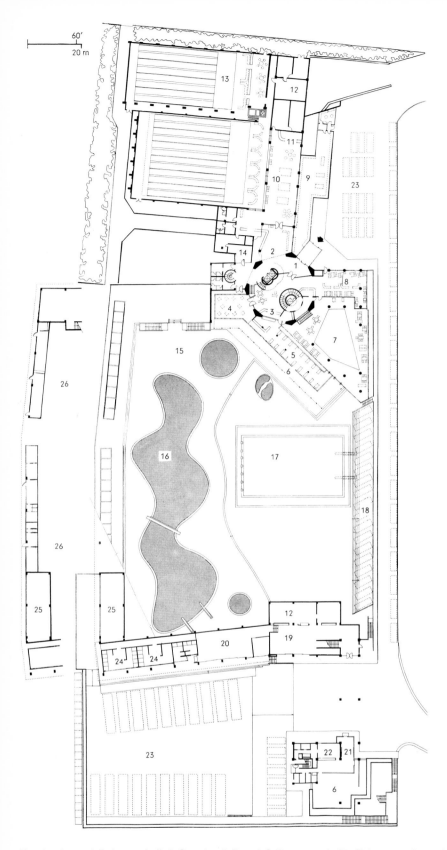

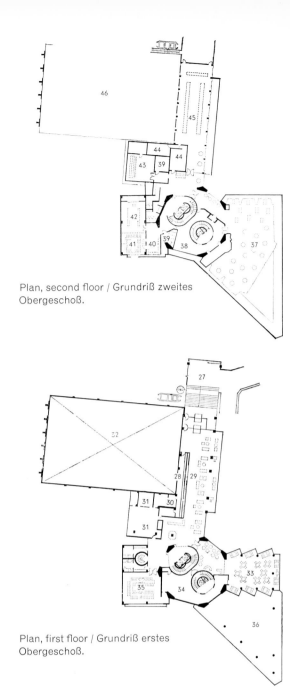

Plan, second floor / Grundriß zweites Obergeschoß.

Plan, first floor / Grundriß erstes Obergeschoß.

◁ Plan, ground floor / Grundriß Erdgeschoß.

4. The seven-sided tower, bathroom pods cantilevered ▷ from the façades.

4. Der siebeneckige Turm. Badezimmergehäuse kragen ▷ von den Fassaden aus.

Key to plans: 1 Entrance hall, 2 Counter, 3 Bar, 4 Grill room, 5 Restaurant, 6 Terrace, 7 Indoor pool, 8 Tea room, 9 Arcade (booths), 10 Bowling alley lobby, 11 Snack bar, 12 Machinery rooms, 13 Bowling alley, 14 Beauty salon, 15 Play deck, 16 Splashing pool, 17 Swimming pool, 18 Covered parking area, 19 Booths, 20 Cafeteria, 21 Drive-in restaurant, 22 Kitchen, 23 Parking area for cars and buses, 24 Lavatories, 25 Storage, 26 Staff wing with lockers, dining room and kitchen, 27 Drive-in porch, 28 Hotel front desk, 29 Lobby, 30 Telephone switchboard, 31 Offices, 32 Void above bowling alley, 33 Restaurant, 34 Main kitchen, 35 Banquet room, 36 Void above indoor

pool, 37 Chinese restaurant, 38 Kitchen, 39 Dressing room, 40 Ceremony hall lounge, 41 Ante-rooms, 42 Marriage ceremony hall, 43 Photo studio, 44 Pantry, 45 Banquet hall, 46 Bowling alley roof.

Legende zu den Plänen: 1 Eingangshalle, 2 Kontrolltheke der Kegelbahn, 3 Bar, 4 Grill, 5 Restaurant, 6 Terrasse, 7 Hallenbad, 8 Tea-Room, 9 Arkade mit Verkaufsständen, 10 Lobby der Kegelbahn, 11 Snackbar, 12 Technische Räume, 13 Kegelbahn, 14 Kosmetiksalon, 15 Spieldeck, 16 Planschbecken, 17 Schwimmbecken, 18 Überdeckter Parkplatz, 19 Verkaufsstände, 20 Cafeteria, 21

Drive-in-Restaurant, 22 Küche, 23 Parkplätze für Pkw und Busse, 24 Waschräume, 25 Lagerraum, 26 Geräte- und Arbeitsraum mit Umkleideräumen, Personal-Speisesaal und Küche, 27 Vorfahrt, 28 Hotel-Empfang, 29 Lobby, 30 Telefonzentrale, 31 Büros, 32 Luftraum über der Kegelbahn, 33 Restaurant, 34 Hauptküche, 35 Bankettsaal, 36 Luftraum über dem Hallenbad, 37 Chinesisches Restaurant, 38 Küche, 39 Garderobe, 40 Lounge des Hochzeitsraumes, 41 Vorräume, 42 Raum für Hochzeitsfeierlichkeiten, 43 Fotostudio, 44 Anrichte, 45 Bankettsaal, 46 Dach der Kegelbahn.

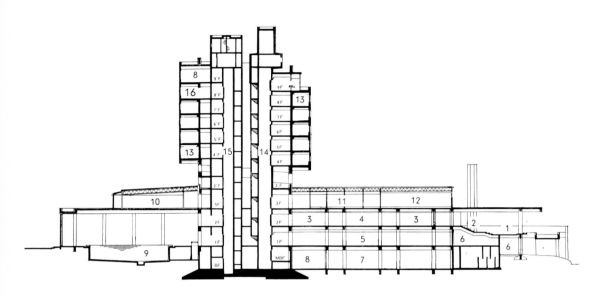

Key to section: 1 Drive-in porch, 2 Hotel lobby, 4 Front desk, 5 Bowling alley lobby, 6 Pump room, 7 Machinery rooms, 8 Kitchen, 9 Indoor pool, 10 Chinese restaurant, 11 Japanese style room, 12 Banqueting hall, 13 Guest-room, 14 Passenger elevators, 15 Service elevator, 16 Roof restaurant.

Legende zum Schnitt: 1 Wagenvorfahrt, 2 Hoteleingang, 3 Hotel-Lobby, 4 Empfang, 5 Lobby Kegelbahn, 6 Pumpenraum, 7 Technische Räume, 8 Küche, 9 Hallenbad, 10 Chinesisches Restaurant, 11 Raum im japanischen Stil, 12 Bankettsaal, 13 Gästezimmer, 14 Gästefahrstühle, 15 Personalaufzug, 16 Dachrestaurant.

5. A glass-walled staircase for guests in the hollow core.
6. Pools: square, round, and irregular. The playdeck, from the guest-room tower.
7. A bathroom. Units are easily removed and replaced in the event of obsolescence.
8—10. Panoramic guest-rooms using the full range of rainbow colors.

5. Ein verglastes Treppenhaus für Gäste, in den hohlen Kern gestellt.
6. Becken als Rechteck, Rund- oder Kurvenform – das Spieldeck vom Turm gesehen.
7. Das Innere eines Badezimmers. Die Einheiten können leicht entfernt und ersetzt werden, sobald sie veralten.
8—10. Gästezimmer mit Panoramablick ,in allen Farben des Regenbogens gehalten.